THE RISE OF
THE SPANISH EMPIRE

IN THE

OLD WORLD AND IN THE NEW

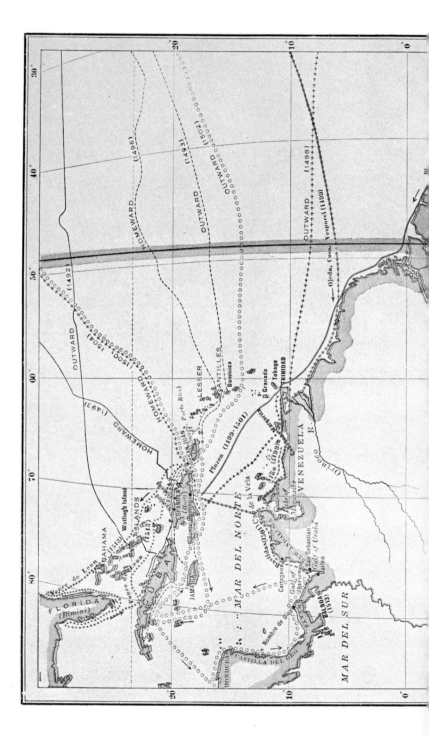

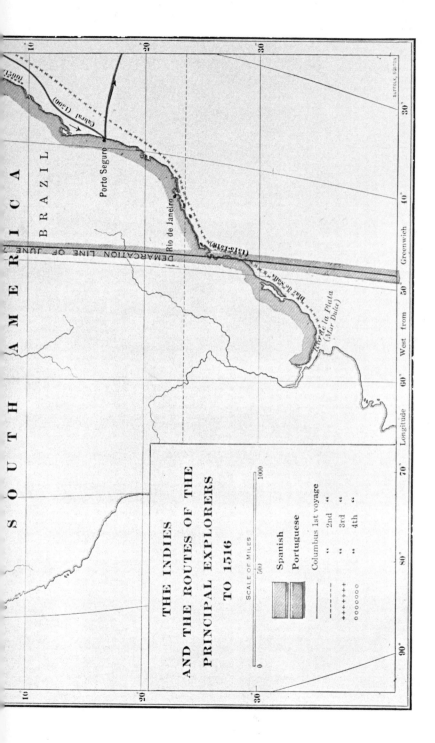

SOUTH AMERICA

BRAZIL

Porto Seguro

(Cabral (1500)

Rio de Janeiro

DEMARCATION LINE OF JUNE

(1515-1516)

Diaz de Solis

Rio de la Plata
(Mar Dulce)

THE INDIES
AND THE ROUTES OF THE
PRINCIPAL EXPLORERS
TO 1516

SCALE OF MILES

0   500   1000

Spanish
Portuguese
Columbus 1st voyage
"   "   2nd   "
"   "   3rd   "
"   "   4th   "

Greenwich

West from   Longitude

30°   40°   50°   60°   70°   80°   90°

SUFFOLK, BOSTON

THE RISE OF
THE SPANISH EMPIRE

IN THE

OLD WORLD AND IN THE NEW

BY

ROGER BIGELOW MERRIMAN

VOLUME II
THE CATHOLIC KINGS

COOPER SQUARE PUBLISHERS, INC.
New York ● 1962

Originally copyright 1918 by The Macmillan Company
Library of Congress Catalog Card No. 61-13267
Printed in the United States of America
Published by Cooper Square Publishers, Inc.
59 Fourth Ave., New York 3, N. Y.

CONTENTS

BOOK III

UNION

CHAPTER XII

v

CHAPTER XIII

CHAPTER XIV

CHAPTER XV

BOOK IV

EXPANSION

CHAPTER XVI

CHAPTER XVIII

CHAPTER XIX

CHAPTER XX

MAPS AND GENEALOGICAL TABLES

MAPS

TABLE

BOOK III

UNION

BOOK III

CHAPTER XII

THE MARRIAGE OF FERDINAND AND ISABELLA

"EVER since the wars began in Castile between King Henry and the nobles of his realm, and before the marriage of King Ferdinand and Queen Isabella, a song used to be sung there by the newcomers within the kingdom; and the words of this song, which was set to very pleasant music, were

'Flowers of Aragon
Blossom in Castile.'

And the children took little bannerets, and, riding on canes and prancing about, cried, 'Standard of Aragon, standard of Aragon!' And I repeated it and repeat it now five times over; for we can now say after our experience of what followed after: 'Lord, out of the mouths of babes and sucklings hast thou perfected praise because of thine adversaries, that thou mightest still the enemy and the avenger.'[1] And to this text we may now reverently attribute a fresh significance over and above the gloss which Holy Mother Church appends to it. And this is to the effect that our Lord observed that His people of Castile were suffering from all manner of pride and heresy, blasphemy, avarice and rapine, wars, tumults and quarrels, thieves and robbers, whoremongers, assassins, gamblers and keepers of gaming tables; from whence it followed that the names of our Lord God and of our Lady, the glorious Virgin Mary, were frequently taken in vain and denied by these evil gamblers,

---

[1] This is an accurate translation of the original Latin of the quotation, which is a curious jumble of Psalms viii, 2, and Matthew xxi, 16.

3

and that the Moors were enabled to murder, plunder, and gain ransoms from Christian folk; and further as a remedy for these evils that our Lord of His infinite mercy and goodness placed it in the mouths of innocent children to proclaim, in the guise of warriors with their standards, and joyously to sing the praises of those who had recently come within the realm, before He put an end to the woes with which the kingdom was afflicted. So that from the flowers and the standard which entered Castile from Aragon for the celebration of the holy marriage of Ferdinand and Isabella, by which the two sceptres of these kingdoms were finally united, there have proceeded so many and such marvellous benefits in the thirty years of their joint reign, that we, who have been witnesses of what our Lord has accomplished in our day and generation, may well take to ourselves the words of our Lord and Redeemer, 'Blessed are the eyes which see the things that ye see.' And thus with the union of the royal crowns, our Lord Jesus Christ visited His wrath upon His foes, and destroyed the murderer and the avenger."

Such are the words in which Andrés Bernáldez, the noted chronicler of the time of Ferdinand and Isabella, describes what he believed to have been an augury of the reign of the Catholic Kings.[1]

It certainly seemed that all the miseries which had afflicted the kingdom of Castile in the later Middle Ages had reached their culmination during the first three-quarters of the fifteenth century, in the reigns of John II and Henry IV.[2] The former had not completed his second year when he ascended the throne; and the regency for him, which was initiated under the wise guidance of his uncle, Ferdinand of Ante-

---

[1] Bernáldez, *Historia de los Reyes Católicos*, cap. vii; cf. also J. Calmette, *Louis XI et la révolution catalane*, pp. 295, note 1, 297, note 1.

[2] D. Clemencin, in *Memorias de la R. A. H.*, vi, pp. 116–134.

quera, was virtually continued, though under far less skilful and devoted hands, until the day of his death. For the king had no aptitude whatsoever for business, nor ability to rule; he was absorbed in the patronage and pursuit of letters, music, and art;[1] when his uncle, the 'good regent,' was called away to the throne of Aragon in 1412, the only question was who should replace him. For a time a council of ministers attempted to continue his work, but its members were for the most part tools in the hands of powerful magnates, or pensionaries of the king's relatives in Aragon and Navarre. Before long, however, a more masterful personality arose, whose proficiency in jousting, dancing, and song insured his favor with his sovereign, while his boundless cupidity and ambition made him aspire to supremacy in the state.[2] From 1420 till 1453, Álvaro de Luna was the undisputed lord of Castile. His audacity impressed; his magnificence dazzled. He was given the office of Constable, and his credit with the puppet monarch mounted so high that all the other counsellors of the realm were soon elbowed aside or overshadowed. The mere fact that the favorite, as well as his master, was the subject of a contemporary chronicle[3] — an honor hitherto almost exclusively reserved for kings — is a significant indication of his preëminence. Nor was it enough that John should hand over the conduct of the government to his all-powerful minister; in the most private actions of his daily life Álvaro's word was law for him; the Constable was even permitted to exercise some measure of superintendence over his marital relations.[4] Needless to say, such prestige as Castile had won during the

[1] *D. I. E.*, xix, pp. 436–454; Puymaigre, *Cour littéraire de Juan II.*

[2] M. J. Quintana, *Vidas de los Españoles Celebres* (Mádrid, 1879, 2 vols.), ii, pp. 1–194; J. Rizzo y Ramirez, *Juicio crítico de Álvaro de Luna* (Madrid, 1865).

[3] *Crónica de Álvaro de Luna*, ed. Miguel de Flores (Madrid, 1784).

[4] Fernán Perez de Guzman, *Generaciones y Semblanzas*, in *B. A. E.*, lxviii, p. 713, col. 2.

comparatively vigorous rule of Henry III was soon thrown away under a régime like this; the waste and corruption at home were only equalled by the weakness and vacillation abroad. The plots to overthrow the favorite were innumerable and kept the realm in an uproar, but one by one they failed; and the state of public confidence and morality is shown by the fact that when the rebels desired to parley with the king and his minister, it was often necessary to find some neutral person of known integrity to preside over the conference, and to furnish him with a large military force as a safeguard against foul play by any of the parties concerned.[1]

In 1418, just at the time that Álvaro was rising into prominence, the king had been married to his cousin Maria, daughter of his uncle and former regent, Ferdinand of Antequera; and three years previously his sister (also named Maria) had wedded Alfonso the Magnanimous; the two branches of the house of Trastamara which occupied the thrones of Aragon and Castile were thus closely connected by a double tie. In 1425 a son, Henry, was born to the king of Castile and his Aragonese wife; but no other children followed, and in 1445 the queen died. It is not necessary to believe the assertions of his enemies that Álvaro was responsible for her demise, but he evidently felt that it was quite within his province to select her successor. Without consulting the king, who apparently desired to wed a French princess, he calmly arranged a marriage for him with Isabella, a cousin of Affonso the African, king of Portugal, and forced his master to conclude it in August, 1447. The motives that inspired the Constable to seek this alliance were probably almost entirely personal; but the match shows that,

---

[1] P. Fernández de Velasco, *Seguro de Tordesillas*, printed in the same volume with Flores's edition of the *Crónica de Álvaro de Luna* (Madrid, 1784).

despite all the struggles and wars of the previous century, Castile still saw the advantages of keeping close to her neighbor on the west. The Portuguese marriage, however, proved the ruin of its originator. Álvaro's arrogance had at last reached a pitch which even John found it impossible to endure. The new queen could not stomach his influence with her husband, which so completely eclipsed her own, and began plotting for his downfall. Finally, after the Constable had refused to listen to a plain hint to retire, he was arrested at his palace at Burgos, and executed two months later in the public square at Valladolid (June 2, 1453). On July 21, 1454, King John followed his favorite to the grave. In addition to his successor Henry, the son of Maria of Aragon, he left two children by his Portuguese wife: Isabella, born April 22, 1451, at Madrigal, who was destined to be the first queen of a united Spain, and Alfonso, born November 15, 1453.[1]

Great expectations were entertained of the new king, who, as Prince of Asturias, had shown commendable energy and vigor; if he had occasionally risen in revolt against his father, he had also valiantly defended the honor of Castile in the battle of Olmedo, in May, 1445, against a hostile combination of factious nobles supported from Aragon and Navarre. He was accessible to his subjects and extremely liberal in giving. A proclamation of war against the Moors of Granada, issued soon after his succession, induced the belief that the infidel was speedily to be driven from the peninsula. But the Granadan war was so slackly conducted that the soldiers mutinied for lack of leadership, and the Emir openly expressed his contempt for his Christian foes; while in internal affairs the young monarch developed

---

[1] Prescott, i, pp. 113–118; and references to the chronicles there given; L. de Corral, *Don Alvaro de Luna*, pp. 29 ff.

an apathy so shameless that he not seldom affixed his signature to public documents without taking the trouble to read them through.   The coinage was debased in shocking proportions in order to furnish material for the royal munificence.   Crime and rebellion stalked unpunished throughout the length and breadth of the land, and the moral degradation of all ranks of society exceeded even the measure common to that licentious age.[1]

The personal aspect and private life of the new monarch were calculated, moreover, to enhance the dissatisfaction created by his career.   "All his Face was disagreeable . . . his Manners and course of Life were wholly addicted to Debauchery and Lewdness."[2]   In 1440, at the age of fifteen, he had been wedded to his cousin, Blanche of Navarre, daughter by a first wife of the future John II of Aragon; but he had been divorced from her thirteen years later on the ground that he had been unable to consummate the marriage.   Examination of the unedifying details of the case leads, however, to grave doubts as to the truth of the pretext alleged; and the fact that negotiations for a second marriage of the Infante with a Portuguese princess were initiated before the first was dissolved is further evidence in the same direction.[3]   It seems highly probable, in fact, that political reasons were at the back of the whole affair.   Castile, as has been already pointed out, had quite as many grounds for wishing to unite with Portugal as with Aragon.   The constant interference of the Aragonese Infantes in the internal affairs of the realm, where as descendants of the house of Trastamara they possessed extensive estates, had been a fertile source of trouble for many years.   Moreover, the second queen of John II, whose influence with her husband had been unbounded, was

[1] Prescott, i, pp. 149–152; A. Rodríguez Villa, *Don Beltran de la Cueva*, pp. 4–7; J. B. Sitges, *Enrique IV y la*   *Excelente Señora*, pp. 41–61, 109–127.
[2] Mariana, tr. Stevens, p. 381.
[3] Sitges, pp. 57–61, 112 f.

a cousin of the lady who was under consideration as a bride for her stepson, and doubtless exerted all her efforts to perpetuate Portuguese influence in Castile. In any case the arrangements for the Portuguese match were pushed rapidly forward during the last months of the reign of John II, and the wedding was finally celebrated, on May 20, 1455, at Cordova, ten months after Henry had ascended his father's throne.[1]

The mass of the nation, however, whose disgust at the fickleness of the new king as a ruler led them the more easily to give credence to uncomplimentary stories concerning his private life, were convinced that the assigned cause of his divorce was the true one; and the fact that the new queen bore no children during the first six years of her married life still further strengthened their belief. The cognomen of *El Liberal*, which had been previously assigned to the king because of his extreme generosity, was now exchanged for the far less flattering one of *El Impotente*. But Joanna of Portugal was sprightly and gay; she had many devoted admirers, prominent among whom was a certain Beltran de la Cueva, a brilliant and handsome young nobleman who had gained complete ascendancy over the mind of the king, and, like Álvaro de Luna, had risen with extraordinary rapidity to the foremost position in the Royal Council. At a feast held in honor of the ambassador of the duke of Brittany, Beltran had held the lists against all comers in defence of the supremacy of the charms of his lady love, whose name he refused to reveal, but whom common report identified as the queen; and when, in February, 1462, Joanna was delivered of a daughter, we are told by the contemporary chronicler Palencia that men generally refused to recognize her as the child of the king, but assigned

---

[1] Sitges, pp. 59–65.

her paternity to the favorite. Whether the popular belief in regard to this matter was correct or not has been the subject of much unprofitable discussion, which from the nature of the case cannot possibly lead to any definite result; yet it is pertinent to observe that it was plainly to the interest of Ferdinand and Isabella, whose rival for the throne of Castile the unfortunate Infanta was subsequently to become, that the tradition of her illegitimacy should be perpetuated, and that the courtly chronicles which were produced in their reign are consequently unsafe guides. Far more important, however, than the actual facts in regard to the paternity of the Infanta, who is usually known as *La Beltraneja*, was the effect which the doubts about it exercised on the state of the realm. This was to deliver over Castile to an orgy of rebellion and lawlessness, which surpassed even the anarchy of the preceding age.[1]

Three months after the birth of the princess, in May, 1462, the king summoned the Castilian Cortes to Madrid, and received their oath of recognition to her as lawful heiress of the realm. Unfortunately we possess no document to tell us what persons signed this oath. It is certain that the king made every effort to secure the names of all the magnates of his realm, but there is strong reason to believe that a number of malcontents were already preparing to take advantage of the doubts which had been cast on the Infanta's origin, as a pretext for a revolt against the crown.[2] Chief among these were Juan Pacheco, Marquis of Villena, and his uncle, Alfonso Carrillo, archbishop of Toledo. The former,[3] who was of Portuguese extraction, and had been

[1] Palencia, *Crónica*, i, pp. 353 ff.; Sitges, pp. 129 ff.; A. Rodríguez Villa, chaps. i and ii, especially pp. 11–13.

[2] Sitges, pp. 129 f.; *Memorias de Enrique IV*, ed. R. A. H., ii. colección diplomática, no. lxxiv.

[3] Not to be confused with Enrique de Villena, the scholar and writer at the court of John II, who was of royal descent, nor with the Infante Henry of Aragon, Marquis of Villena, who died in 1445.

introduced into the Castilian royal household through the good offices of Álvaro de Luna, was a restless, intriguing spirit, who delighted to fish in troubled waters. Honor and loyalty were strangers to him. His own advancement was his sole aim, and he cared not what means he employed to attain his ends. The archbishop, who could claim few clerical attributes save his title, was another characteristic product of the age — ferocious in his hatreds, formidable on the battlefield, and exceedingly valuable to any cause which he should elect to espouse, on account of the vast resources which he commanded as primate of Castile.[1] Both these men, who had expected to rule in the counsels of the young king, had fiercely resented the sudden rise of Beltran de la Cueva and the consequent eclipse of their own fortunes. They had been deeply dissatisfied with the way in which the new favorite had carried on the government; now, with the birth of La Beltraneja and the questions that had been raised concerning it, they saw their opportunity for revenge.

How much they could have accomplished by their own resources is exceedingly doubtful; but it so happened that powerful outside support was close at hand. The restless King John of Aragon, who had never ceased to covet the throne of Castile for his own family, had dreamed ever since 1457 of a marriage of his son Ferdinand, the offspring of his second wife, to Isabella, the half-sister of King Henry, as a means to secure that end.[2] The recognition of La Beltraneja as the lawful heiress of the Castilian throne would spell ruin for his plans; and the prospect of it threw the Aragonese king into the arms of the Pachecos. The growing cordiality of the courts of Castile and Portugal, which had been a marked feature of recent years, was also

---

[1] Pulgar, *Los claros varones de España*, tits. vi, xx.   [2] Sitges, p. 131.

most unwelcome to John, with his aspirations for an ultimate union of Castile and Aragon; and his apprehensions were redoubled when he learned in 1464 that negotiations were on foot for a marriage of the Princess Isabella to Affonso the African — a union which would naturally cut the ground from beneath his feet in another way.[1] Finally, Henry the Impotent had contrived to give offence to the king of Aragon by sending aid to the latter's rebel subjects in Catalonia in the winter of 1462–63; while a year later he had filled the cup of the wrath of the Pachecos by raising the detested Beltran de la Cueva to the coveted dignity of grand master of Santiago.[2] All these things combined to unite the Castilian rebels and the king of Aragon. They had numerous objects in common, and the advantages of coöperation were obvious.

On May 16, 1464, Carrillo and Pacheco, together with the latter's brother, the grand master of Calatrava, solemnly bound themselves together to provide for the security of the Infanta Isabella and of her brother Alfonso, whom they represented as in danger from some frightful conspiracy. A little later (the exact date is not possible to ascertain) the king of Aragon joined with them and with other lords and prelates of the realm to propound to King Henry certain measures which would redound to his good service and to the weal of his kingdom.[3] A public pronouncement of their intentions, which the confederates issued at Burgos in the following September, reveals what these measures were: the recognition of Alfonso in place of La Beltraneja as lawful heir to the throne, and the appointment of a committee of five to consider the state of the realm.[4] At a conference

[1] Diego Enríquez del Castillo, *Crónica del Rey Enrique el Cuarto* (in *B. A. E.*, lxx), caps. lv and lvii.

[2] Sitges, pp. 72–108; A. Rodríguez Villa, pp. 24 f. Beltran soon after resigned this office.

[3] *Memorias de Enrique IV*, ii, nos. xcii, xcv; Sitges, pp. 133–136.

[4] *Memorias de Enrique IV*, ii, no. xcvii.

with King Henry, moreover, the rebels secured the person of the prince, and they furthermore extorted from the king a promise to acknowledge him as his heir, on condition that he should marry La Beltraneja. Subsequent events, however, persuaded them that Henry had no intention of abiding by any concessions which he might temporarily be induced to make, especially as they had entirely failed to persuade him permanently to dismiss Beltran de la Cueva.[1] The revolt had, in fact, gone too far to be settled by negotiation, and as the king showed no disposition to fight, the conspirators soon became convinced that their only hope of effecting their ends was by violently and publicly humiliating him. At Ávila accordingly they "resolved upon a most Barbarous Action, to the Eternal Infamy of Spain; Without the Walls of that City they Erected a Scaffold, and placed on it the Statue of King Henry in his Royal Robes on a Throne with his Scepter and Crown. Thither the Villanous Nobles, and a Multitude of People, resorted. Then a Cryer proclaimed Sentence against the King, laying to his Charge many horrid Crimes. Whilst the Sentence was reading, they leasurely stripped the Statue of all its Robes, and at last, with Reproachful Language, threw it down from the Scaffold. This Villany was acted upon *Wednesday* the 5th of *June*. Immediately Prince *Alonso,* who had been all the while present, was brought upon the Scaffold, there lifted upon the Shoulders of the Nobles, and proclaimed King, the Royal Standard being Displayed in his Name, as was the Custom at the Inauguration of Kings. The Multitude presently cryed, *God Save King Alonso,* which was ingaging themselves in the Quarrel." [2]

[1] Enríquez del Castillo, caps. lxvi, lxvii; Sitges, pp. 148–154.
[2] This account is taken from Stevens's Mariana, p. 407. Other descriptions may be found in Valera's *Memorial de diversas Hazañas,* cap. xxviii (in *B. A. E.,* lxx); in Enríquez del Castillo, cap. lxxiv; and in A. de Palencia,

The opinions of Spanish jurists and historians differ widely as to the rights and wrongs of this dramatic act, but the majority condemn it as an unwarrantable revolt against the constituted authority of the crown.[1] Terrible disruption in the realm was certainly its immediate result. For neither the king's partisans nor those of the revolutionists were strongly preponderant. A list of the grandees which followed the rival standards indicates that the two sides were evenly balanced; a prolonged struggle seemed therefore inevitable, to the ruin of the peace of the realm.[2] The king was supported by Beltran de la Cueva, whom he promptly raised to the new dignity of Duke de Albuquerque; he also sought the support of the papacy, which he urged to fulminate against the rebels the censures of the church; he even sent the queen to Portugal to continue the negotiations of the previous year for the marriage of Isabella to Affonso the African, and to demand aid and support from the latter in his distress. A treaty was actually signed between the queen and the Portuguese monarch to that effect; but at the last moment King Henry drew back and refused to ratify it, on the ground that Affonso had put too high a price upon his alliance.[3] The fact really was that the Castilian sovereign still fervently hoped to find a way out of his difficulties without an appeal to arms. The rebels had certainly given him every pretext for attacking them, not only by the deposition at Ávila, but also by the violent and abusive proclamations which they subsequently caused the young Alfonso to issue in justification of his assumption of the kingship.[4] The forces at their disposal were no greater than Henry's; there had recently been some desertions

Crónica de Enrique IV, ed. A. Paz y Melia, i, pp. 455 ff.
[1] Sitges, p. 155.
[2] Valera, cap. xxx.

[3] *Memorias de Enrique IV*, ii, nos. 124, 128; Sitges, pp. 156–158; Rodríguez Villa, pp. 164–166.
[4] *Memorias de Enrique IV*, ii, no. cxix.

from their ranks to those of the crown,[1] and John of Aragon
was at the moment too fully occupied in Catalonia to give
them any aid. A vigorous thrust by the royal party at
this stage would in all probability have compassed their
defeat; but King Henry preferred negotiation, and in the
spring of 1466 he entertained a proposal to detach the
Pachecos from the insurgents by the marriage of the Princess Isabella, whose union with the king of Portugal was
now regarded as impossible, to the grand master of the
order of Calatrava, the brother of the Marquis of Villena.
Despite the entreaties of the princess, who was apparently
resolved to die rather than submit to the match, the preparations for it were hurried through. Applications were made
to Rome for the grand master's dispensation from his vows
of celibacy; magnificent presents were purchased for the
bride; but the wedding was prevented at the last moment
by the sudden death of the bridegroom, while on his way to
Madrid for the ceremony, on May 2, 1466. The nature of
the illness that carried him off was impossible to ascertain,
and at least one authority attributes his demise to poison;
but if poison it was, there is no reason to lay the responsi-
bility at the door of the still youthful Isabella.[2]

The death of the grand master, however, did not break
off the negotiations, which continued till the year 1467,
though without success. A number of betrayals and
desertions characterize this state of the proceedings,[3] but
before long it became obvious that a trial of strength on the
field of battle was sooner or later inevitable. It occurred
at last, on August 20, 1467, on the plain of Olmedo, close to
the spot where John II of Castile, twenty-two years before,
had triumphed over his subjects. Many deeds of reckless
valor were performed on both sides — the most dramatic

---

[1] Sitges, p. 160.   [2] Sitges, pp. 160 f.; Prescott, i, p. 169.   [3] Sitges, p. 162.

being perhaps the action of Beltran de la Cueva, who, on learning that forty knights in the opposing ranks had sworn to slay him if he ventured to show his face in the fight, promptly notified his foes of the garb he intended to wear, in order that they might not be at a loss to find him. The king's forces, which were the more numerous, retained possession of the field at the end of the day; but Henry had not the energy to follow up his victory, and less than a month later he permitted Segovia, his favorite town, to fall into the hands of his foes, without striking a blow in its defence.[1] Again the hope of detaching the Marquis of Villena from the confederates led to a renewal of fruitless negotiations, with the usual series of betrayals and counter-betrayals as their inevitable accompaniment. This time a new element was introduced by the fact that the young Prince Alfonso, who had hitherto surrendered himself to the dictates of the grandees, had begun to give signs of independence and vigor, which promised to leave small room for the continuation of baronial tutelage. "This youth," exclaimed one of the magnates, "although in the hands of others and under our guardianship, is gaining far too much arrogance for such tender years! If we are to avoid ruin, we shall have to seek means to control him, either by dissipation or some other yoke."[2] On July 5, 1468, the prince died, after an illness of four days' duration. When we consider the state of the realm and the prevalence of foul play, we cannot wonder that the majority of the contemporary historians incline to attribute his death to the characteristic fifteenth-century cause: Pulgar alone states categorically that he was carried off by the pestilence.[3] In view of the nature of the evidence, we shall probably do well to follow

---

[1] Palencia, ii, pp. 59–73; Sitges, pp. 162–166.

[2] Palencia, ii, p. 112.

[3] Sitges, pp. 167 f.

the example of the chronicler Castillo and not attempt to give too definite a verdict; but the words in which that prudent writer comments on the event make it perfectly plain what he believed. "It was assuredly," he avers, "a most marvellous fact that three days before he died, the prince's death was divulged throughout the whole realm." [1]

With Alfonso gone, everything depended on the Princess Isabella, who had been in the camp of the insurgents ever since the fall of Segovia in the previous year, and had recognized the late prince as the lawful occupant of the Castilian throne.[2] If she insisted on being acknowledged as queen, and could prevail upon a sufficient number of the insurgents to support her, a continuation of civil war and anarchy would be inevitable; on the other hand, a compromise would infallibly be welcomed by Henry and would probably go far to preserve the peace of the realm. At a meeting held on August 17 to deliberate about the situation, a rift appeared in the ranks of the confederates; the archbishop of Toledo being clearly in favor of immediately recognizing Isabella as queen, while the Marquis of Villena counselled a reconciliation with the king. Isabella, quite as much from policy as from unselfishness, soon decided that if possible she would pursue the latter course. She had no intention of renouncing what she regarded as her just title as queen of Castile, but she plainly perceived that her reign would be far happier, and the kingdom more united, if she could obtain Henry's approval. She therefore consented to hold an interview with her half-brother, not indeed as the titular head of a rebel faction suing for peace, but as lawful queen of the realm, willing for the sake of internal quiet to permit him during his life to retain the dignity of king, provided her own right to succeed him was unequivocally recog-

---

[1] Enríquez del Castillo, cap. cxiv   [2] Sitges, pp. 165, 171–174.

nized.[1]   The interview took place on September 19, 1468, at Toros de Guisando, southwest of Avila, in the presence of the archbishop of Toledo, the Marquis of Villena, and other grandees.   It ended in an agreement substantially in accord with the Infanta's contentions, Henry being allowed to live out the remainder of his days on the throne of Castile, while Isabella was recognized and sworn to as princess and heiress of the realm to the prejudice of the claims of La Beltraneja.[2]

At this point we must leave the narrative of Castilian events, in order to bring the affairs of the eastern kingdoms up to date.

John II of Aragon, the younger brother of Alfonso the Magnanimous, and the father by his second wife of Ferdinand the Catholic, was unquestionably one of the most remarkable sovereigns of the fifteenth century.   Compact and vigorous in body, and inured to toil, he was filled to the brim with nervous energy and power; even the painful cataract which afflicted him in the latter part of his life, and, until it was removed by an operation in 1468, rendered him at times almost totally blind, was unable to diminish his extraordinary vitality.   His physical qualities were fully matched by those of his mind and character.   Unceasingly ambitious, a past master of diplomacy and intrigue, he was held back by no moral scruple from the relentless pursuit of his own ends.   Had he lived in Italy, half a century later, Machiavelli might well have utilized him instead of Caesar Borgia as a model and pattern for *The Prince*.[3]

[1] Palencia, ii, pp. 177–199; Sitges, p. 175.

[2] The text of the *concordia* is published in the *Memorias de Enrique IV*, ii, no. clii; also in Sitges, pp. 178–189, with the comments of the contemporary chroniclers.   It is not improbable that the clauses in the treaty which connote a recognition by Henry that La Beltraneja was not his daughter were inserted subsequently, under Ferdinand and Isabella.

[3] Calmette, *Louis XI et la révolution catalane*, p. 42; Desdevises du Dezert,

During the last years of the reign of his father, the good King Ferdinand, John had hopes, as we have already seen, of securing for himself the succession in Sicily, but his elder brother, Alfonso the Magnanimous, had no wish to see him established there, and in 1419 succeeded in diverting his attention in another direction by arranging a marriage for him with Blanche, widow of Martin the Younger of Aragon, and daughter of the king of Navarre.[1] We have not had occasion to deal with this little saddlebag realm since the early days of the Reconquest, when it was alternately involved in the affairs of Aragon and Castile. Suffice it to say that after remaining for a long time in the hands of a separate Spanish dynasty, which, however, was closely related to the royal lines in the other Iberian kingdoms, it had passed in the year 1234 to the French family of the counts of Champagne, thence in 1284 to the French crown, and finally, in the early part of the fourteenth century, to the French feudal house of the counts of Évreux; the wife of John of Aragon was the daughter of the third of the Évreux kings of Navarre. During this long period of subjection to French influence, the Navarrese had maintained their pristine independence, and sturdily insisted on the rigorous observance of all their ancient privileges. It is true that some new institutions, notably a *Chambre des Comptes*, were introduced by the sovereigns of the Évreux line, but the inhabitants were more than ever averse to having their desti-

---

Don Carlos d'Aragon, p. 94. The number of John's enemies who died at the most convenient possible moment for John has naturally given rise to accusations of poison. Seemingly no one could cross his path with impunity. His son Charles, his daughter Blanche, Pedro the Constable of Portugal, John of Calabria, Alfonso the Infante of Castile, all died at the very moment when their continued existence would have seriously embarrassed the king of Aragon. It is impossible, on the evidence that has come down to us, to substantiate the poison theory in any one of these cases; on the other hand the absence of evidence may simply show that John did his work skilfully. Cf. L. Comenge, *Apuntes históricos. Clínica egregia* (Barcelona, 1895), *passim*.

[1] Cf. Vol. I, p. 411, and Desdevises du Dezert, *op. cit.*, pp. 95–106.

nies shaped by their more powerful neighbors; and they had thus far succeeded in imbuing the foreign sovereigns whom dynastic changes had brought them with their own zeal for the preservation of their autonomy.[1]

The marriage treaty of John of Aragon and Blanche of Navarre was apparently inspired by the idea of a sort of federation of the little Pyrenean realm with the kingdoms of Spain, and was welcomed by the Navarrese as a guarantee of their independence against the French influences which had been preponderant there for the past two centuries.[2] John of Aragon, however, regarded the matter in a somewhat different light. Elbowed out of Sicily, he was keenly desirous to possess a crown of his own; since it was improbable, at that period, that he would ever be the heir of his brother Alfonso in Aragon, he welcomed the opportunity to satisfy his ambitions in Navarre. But that was not all. Though his accession in Aragon was improbable, it was, to say the least, possible; he was, moreover, exceedingly influential in Castile, and was constantly meddling in its affairs.[3] If fortune favored him, there was certainly a chance that from Navarre as a centre he might ultimately unite all the different kingdoms of Spain under his own or his children's rule, as they had once been united four centuries before under the sceptre of Sancho the Great. Just when an idea of the possibility of an Iberian unity first took shape in the mind of John of Aragon, it is impossible to say. It was clearly the guiding motive of his declining years, and may well have been dimly conceived of even at this early stage. But the indispensable preliminary was that he should make good his hold on the little mountain kingdom whose heiress had

---

[1] A good account of Navarrese institutions is given in Desdevises du Dezert, pp. 57–87: cf. also J. A. Brutails, *Documents des archives de la Chambre des Comptes de Navarre* (Paris, 1890).
[2] *D. I. A.*, xxvi, pp. 283–358; Desdevises du Dezert, pp. 99–105.
[3] Cf. *ante*, pp. 11 ff.

become his wife; and his prospects of accomplishing this were not at first encouraging. In his marriage treaty with Blanche of Navarre, he had been unable to prevent the insertion of numerous provisions which seriously limited his political authority in that realm. The Navarrese had no intention of making him really king; they expressly stipulated that he should have no sovereign rights apart from his wife, and that, if she predeceased him, her eldest child, whether male or female, should inherit the throne to the prejudice of her husband. The treaty, however, failed specifically to state at what age under these circumstances the royal power and authority should be fully surrendered to the heir; and, as things worked out, this omission ultimately afforded John an opportunity, of which he was not slow to avail himself, to get the government into his own hands.[1]

A son, Charles, was born to John on May 29, 1421; and two daughters, Blanche and Eleanor, followed in the succeeding years. In 1425 Charles the Noble, the old Evreux king of Navarre, died, so that John, as husband of the late monarch's daughter, became titular king of the realm; but the Navarrese were so violently opposed to granting him any real political power that he soon desisted from any effort to make his authority felt, and left the conduct of the government in the hands of his wife. During the next fifteen years he was almost exclusively occupied in Aragon and Castile; in the former, as lieutenant and representative of his absent brother, Alfonso the Magnanimous; in the latter, as an ambitious intriguer, head and centre of all the various baronial coalitions which aimed to curb the omnipotence of Álvaro de Luna.[2] Finally, in May, 1441, Blanche of Navarre died, leaving the throne of the realm, in con-

---

[1] Desdevises du Dezert, pp. 102–105. [2] Ibid., pp. 107–113.

formity with her marriage treaty, to her son Charles, Prince
of Viana, but begging him not to assume the title of king
"without the consent and blessing of his father." [1]   If the
queen hoped in this way to reconcile her son and her husband,
she was grievously in error ; what she had really done was to
render a conflict between them inevitable.   Had she left the
delicate matter entirely alone, John would probably never
have dared to assert any claims at all ; as it was, he reappeared in Navarre soon after the death of his wife, and demanded that Charles recognize him as king.   After a long
struggle, in which he was far more vigorously opposed by
the Navarrese Cortes than by his gentle and modest son, he
gained his ends ; though Charles drew up a secret protestation against the validity of his father's title to the crown.
Ostensibly, however, the victory lay with John, who soon
returned to his intrigues in Castile, leaving Charles to govern
Navarre as his lieutenant and representative in his absence.[2]

In September, 1444, John of Aragon was betrothed to
Joanna Enríquez, the brilliant and charming daughter of the
Admiral of Castile, and great-great-granddaughter of King
Alfonso XI ; their marriage was celebrated in the summer of
1447.[3]   This union was a significant evidence that, despite
his recent defeat at Olmedo in 1445, John of Aragon had by
no means renounced his ambition to make capital for himself out of the domestic discord in Castile.   The Admiral
Enríquez was the most powerful of the opponents of Álvaro
de Luna, and his alliance would mean everything to John
in case the latter decided to renew the contest in the western
kingdom.   Meantime in Navarre the news of John's second
marriage was received with universal apprehension and dis-
approval.   According to the fueros, he was thereby deprived

---

[1] Desdevises du Dezert, pp. 126–129.
[2] *Ibid.*, pp. 129–137.   [3] *Ibid.*, pp. 196 f.

of the last remnant of legal right to the Navarrese throne;[1] but the inhabitants knew him too well to think for one moment that he would acknowledge this, and their worst fears were confirmed, in the autumn of 1449, when he re- appeared in the realm, bringing with him a host of Castilian and Aragonese followers, whom he promptly installed in posts of profit and authority, to the prejudice of the Navar- rese.[2] Despite the pliant nature of Charles, it was clear that the differences between father and son could only be settled by war. The mass of the Navarrese supported the prince; so did the dominant party of Álvaro de Luna in Castile; in law-respecting Aragon also warm sympathy was manifested for his side.[3] But Navarre itself was so disrupted that John was not entirely without adherents there; that the powerful family of the Beaumonts had decided to throw in their lot with Charles was sufficient reason why their tradi- tional rivals, the Agramonts, should range themselves on the side of his father. In late October, 1451, the rivals met at Aybar, south of Sanguesa. After they had almost succeeded in reaching a satisfactory compromise by parleying, the im- patience of their rival partisans reached the breaking point; battle was joined before the opposing chiefs could prevent it, with the result that the young prince was defeated and made prisoner.[4] The Cortes of Aragon showed a disposition to offer mediation between father and son,[5] but John would have none of it. Later a plan was broached for placing the settlement of the affair in the hands of Alfonso the Magnanimous, and pending the latter's decision the prince was permitted, under harsh conditions, to return to Navarre, in June, 1453, but as the terms on which he had been liberated were not fulfilled, the hope of a peaceful solution of the difficulty vanished,

[1] Desdevises du Dezert, p. 198.
[2] Ibid., pp. 200 f.
[3] Ibid., pp..212, 232.
[4] Ibid., pp. 226-228.
[5] Ibid., pp. 232-234.

and war blazed forth again between the rival parties. Meantime, in the midst of all these broils and battles, John's new wife had borne him a son, the future Ferdinand the Catholic, on March 10, 1452, in the little town of Sos. When the baby was christened in the cathedral of Saragossa on February 11, 1453, it was observed that the utmost pomp and magnificence were displayed, "just as if he had been the heir of all these kingdoms." [1]

It will be readily understood that the birth of Ferdinand was not calculated to diminish the animosity between John and Charles. The chance, which had been slight in 1420, that John might some day succeed his brother Alfonso in Aragon, was now far greater. The disruption in Castile promised well for the ultimate success of his intrigues in that direction, especially in view of his marriage with Joanna Enríquez. If he could but establish his own authority in Navarre, and hand it on unchallenged to Ferdinand, the latter might some day actually realize his father's dreams of a union of all the Spanish realms under a single sceptre. And so the struggle between John of Aragon (who most of the time was represented in Navarre by his indomitable wife) and the unfortunate Prince of Viana continued from 1453 to 1456, with occasional interruptions for diplomatic purposes; but the tide turned steadily against the prince, so that he finally abandoned the unequal fight, and, travelling by way of France and northern Italy, sought refuge at the court of his uncle, Alfonso the Magnanimous, in Naples.[2] The latter had little relish for the ways of his brother;[3] on the other hand he had deep sympathy and a high regard for his unfortunate nephew, whose literary and artistic tenden-

[1] Zurita, iv, f. 10.
[2] Desdevises du Dezert, pp. 234–246, 251 f.
[3] Zurita, iv, f. 44, tells us that he used to say, "Mi hermano el Rey de Navarra, è yo nacimos de un vientre, è non somos de una mente."

cies must have strongly appealed to him; and he was busily
engaged in an attempt to reconcile father and son on a
basis satisfactory to the latter, when he died, on June 27,
1458.[1] The Neapolitans offered their crown to Charles, in
prejudice of the rights of Alfonso's illegitimate son, Ferrante,
to whom the Magnanimous King had left it; but the prince
had too much respect for the memory of his uncle to accept,
and soon passed over to Sicily, where he hoped to find peace
and quiet, if not active support and sympathy in his misfortunes.[2]

The ultimate result of the death of Alfonso the Magnanimous was to widen the scope of the quarrel between Charles
and his father, and also to bring it to a head. John succeeded his brother in Sicily, Sardinia, and in his Spanish
realms, so that his dreams of Iberian unity were brought
measurably nearer realization than ever before; yet, on the
other hand, Charles became the legal heir-apparent in all
these kingdoms at the same time. If the new king of Aragon
desired to pass on all his dominions to his beloved Ferdinand,
the Prince of Viana must somehow be set aside. The latter's
presence in Sicily, moreover, was profoundly disquieting to
John; for the natives, who retained the happiest memories
of the prince's mother, Blanche of Navarre, and had not
ceased to aspire to the possession of an independent sovereign, were obviously desirous to make Charles their king.
The upshot of the matter was that in the spring of 1459
John sent over a special messenger to Sicily to order his son
to repair to Majorca, where the latter finally arrived on
August 20.[3] Meantime negotiations had been in progress
between the prince and his father. The former was, as
usual, willing to go to any lengths to obtain peace; but his

[1] Desdevises du Dezert, pp. 253–
259; Ametller, ii, pp. 839–849.

[2] Desdevises du Dezert, pp. 259–265.
[3] Ibid., pp. 265–274.

cause had of late been vigorously espoused by the liberty-loving Catalonians, who rivalled the Navarrese in their respect for the law, and, detesting the way in which John had dared to override it, urged the prince to make a strong stand for his rights. On the other side, the king and his wife conducted the negotiations with the greatest skill and duplicity; and, pressing their advantage to the utmost, finally extorted from Charles in January, 1460, an agreement by which the latter delivered to his father the principal fortresses of Navarre, allowed his rights as heir in that realm and in Aragon to be passed over in silence, and received in return merely his father's pardon for faults which he had never committed, and the permission to reside wherever he wished, save in Sicily and in his native land. Two months after the conclusion of this agreement, the prince arrived at Barcelona. where the population, who had followed his fortunes with increasing affection and solicitude, joyously welcomed him as *Primogenit,* or heir to the throne.[1] Clearly they thought that the fact that his title had been passed over in the recent treaty meant that John had intended to concede it to him; but they were enlightened on this point a few days later in most unsatisfactory fashion by a letter from the king to his chancellor, the bishop of Gerona, in which they were strictly forbidden to treat or address the prince as the heir or successor of his father.[2]

This mandate was taken by the Barcelonese as a violation of their constitution. They resolved to defend the rights of the prince; and from that moment the scene of interest in this singular drama shifts from Navarre to Catalonia. The events of the summer of 1460 served further to widen the breach between father and son. In order to strengthen himself for the struggle which he now foresaw was inevitable,

[1] Desdevises du Dezert, pp. 275-284.   [2] *Ibid.*, pp. 293-295.

Charles made overtures for the hand of the Infanta Isabella of Castile — a plan doubly distasteful to his father, because the accomplishment of it would necessarily render impossible what was already the darling project of the latter's heart, namely the marriage of Isabella to his son Ferdinand. In order to prevent it, the king suddenly appeared in Catalonia, where he was received with a coldness which contrasted strongly with the popularity of the prince; and on December 2, at Lerida, where John was holding the Catalonian Cortes, Charles was suddenly arrested and ordered into confinement.[1] But the liberty-loving Catalonians rushed to the rescue of the captive. The Diputación General took his case under its protection, and after the failure of a number of embassies despatched to the king to demand his release, proclaimed the Somatent on February 8, 1461, "against the evil counsellors of the crown."[2] Taken entirely by surprise, John was forced to yield. After a vain attempt to extricate himself from his difficulties by diplomacy, he liberated Charles, who in March returned to Barcelona amid the cheers of the enthusiastic populace; and in the following June he signed a treaty which was virtually an admission of defeat. But the prince did not live long to enjoy the victory which the valorous Catalonians had won for him; on September 23, 1461, he fell ill and died at Barcelona.[3]

The death of Charles, however, was by no means the end of the difficulties of the king of Aragon. In Navarre, the prince's two younger sisters, Blanche and Eleanor, still remained — a bar to the succession of the Infante Ferdinand, if not to John's own possession of the throne during his lifetime;[4] while in Catalonia the prince's demise, which was universally believed to have been caused by foul play, in-

---

[1] Desdevises du Dezert, pp. 295-308.
[2] Calmette, pp. 43-45.
[3] Calmette, p. 53; Desdevises du
Dezert, pp. 390-399, who rejects the theory that he was poisoned.
[4] Calmette, pp. 32, 71, note.

sured the continuance and increase of the rebellion. But before we examine the way in which John handled these two
problems, we must pause to introduce upon the stage another
actor, whose character bears striking resemblance to that of
the king of Aragon, though their aims were diametrically
opposed — the redoubtable Louis XI of France, who had
succeeded his father on the throne of that kingdom on
July 22, 1461. The fundamental idea of the policy of this
monarch was to increase the domains of the crown of France
at home at the expense of his feudal vassals, and abroad
at the expense of the neighboring realms; in Spain he
specially coveted the county of Catalonia.[1] Memories
of the days of the Spanish Mark furnished some historical
justification for this ambition; the acquisitions of St.
Louis at the expense of James the Conqueror were even
fresher in men's minds; a French reconquest of Cerdagne
and Roussillon, and if possible of further territories to the
south of them, would be a fitting sequel to the treaty of
Corbeil.[2] The outbreak of the Catalonian revolt also,
which so nearly coincided with Louis's accession, apparently afforded a particularly favorable opportunity for
the prosecution of his plans. The question was, how would
he take advantage of it? Would he support the revolutionists and ultimately attempt to make himself their
sovereign? Or would he support King John against them
and make the king of Aragon pay liberally for his aid?[3]

A brief testing of the first of these alternatives convinced
Louis of its futility from his point of view. The Catalans
were bent on the assertion of their rights, but they were not
willing to renounce their allegiance to the king of Aragon,
and still less to accept the sovereignty or tutelage of the
king of France.[4] The latter was consequently thrown back

[1] Calmette, p. 380.   [2] Vol. I, pp. 289 ff.   [3] Calmette, p. 55.   [4] Calmette, pp. 63 f.

on the policy of supporting John, and on April 12, 1462, signed with him a treaty at Olite, on the basis of mutual guarantees in the possession of their respective states.[1] But in addition to being a general agreement of friendship and alliance between France and Aragon, the treaty of Olite contained special provisions relative to the kingdom of Navarre, where Louis was quite ready to coöperate with John provided he could thereby facilitate his own aims in Catalonia. John's problem in Navarre was how to deal with the two surviving sisters of the late prince: of whom the elder, Blanche, the divorced wife of Henry the Impotent of Castile, had been pronounced heiress of the realm in her brother's will, while the younger, Eleanor, had strengthened herself by a marriage with her powerful French neighbor, the brilliant Gaston de Foix.[2] Realizing that he could not possibly hope to dispose of both these princesses at once and thus clear the way for Ferdinand's succession in Navarre, John had made a virtue of necessity, and adopted the policy of allying himself with the younger, for whose vigorous husband he had a wholesome respect, against her elder sister. Since 1455 he had drawn close to Gaston and Eleanor de Foix, by an agreement which assured to them the Navarrese succession, and to himself the tenure of the throne during his lifetime.[3] Now by the treaty of Olite John obtained Louis's support in this arrangement, and received the French king's promise to aid him in the conquest of such places in Navarre as held out against him; it was further stipulated that the unfortunate Blanche should be placed in the hands of her sister Eleanor, as a guarantee against her asserting her own rights to the Navarrese throne.[4] The very day after the signature of this compact, the un-

[1] Calmette, pp. 69 f.

[2] Cf. H. Courteault, *Gaston de Foix*, pp. 29 f., 84.

[3] Calmette, pp. 32 1.; *D. I. E.*, xl, p. 541.

[4] Calmette, p. 71.

happy lady was informed that she must go to France, in order, so she was told, that she might be wedded to the Duke of Berry. The pretext did not deceive her, and she protested violently, but in vain; her father was obdurate. Two months later she was virtually a prisoner in her sister's hands at the castle of Orthez, whence she was subsequently removed to Lescar; and there, on December 2, 1464, she died, not improbably a victim of poison.[1] On April 30, 1462, during her journey northward, and with a full realization of the fate that was in store for her, she had bequeathed all her rights to Navarre under her brother's will and the law of the land to her quondam husband, King Henry of Castile, and his successors, to the prejudice of the claims of Eleanor and her heirs; and Ferdinand the Catholic subsequently adduced this bequest in support of his own pretensions to Navarre by right of his wife Isabella.[2] At this point the Navarrese question falls into the background; and we may leave it in order to return to Catalonia, merely remarking, as we pass on, that the memory of John of Aragon's desperate struggles to gain for himself full control of the little mountain kingdom furnishes the key to the otherwise inexplicable lengths to which Ferdinand the Catholic subsequently went to regain it. That monarch had been brought up with the idea that Navarre was one day to be his, and it never ceased to haunt him until he had taken measures to realize it.[3]

Less than a month after the signature of the treaty of Olite, which dealt with the affairs of Navarre, the kings of Aragon and France made another and more important pact (May 9) at Bayonne, relative to the revolt in Catalonia. It provided that Louis should furnish John military aid

[1] Courteault, *Gaston de Foix*, pp. 246–249.

[2] Calmette, p. 72, note 4.
[3] Calmette, p. 72.

against his rebel subjects, carefully defining its nature and the amount of the money compensation to be paid for it, and further stipulated that as soon as the revolt should have been suppressed, the two border counties of Cerdagne and Roussillon — the only Aragonese lands remaining north of the Pyrenees — should be handed over to the king of France until the payments due from the king of Aragon should have been completed.[1] An entering wedge had thus been driven for the French occupation of Catalonia — the ultimate goal of the ambition of Louis XI. On the other hand, the news of the alienation of the counties naturally completed the measure of the wrath of the Catalonians against their king. Hitherto the revolt had been conducted for the defence of the fueros, but without any thought of the deposition of the monarch; now John and his wife were solemnly declared public enemies and deprived of their royal rights, and the Diputación General arrogated to itself supreme power in Catalonia, on the plea that it must act as regent for the ten-year-old Ferdinand. It was, in fact, only a thinly veiled move for independence, and by the following August even the farce of recognizing the rights of the Infante was abandoned;[2] the ancient traditions of the county, together with its extraordinary economic prosperity, combined to give it the strength and prestige to venture thus early on a struggle for complete freedom. And the deeds of the revolutionists were fully worthy of their declarations. The Diputación General pushed forward its preparations for military defence with energy and success. At the opening of hostilities the queen and her son were besieged in Gerona, and it was only with great

---

[1] Calmette, pp. 84–92, 385–401, 429–439.

[2] Calmette, pp. 94–98, 171 f.; D. I. A., xxi, passim, and xxii, p. 445;

Manual de novells ardits vulgarment apellat Dietari del Antich Consell Barceloní, ii, pp. 408 ff.

difficulty that the rescuing armies of Louis XI and Gaston de Foix effected their deliverance on July 23. A siege of Barcelona in the following autumn by a Franco-Aragonese army under King John was a complete failure. The most important result of the campaign had been to put Louis's army in practical possession of Cerdagne and Roussillon, and in the early months of 1463 the king of France took advantage of it. On March 2 he replied to a delegation of the inhabitants, who came to inquire what his intentions were in regard to the counties, with a series of casuistic arguments justifying his annexation of them.[1] He had already gone much further than any interpretation of the treaty of Bayonne could possibly have warranted; he was treating Cerdagne and Roussillon as if they were to be permanently an integral part of the kingdom of France.[2]

The occupation of the two border counties by the forces of Louis XI, culminating in this declaration of their annexation, was most displeasing both to John and to the Catalan revolutionists. It enlightened the former as to the true character of his treacherous ally, while it gave the latter their first inkling that their independence was quite as much in danger from France as from Aragon. Revenge was for the moment quite out of the question for John, but the insurgents' reply to the French invasion was to throw themselves into the arms of King Henry of Castile.[3] The latter had many causes of quarrel with the king of Aragon. The fact that Blanche of Navarre had declared him her heir in that realm created another bone of contention between the two sovereigns, and also between the Castilian monarch and Louis XI; and the latter's failure promptly to ratify and continue at his accession the traditional

[1] J. Vaesen, in *Révue d'histoire diplomatique*, i, pp. 441 ff.

[2] Calmette, pp. 167–169.
[3] Sitges, pp. 73 ff.

Franco-Castilian alliance was another factor which tended to embroil them.[1] Indeed, as far back as August, 1462, when the French armies had been in Cerdagne and Roussillon only one short month, an ambassador was despatched by the Diputación General of Barcelona to the court of Castile formally to offer the sovereignty of Catalonia to Henry the Impotent. In September the latter accepted it, and promised to send an army to the aid of his new vassals; in December Castilian troops arrived on the confines of Aragon.[2] For the French king this development was most unwelcome. If the Castilian army should succeed, as there was good reason to think it might, in completely dispossessing the king of Aragon, Louis would have had all his trouble for nothing, and would stand little chance of retaining Cerdagne and Roussillon. At all costs he must eliminate the king of Castile, and with this end in view he put himself forward as arbitrator in the quarrel between John and Henry; he hoped that a peaceful solution of their difficulties would induce the latter to retire to his own realm.[3] To Louis's proposal both sovereigns agreed — John as a means of gaining time, Henry out of natural indolence and desire to avoid war; and in the end of April, 1463, Louis gave sentence at Bayonne to the effect that Henry should abandon the Catalans, and John give up to Henry the revenues of his Castilian estates and certain disputed territories in Navarre.[4] The French king had thus got rid of the Castilians, though at the cost of incurring their increased enmity; for they were deeply dissatisfied with his award, and were subsequently to show it to his discomfiture.[5] He had also diminished the difficulties of John of Aragon, ostensibly still his ally but really his enemy, in Catalonia;

[1] Calmette, pp. 60, 170 f.
[2] Calmette, pp. 172–174.
[3] Calmette, p. 176.
[4] Calmette, pp. 186–189.
[5] Calmette. pp. 189 f.

and yet, on the other hand, he had added to his irritation by the concessions which he had obliged him to make in Castile and Navarre. In other words, he had substantially increased the causes that would naturally lead John to seek ultimately to take revenge on himself; he had also paved the way for that revenge.

John had to bide his time, however, for many years to come; his path was still blocked in a number of different directions. In June, 1463, the Catalans, deserted by Castile, applied to Louis XI, to see if he could be induced to abandon his alliance with the king of Aragon and aid them to win their independence. At first the French king held out the highest hopes to the ambassadors, but his deeds belied his words; and it was not long before the emissaries became firmly convinced that he cared nothing whatsoever for their liberties, and that the real object of his policy was to unite Catalonia to his own domains.[1] The farce of continuing the negotiations was kept up through the remainder of the year, owing to the reluctance of both parties to come to any definite decision; but all real hope of an accommodation had vanished long before. Meantime another power had become involved in the struggle, through the action of the Catalans in offering their sovereignty to Dom Pedro, the Constable of Portugal, whose maternal grandfather had been one of the unsuccessful candidates for the Aragonese throne after the death of King Martin in 1410. This prince arrived in Barcelona on January 22, 1464; but he was feeble and ineffective to the last degree, and under his unhappy tutelage the cause of the revolutionists went from bad to worse till his death on June 29, 1466.[2] With the story of the Constable's misfortunes we are not particularly concerned, but the episode of his inter-

[1] Calmette, pp. 203–232.   [2] Calmette, pp. 236–264.

vention had an important bearing on the relations of Aragon and Castile. The resentment which the sovereigns of these two states had cherished against one another for many years past had visibly cooled since Louis XI's attempt to arbitrate between them in 1463. Many of their mutual grudges had been forgotten in the heat of their common anger against the arbitrator, and now the process of rapprochement between the two Spanish courts, which the French king had unwittingly initiated, was still further advanced by this affair of Dom Pedro. It was of the utmost importance to John that Henry should bear no aid to the new sovereign of the rebel Catalans; if on the other hand the king of Aragon could induce the king of Castile definitely to abandon the Constable, it would be a long step towards ruining the entente between the Castilian and Portuguese courts, whose recent progress had so greatly worried John. On June 9, 1464, the king of Aragon gained his end by the signature at Pamplona of a treaty with the king of Castile, in which the two monarchs promised one another mutual aid against their respective enemies. Castilian support of the Constable, which had been more than possible a few months before, was henceforth out of the question.[1] To be sure, the king of Aragon was not yet certain enough of the loyalty or power of Henry the Impotent to trust his fortunes exclusively to him; and he had by no means abandoned his own intrigues with the malcontents in Castile. Indeed, at the very moment that he was negotiating for the treaty of Pamplona, he was in active relations with the Pachecos;[2] the double game was ever dear to the heart of John II. But, for all that, the signature of the treaty of Pamplona was an interesting evidence of the real tendency of the times, though contemporaries do not seem to have comprehended

[1] Calmette, p. 253, note 1.   [2] *Ante*, pp. 11 ff., and Calmette, pp. 293 f.

its meaning.   It was a milestone on the road to the marriage of Ferdinand and Isabella.

Fresh complications ensued on the death of the Constable of Portugal in 1466, when the Catalans offered their sovereignty to a new protector — René the Good of Anjou and Provence — of whom they expected better things.[1] Though too old himself to embark upon such a perilous venture, this 'titular sovereign of half a dozen empires'[2] had a son, the gallant John of Calabria, whom he could send to the Catalans as his representative.   Though he did not actually possess a rood of the land that he claimed in Sicily, Italy, and Jerusalem, he was solidly established in his French dominions, and his tenure of Provence, which had so many historical and commercial connections with Catalonia, rendered him a particularly valuable ally for the revolutionists.   He was also descended, through his mother, Violante, from the old line of the counts of Barcelona, and was therefore not without hereditary claims;[3] while, on the other hand, he was the head of a family that had been the consistent opponent of the house of Aragon in Sicily and the Mediterranean since the time of the Sicilian Vespers, and had himself fought with Alfonso the Magnanimous over the succession in Naples.[4]   Finally the new candidate received after some little delay a promise of support and coöperation from his nephew, King Louis of France, who had begun to realize that he could never hope to attain his ends in Catalonia through alliance with John, and therefore quite characteristically had determined to reverse his policy; the Italian ambitions of the French king also combined at this juncture to induce him to favor the new pretender.[5]   Indeed, René's acceptance of the sovereignty of

[1] Lecoy de la Marche, *Le Roi René*, i, pp. 366–379.
[2] Prescott, i, p. 141.
[3] Calmette, p. 265.
[4] Cf. Vol. I, pp. 419, 422.
[5] Calmette, pp. 271–274.

Catalonia and its results may be regarded as a link in the chain that binds the Angevin-Aragonese struggle of the two preceding centuries to the Franco-Spanish wars of the succeeding age. It fills the gap between the triumph of Alfonso the Magnanimous and the raid of Charles VIII.

The Catalan question, in fact, was rapidly becoming a European one, in which all the various powers were to take sides either for or against the king of Aragon. The Angevin military occupation of the county, which began in the spring of 1467, was checked, though not wholly prevented, through the skill and intrepidity of Joanna Enriquez and of the Infante Ferdinand, who received in this campaign his baptism of fire;[1] but the military events are of far less consequence for our purposes than the diplomatic ones. Here, as may be imagined, it was the old king of Aragon who took the lead; and though he was terribly hampered by his blindness,[2] and weakened in the winter of 1468 by the death of his valorous wife, his efforts were extraordinarily success-ful. At the crisis of his political fortunes, he was found at his very best. His object was to draw near to any and every power which could possibly be made an enemy of France and Anjou, and his agents all over Europe were busy in effecting this end. In Italy he managed to win the support of the duke of Milan — the more important because Louis had counted the Sforza as an ally of his own.[3] He also approached Charles the Bold of Burgundy and Edward IV of England.[4] But unquestionably his most brilliant victory was won in the kingdom of Castile. He had keenly ob-served the course of events in that realm since the signature

---

[1] Calmette, pp. 275–283; Lecoy de la Marche, *Le Roi René*, i, pp. 374–378.

[2] It was at its worst in this period. An operation for cataract was success-fully performed by a Jewish doctor, named Caixcas Abiabar, in September, 1468. Cf. Calmette, p. 296, note 4.

[3] Calmette, pp. 287–289.

[4] Calmette, pp. 290 f.

of the treaty of Pamplona in June, 1464 : the triumph of the rebels and the humiliation of the king of Ávila in 1465, the subsequent waverings of the policy of the crown and the project of the marriage of the Infanta Isabella to the grand master of Calatrava, the second battle of Olmedo, the sudden death of the Infante Alfonso, and finally the reconciliation of Toros de Guisando ; so rapidly did fortune change between the conflicting factions that the king of Aragon must have been exceedingly thankful that he had kept in touch with both sides. Still it would obviously be preferable for him if possible to gain his ends in alliance with the *de jure* power in Castile, rather than in opposition to it ; and whatever the internal state of the western kingdom, the course of its foreign policy in the last two years had been such as to give John of Aragon good reason to hope much from the attitude of Henry the Impotent. Two features of the situation were especially encouraging. The first was the Castilian king's refusal to ratify the treaty with Portugal which his queen had drawn up in 1465 and which provided for the marriage of the Princess Isabella to Affonso the African.[1] The second was his conclusion, in the summer of 1467, of an alliance with Edward IV of England, which marked the definite breach of the traditional entente between Castile and France.[2] Indeed, it is by no means fantastic to suppose that the king of Aragon may have contributed to both these results, though we have no positive evidence of it. And now, with the death of Alfonso and the subsequent recognition of the Princess Isabella as the lawful successor to her brother's throne, the time had come for vigorous and decisive action. The acknowledged heiress of Castile could not in the nature of

[1] Cf. *ante*, p. 14.
[2] Daumet, *Étude sur l'alliance de la France et de la Castille*, pp. 109 f., and Calmette, p. 294, who misdates the treaty September 1 ; it should be July 1.

things remain unwedded long. If her marriage to the Infante Ferdinand — the cornerstone of the whole policy of John II — was ever to be realized, there was not a moment to be lost.

The king of Aragon and his son did not even wait for the news of the interview at Toros de Guisando to make overtures for Isabella's hand; an ambassador was despatched to Castile carrying the formal proposals for it in July, 1468, as soon as the death of Prince Alfonso was known.[1] Isabella, who was fully alive to the political advantages of the match, and had received most favorable reports of Ferdinand's personal charms, accepted at once, and the marriage treaty was drawn up and duly signed in January, 1469.[2] But serious opposition both abroad and at home remained to be encountered and overcome before the union of the royal pair could be actually accomplished. Louis XI of France, aroused too late to a realization of the results of his neglect of Castilian affairs, made haste in the spring of 1469 to despatch to Henry's court a special ambassador, Jean Jouffroi, bishop of Albi, charged with the double duty of revamping the old Franco-Castilian alliance at the expense of the more recent Anglo-Castilian one, and of offering Louis's brother, the Duke of Guienne, as an alternative candidate for Isabella's hand. In the first of these errands the bishop was successful, owing to the vacillations of Henry IV; but in the second and more important one he utterly failed, despite several interviews with the Infanta herself.[3] The marriage which was to unite the Spanish realms was thus accomplished in the teeth of the displeasure and opposition of the king of France; but it had also been greatly facili-

[1] Sitges, p. 194.
[2] Sitges, p. 196. Ferdinand had been raised by his father to the dignity of king of Sicily on June 18, 1468, very likely with a view to the Castilian match. Zurita, iv, ff. 156–157.
[3] Daumet, op. cit., pp. 110 f.; Sitges, pp. 192 f.; Calmette, pp. 295 f.

tated by the mistakes of Louis's whole Spanish policy in earlier years; so that the Catholic Kings came to the throne with a tradition of hostility to France behind them, which was to bear terrible fruit in the succeeding age.

But John and Ferdinand had other things that worried them far more, for the time being, than the abortive opposition of the king of France. Chief of these was the hostility which the prospect of Isabella's marriage aroused in Castile. No sooner were the intentions of the princess known, than the majority of the grandees, foreseeing the end of their independence if the monarchy was suffered to become too strong, forgot the reconciliation of Toros de Guisando, and prepared to espouse the cause of La Beltraneja. Nay more, with the aid of the treacherous Marquis of Villena, they won over the fickle king to support them, and still further strengthened their hands by reviving the project of earlier years, that the Princess Isabella should be wedded to Affonso of Portugal.[1] This last plan was wrecked on the firm refusal of the Infanta to entertain it; moreover a considerable number of the grandees, among whom the most prominent was the archbishop of Toledo, rallied to her side, while the popular sympathy for her cause was manifested on every hand in no uncertain tone. Still, her situation in the spring of 1469 was critical in the extreme. She held her court, virtually unprotected and alone, at first at Ocaña, near Toledo, and afterwards at Madrigal, south of Valladolid. She was being constantly spied upon by her numerous foes, and was subject at a moment's notice to capture and imprisonment. In the end of August, while her brother and the Marquis of Villena were on a progress in Andalusia, they directed the archbishop of Seville to march with sufficient forces to her residence and seize her; but the plan was

[1] Sitges, pp. 189 f.; Zurita, iv, ff. 161–162.

frustrated by the energy of her friend the primate, who was never found wanting if a battle of any kind was to be fought, and succeeded in carrying her off in triumph to the friendly shelter of Valladolid.[1]

Nothing, however, could permanently secure the Infanta's safety so effectively as the speedy completion of her marriage. Envoys were therefore despatched to Aragon to urge Ferdinand to come and claim his bride. As John, in the throes of his struggle with the rebels in Catalonia, was utterly unable to furnish his son with a military force sufficient to cope with his foes, the Infante was obliged to undertake the perilous journey with only a few attendants, disguised as merchants, and at night; not until he reached Burgo de Osma did he receive the protection of the partisans of his betrothed, and it was later still before he was able to throw off all concealment. In the evening of the fifteenth of October he reached Valladolid and held his first interview with the princess; and on the nineteenth, at the private residence of Juan de Vivero, they were married. So great was the poverty of bride and groom that they were apparently obliged to borrow money to pay the expenses of their wedding and of the simple ceremonies which followed it; and the contemporary chroniclers, who usually wax eloquent in their descriptions of such events, are almost silent about the whole affair. But no outward pomp or circumstance could possibly have added lustre to the union which created the mightiest nation of the sixteenth century and laid the foundation for one of the two greatest empires of modern times. The real celebration of the marriage of Ferdinand and Isabella was the glorious epoch in Spanish annals which it introduced.[2]

[1] Sitges, p. 197.
[2] Palencia, ii, pp. 281–285; Prescott, i, pp. 188–193; Calmette, p. 297; Sitges, pp. 198–205.

The characters of the monarchs whose wedding had been solemnized under such unusual circumstances have been so often and so fully described[1] that it is difficult to add anything more; but as the period of their reign was that in which above all others the personalities of kings determined the policy and prestige of kingdoms, it is impossible to pass over the subject in silence. The contemporary chroniclers are absurdly loud in their praises of both sovereigns, particularly of Isabella; and even some of the modern historians have not entirely avoided exaggeration. Piety, dignity, inflexible determination and high courage, both moral and physical, were the outstanding virtues of the queen; intolerance and excessive fondness for pomp and display her most obvious faults. Her main aim in life was to reduce her kingdom to internal peace, order, and union, and to level all barriers and distinctions under the throne; and for the accomplishment of that mighty task her character and abilities preëminently fitted her. No less heroic a figure could possibly have humbled the rebel baronage, or invested the administration of justice with the majesty which should be inseparable from the law. Her husband, on the other hand, was essentially cosmopolitan in his talents and qualities — as distinctively the product of the land whose main attention had been directly to foreign affairs, as was Isabella of a country which had been chiefly occupied at home. Cautious, calculating, and persistent; parsimonious, though to good purpose, like his contemporary Henry VII of England;[2] he never acted impulsively, never struck unless he was well able to follow

---

[1] Notably by Clemencin, in *Memorias de la R. A. H.*, vi, pp. 1–54; by Prescott, iii, pp. 173–194, 369–382; and by Lea, *Inquisition of Spain*, i, pp. 20–24.

[2] " Il Re di Spagna presente, se fusse tenuto liberale, non arebbe fatto nè vinto tante imprese." Machiavelli, *Il Principe*, cap. xvi.

up the blow. Deficient in frankness, generosity, and other qualities which win men's affections, he was on the whole less highly esteemed than was the queen, and was not unnaturally detested by the victims of his political triumphs; but the real man, as revealed by his correspondence, steadily improves on closer acquaintance. Diplomacy was unquestionably his forte; and as the diplomacy of the time consisted chiefly in lying, we need not wonder that Machiavelli held him up as a model for princes in his skill at "playing the fox." [1] Ferdinand himself was quite aware of his abilities in this regard and gloried in them. It is said that on learning that Louis XII of France had complained that he had deceived him for the second time, he promptly replied, "He lies, it's the tenth." Other subsidiary merits and defects of the royal pair will be indicated in the succeeding pages; for the present we need only remark that the above mentioned qualities in each formed the most complete and perfect counterpart of those of the other. Ferdinand and Isabella supplemented one another at every point; where the one was weak, the other was strong, and vice versa. Between them they possessed talents which would make it possible for their united realms to follow up each and all of the multifarious paths of activity that opened before them on every side. At the most critical stage of her development, Spain was thus enabled to pursue all the national objects which had previously animated her component parts, and to assume many fresh burdens besides.

[1] Machiavelli, *Il Principe*, cap. xviii.

BIBLIOGRAPHICAL NOTE

See notes at the end of Chapters II and IX in Volume I, and add :

Contemporary Authorities. — *Memorias de Don Enrique IV de Castilla*, vol. ii, ed. R. A. H. (printed in 1835–37, but not published till 1913), contains a valuable collection of documents. The first volume, which will comprise a new edition of the chronicles of Palencia and Castillo, has not yet appeared. *Levantamiento y guerra de Cataluña en tiempo de Don Juan II*, ed. Prospero de Bofarull y Mascaro and Manuel de Bofaruli y de Sartorio (in *D. I. A.*, vols. xiv–xxvi : Barcelona, 1858–64), is the most important collection of documents on the subject with which it deals. The *Crónica de Juan II* (Logroño, 1517; Seville, 1543; Pamplona, 1591; Valencia, 1779; and Madrid, in *B. A. E.*, vol. lxviii, pp. 277–695, 1877) and the *Crónica de D. Álvaro de Luna* (ed. J. M. de Flores, Madrid, 1784) are fundamental for the history of Castile in the first half of the fifteenth century. Alonso de Palencia, *Crónica de Enrique IV* (Spanish translation by Antonio Paz y Melia in the *Colección de Escritores Castellanos*, Madrid, 1904–09, 5 vols.), and Diego Enríquez del Castillo, *Crónica del Rey Don Enrique el Cuarto* (ed. Flores, Madrid, 1787, and also in *B. A. E.*, vol. lxx, pp. 99–222, Madrid, 1878), are the standard authorities on that reign; on these two writers cf. Prescott, i, pp. 216–218; Sitges, pp. 14–19. Diego de Valera, *Memorial de diversas Hazañas* (in *B. A. E.*, lxx, pp. 3–95, Madrid, 1878), and Hernan Pérez del Pulgar, *Claros Varones de España* (Madrid, 1775, 1789, etc.), give a number of interesting details.

Later Works. — Diego Clemencin, *Elógio de la Reina Católica Doña Isabel* (*Memorias de la R. A. H.*, vol. vi, Madrid, 1821), is a valuable series of essays on different phases of Isabella's government, with a useful appendix of documents. W. H. Prescott, *History of the Reign of Ferdinand and Isabella* (4th edition, London, 1846, 3 vols.), was first put forth in 1837, and is still the standard history of the period. J. B. Sitges, *Enrique IV y la Excelente Señora* (Madrid, 1912), is a scientific study, based on the sources, with a valuable critical bibliography. Joseph Calmette, *Louis XI, Jean II, et la révolution catalane (1461–1473)* (Toulouse, 1903), is an indispensable work by a recognized master of the period, with full references and a list of authorities. Antonio Rodríguez Villa, *Bosquejo biográfico de Don Beltran de la Cueva* (Madrid, 1881), and Henri Courteault, *Gaston IV, Comte de Foix* (Toulouse, 1895), are both sound biographical studies, which bear indirectly on the field covered in this chapter. Fernando Ruano Prieto's more recent *Don Juan II de Aragón y el Príncipe de*

Viana (Bilbao 1897) adds little to *Don Carlos d'Aragon* by Georges Desdevises du Dezert (cf. Calmette, p. 32, note). The lives of Álvaro de Luna by M. J. Quintana (in *Vidas de los Españoles Celebres*, Madrid, 1879, 2 vols., ii, pp. 1–194), by Juan Rizzo y Ramirez (Madrid, 1865), and by León de Corral (Valladolid, 1915), are also useful.

CHAPTER XIII

THE STRUGGLE FOR THE THRONES AND THE CONQUEST OF GRANADA

THE union of the Spanish kingdoms, which was the ultimate object of the policy of John of Aragon, was far from being fully accomplished by the marriage of Ferdinand and Isabella. The best possible start had already been made; but there was still much more to be done before the future sovereigns could call their thrones their own. Castile had to be pacified and united, the power of the factions abased, and that of the monarchy exalted. Hostile France and Portugal had to be dealt with, and their recognition won. The Catalan insurrection had to be put down, and the kingdom of Granada conquered from the Moors. The narrative side of the story of these events will occupy us in the present chapter; the social and constitutional aspects will be treated in the two succeeding ones.

The news of the marriage of Ferdinand and Isabella was most displeasing to Henry IV; while Louis XI of France, who had awakened too late to the true state of affairs in Spain, could not at first believe that his tardy efforts to prevent it had been unsuccessful.[1] The two kings were naturally drawn close together by their common enmity to the newly wedded pair, and speedily prepared to join forces against them. Within a year of the marriage of his sister, the Castilian sovereign, in flagrant defiance of the pact of Toros de Guisando, made oath to the legitimacy of La

[1] Sitges, p. 194.

Beltraneja, once more acknowledged her as lawful heiress
of his throne, and finally caused her to be married by proxy
to Louis's brother, the Duke of Guienne, who shortly before
had been suing for the hand of the Princess Isabella.[1] This
combination, supported as it was by a large number of the
Castilian grandees, boded ill for the cause of Ferdinand and
his bride; but there were two serious weaknesses in it
which ultimately effected its ruin.   In the first place, it was
largely the work of Louis XI, a foreign monarch, and if it
attained its ends, it was bound to carry the sovereignty of
Castile across the Pyrenees. This fact naturally elicited
vigorous opposition among those whose patriotism was not
entirely subordinated to their desires for personal aggrandizement; and it is highly significant that as soon as the
news of it was made public, the inhabitants of the northwestern provinces — the traditional cradle of Spanish independence — went over to support the cause of Ferdinand
and Isabella.[2] Secondly, and even more important, the
entente cordiale between Louis and his brother, which underlay the entire scheme, was only temporary.   In less than a
year after his proxy marriage, the Duke of Guienne had
applied to the Pope for dispensation alike from the oath of
fidelity which he had made to the king of France and from
his union with his Spanish bride.[3] He was already negotiating with Charles the Bold of Burgundy, in whom he discerned
a far more powerful ally than the Impotent King of Castile.
In the autumn of 1471, he had even gone so far as to apply
for the hand of Charles's daughter, Mary. But before he
could make much progress with this new plan he died, on
May 25, 1472.[4] His removal served to relieve Louis XI from
serious embarrassments at home, but it also terminated the

[1] Sitges, pp. 207–228.
[2] Prescott, i, p. 197.
[3] *Lettres de Louis XI*, ed. Société de
l'Histoire de France, iv, pp. 265,
306.
[4] Sitges, p. 228.

project of French interference in Castile, of which his marriage with La Beltraneja had been the corner stone. If the French king continued to desire to breed trouble for Ferdinand and Isabella in Spain, he would have to find other methods.

Meantime in Castile everything was in turmoil and confusion. Ferdinand and Isabella held their little court at Dueñas, but were so destitute of resources that they were unable to take arms against their foes. In fact, down to the death of Henry the Impotent, they did everything, short of renouncing their rights to the succession, in order to maintain friendly relations with him.[1] But the king would not abandon La Beltraneja, nor desist from his efforts to find a husband for her. After the summer of 1471, when the match with Guienne had become practically out of the question, he dallied with schemes for wedding her to Frederic, the son of Ferrante of Naples; to Henry of Aragon, a nephew of John II; and finally to Affonso the African of Portugal.[2] None of these projects was realized — at least not in Henry's day — but the negotiations for them, and the fact that there was no prospect of a permanent reconciliation between Henry and his sister, served to keep the realm in an uproar during the last three years of the Impotent King. Andalusia was devastated by the bloody feuds of the Ponce de Leons and the Guzmans.[3] All the highways in the realm were infested with robbers and thieves; even the *hermandades* seemed temporarily powerless.[4] Late in the year 1473, Henry and Isabella held an interview at Segovia, during which they manifested every evidence of outward friendship and cordiality. At Epiphany, 1474,

[1] Prescott, i, pp. 197–201. In 1473, moreover, Ferdinand was summoned to Catalonia to help his father against the revolutionists there.

[2] Sitges, pp. 229–231.
[3] Bernáldez, caps. iii, iv.
[4] J. Puyol y Alonso, *Las Hermandades*, pp. 89–90.

Ferdinand was also received by the king of Castile, and in the succeeding months there were other meetings. Still, no understanding was apparently reached on the crucial question of the succession to the throne, and "since many things which it were perilous to set down were alleged concerning each party, it was impossible to make peace between them."[1] Finally, on December 11, 1474, King Henry died in his palace at Madrid. A careful comparison of the statements of contemporary chroniclers and of the documents bearing on the case points to the probability that he left no formal or written will; but it seems clear that he declared verbally on his deathbed that he recognized La Beltraneja as his daughter and as lawful heiress of his throne. There can be little doubt that she was the legal successor. She was unquestionably the daughter of the queen of Castile, born in the royal palace; and the allegations of her foes in regard to her paternity were never definitely proved. Finally, she had been formally acknowledged and sworn to by the Castilian Cortes as the heiress of the realm, and had been recognized as such by King Henry.[2]

But if the strict letter of the law was on the side of La Beltraneja, expediency and the political interests of the kingdoms of Spain dictated the recognition of Isabella, who was solemnly crowned queen of Castile in Segovia two days after her brother's death.[3] She already represented, in fact, the nascent idea of Iberian unity, and the principle of freedom from foreign intervention. It was for these reasons, rather than because of any legal argument which she advanced in

[1] Sitges, pp. 245-247; Enríquez del Castillo, *Crónica*, cap. clxiv (*B. A. E.*, lxx, p. 218).
[2] Sitges, pp. 8, 129 f., 248-254; Prescott, i, pp. 213-215. The latter (i, p. 220) says that the acknowledgment by the Cortes of La Beltraneja's right to the succession was reversed by that body's subsequent recognition of Isabella at Ocaña, but Sitges (p. 190) rightly points out that this statement rests solely on a protestation of Isabella in 1471, the veracity of which it is permissible to doubt.
[3] Sitges, p. 253.

support of her claims, that the majority of patriotic Castilians rallied loyally to her standard. Many of the nobles, also, began to waver in their allegiance to La Beltraneja, and sought reconciliation with Isabella. The prospect of her strong rule was probably no more palatable to them than before, but they had begun to discern that the ultimate victory would probably rest with her, and they did not care to be found in the ranks of her foes. Among them were the Duke of Albuquerque, reputed father of La Beltraneja, and the powerful house of Mendoza; even the treacherous Marquis of Villena apparently made secret overtures to the queen at this period, though the parties were unable to come to any definite agreement. On the other hand, the archbishop of Toledo, angered at a slight at the hands of Ferdinand, deserted the cause of his spouse, declaring that 'as he had released her from spinsterhood, so he would send her back to the distaff again.' [1] As long as this sort of sentiment was rife in the realm, Isabella could not be said to hold the throne of Castile. And the forces of the opposition were the more to be reckoned with, because they were to receive ardent support at the critical moment from King Affonso the African of Portugal.

This impetuous monarch, as we have already seen, had previously entertained high hopes of winning the Castilian succession by marrying either Isabella or her niece, La Beltraneja. As soon as the news of Henry IV's death reached him, he prepared to return to the charge. In early January, 1475, he had resolved to gather his forces, invade Castile, and, after wedding La Beltraneja, to incorporate it in his own dominions.[2] On the eighth of that month he wrote to solicit the aid of Louis XI of France, who, after considerable delay and tentative negotiations with the other

[1] Sitges, pp. 264–266, 277.   [2] Sitges, p. 267.

side, agreed in September to support him.   Meantime, during the early days of May, Affonso entered Castile with a small but efficient army, joined forces with the Marquis of Villena, was solemnly affianced to La Beltraneja, and was recognized with her by their adherents as lawful sovereign of the realm.[1] But the Portuguese monarch was as unaccountably dilatory in substantiating his claims to the Castilian throne as he had previously been precipitate in advancing them.   At the moment of his invasion, Ferdinand and Isabella were totally unprepared to resist him.   Had he struck at once, before they had had an opportunity to collect their forces, he might possibly have compassed their defeat.   But instead he waited idly for reënforcements from his Castilian confederates, and thus afforded his rivals a precious respite, which they well knew how to utilize. Proposals for a settlement of their differences by personal combat between Affonso and Ferdinand, and also for peace on the basis of the cession to the former of Galicia, Toro, Zamora, and a large money indemnity were exchanged, but ended in nothing;[2] and in the meantime, by superhuman exertions, Ferdinand and Isabella recruited every available soldier from those portions of the realm which remained loyal to them.[3] Finally Ferdinand made a move to capture the town of Zamora on the Douro, so as to cut his enemy's communications, and thus brought Affonso to bay;   the Portuguese monarch, who had recently received considerable reënforcements under his son, was obliged to accept battle on March 1, 1476, on a wide plain to the east of the city of Toro.[4] It was "a noble combat of the ancient sort," as one of the Portuguese historians remarks with satisfaction, "for in spite of the presence of artillery and gunpowder,

---

[1] Sitges, pp. 267 f.; Bernáldez, caps. xvii, xviii, xix.
[2] Sitges, pp. 302 f.
[3] Prescott, i, pp. 230–235.
[4] Sitges, pp. 305 f.

destined to revolutionize the art of war," it was decided for
the most part by hand-to-hand conflicts with swords, "making the whole a contest rather of physical strength than of
skill." Night and a deluge of rain put an end to the fighting,
and the Portuguese writers are fond of pointing out that as
Affonso's son remained in possession of the battleground
till the following morning the conflict can scarcely be regarded as a defeat for his side.[1] But if the forces of Ferdinand and Isabella were denied the glory of a complete victory
in the field, they certainly succeeded in gathering all the
fruits of it. The military and political prestige of their
rival was shattered beyond repair. Zamora surrendered on
March 19; in June Affonso retired with La Beltraneja to
Portugal, and the remnants of his army were soon dispersed.
On the other hand, Ferdinand and Isabella did everything
in their power to make all men believe that they had won
an overwhelming victory. Processions and thanksgiving
services were ordered in the chief towns of the realm. The
captured standard of Affonso V was solemnly laid on the
tomb of John I of Castile, in reparation for the great defeat
of Aljubarrota ninety-one years before. The convent
church of San Juan de los Reyes at Toledo was founded to
commemorate their triumph.[2]

But the fiery king of Portugal was unwilling to desist from
his Castilian project without one more attempt to retrieve
his fortunes. French aid, as he now clearly realized, was
more than ever indispensable to success; and with the
object of securing it, he repaired in the summer of 1476 by
way of Ceuta and the Mediterranean Sea to the court of
Louis XI.[3] But in the meantime that crafty monarch had

[1] Antonio de Lebrija, decad. i, lib.
v, cap. vii; Prescott, i, pp. 235–244;
Oliveira Martins and other writers,
cited in Sitges, pp. 306–312, especially

Sousa Viterbo, *A Batalha de Touro*
(1900).
[2] Sitges, p. 312.
[3] Ruy de Pina, *Chronica d' El-Rei D.*

taken the measure of Affonso's incompetence. His own troops, sent to the succor of his Portuguese ally, had failed to make any impression in the north of Castile. He had begun to realize that he stood little chance of successfully opposing Ferdinand and Isabella, and that he had better make haste to treat with them.[1] He therefore put off the requests of Affonso with various excuses, and soon after permitted him to visit the court of his rival. Charles the Bold, ostensibly for the purpose of mediating between Burgundy and France. Charles, who was Affonso's cousin, did not take long to convince him of the faithlessness of Louis; and on January 21, 1477, the Portuguese monarch was back again at Paris, where he received news of the Burgundian duke's defeat and death in the battle of Nancy sixteen days before.[2] For some months more he hung about the French court, wasting his time in fruitless negotiations for a papal bull of dispensation for his marriage to La Beltraneja; when at last he was roused to a sense of the ridiculous and humiliating situation in which he had placed himself, he suddenly resolved to resign the throne of Portugal in favor of his son, and end his days in a monastery in Jerusalem.[3] But the protests of his friends and of the king of France prevented the execution of this project; in the autumn of 1477 the unhappy monarch returned to his own dominions, where his son, who had already assumed the crown, made haste to relinquish it in his favor.[4] Once more Affonso prepared to try his fortunes by the sword. He collected his forces, notified the king of France of his intentions, and in the early

Affonso V, caps. cxcii–cciii; Damião de Goes, Chronica do Príncipe D. João, cap. lxxxix; Sitges, p. 314.

[1] Pulgar, Crónica de los Reyes Católicos, pt. ii, caps. liii, liv (B. A. E., lxx, p. 306).

[2] Sitges, p. 315. On the relations of Ferdinand and Charles the Bold at this juncture, cf. J. Calmette in B. H., vii, pp. 34–37.

[3] Sitges, pp. 315 f.; Pulgar, Crónica, pt. ii, cap. lxxxv (B. A. E., lxx, p. 341).

[4] Sitges, pp. 316–320.

months of 1479 again invaded Castile. But his chances of success, slight three years before, had by this time dwindled to nothing. Ferdinand and Isabella had already begun to reorganize their kingdom. They had received the submission of the majority of the rebel nobles. A treaty with Louis XI, though not yet actually signed, was inevitable in the near future.[1] The only battle of the ensuing campaign was fought near Albuera, February 28, 1479; before hostilities could proceed any further, negotiations for a settlement had begun between Isabella and Affonso's sister-in-law, the Infanta Beatrice of Portugal. In the following September, two treaties, reiterating and confirming the ancient peaces, were concluded by the accredited representatives of both kingdoms.[2] One of them further provided for a mutual restoration of conquests along the Castilian-Portuguese border; since, however, its main interest for us lies in its stipulations with regard to the Canaries and the west coast of Africa, it may be most conveniently reserved for consideration in another place.[3] The other, which more immediately concerns us, dealt directly with the dynastic question. It decreed that Affonso should abandon the title of king of Castile, and Ferdinand and Isabella that of sovereigns of Portugal; that the king and queen of Castile should pardon and restore to their estates such of their subjects as had supported the Portuguese in the recent war; that their daughter Isabella should wed Affonso, the little grandson of the king of Portugal, to cement the union and concord between the two realms; and, finally, that La Beltraneja should either be married to John, the infant son of Ferdinand and Isabella, or else take the veil.[4]

---

[1] Sitges, pp. 321–332.
[2] Balaguer, *Reyes Católicos*, vol. i, pp. 391–419, *passim*; Fernández Duro, *Marina de Castilla*, p. 262.

[3] Cf. *infra*, pp. 173 f.
[4] Ruy de Pina, *Chronica*, caps. ccvi, ccvii, ccix; Pulgar, pt. ii, cap. xci (*B. A. E.*, lxx, pp. 347 f.). The text of

That unfortunate lady was not long in choosing between the alternatives which had been set before her.
Thoroughly tired of being the sport of factions, she entered
the convent of Santa Clara de Coimbra, with the full
approval, if not at the positive exhortation, of Ferdinand
and Isabella; and the wretched king of Portugal, equally
weary of the cares of state, was only prevented from retiring to a monastery by his death at Cintra, August 28, 1481.[1]
Seldom, if ever, has a royal career so gloriously begun had a
more utterly farcical termination.

Thus was the union of Aragon and Castile consummated,
as it were, in the teeth of the opposition of Portugal. Accident rather than design was responsible for the way things
had worked out. Geographically and historically, as we
have already seen, Portugal possessed many more ties with
Castile than did the eastern kingdoms, at least down to the
accession of the house of Trastamara to the thrones of the
realms of Aragon; and linguistically, when we remember
that Catalan, Valencian, and Italian, rather than Spanish,
were spoken in the bulk of the Aragonese dominions, she
was scarcely further apart from Castile than were they
Throughout the later Middle Ages Castile had sought
alliances with the royal house of Portugal quite as often
as with that of Aragon, and it was largely by alternative
plans of union with Portugal that the enemies of Ferdinand
and Isabella attempted to subvert the ends for which their
marriage stood. That Castile turned eastward rather than
westward when the decisive moment came, was a fact of
the gravest import for her future career. Had she united
with Portugal rather than Aragon, she would probably
have avoided entanglement in all the weary European

the treaty is printed in Sitges, pp. 409–
463.

[1] Ruy de Pina, *Chronica*, cap. ccxii;
Prescott, i, p. 251; Sitges, p. 335.

wars and diplomacy which issued out of the struggle over the Neapolitan inheritance. She might well have been able to devote herself exclusively to the upbuilding of a great imperial domain on the Atlantic. She might have avoided that multiplicity of conflicting interests, powers, and responsibilities, which, though it doubtless served to enhance her prestige for a time, proved ultimately to be a potent cause of her decline. To speculate on what might have been is proverbially idle; but in the light of our present knowledge it certainly seems that the union of Castile and Aragon, though attended for the time being by most brilliant results, was ultimately productive of effects far less beneficent than would have followed a union of Castile and Portugal. There can be no question that it diverted both parties to the bargain from their normal and traditional lines of development. It forced Castile into Mediterranean politics and Aragon into expansion in the New World; and the final result of it was to create an organism so vast, so complicated, and so cumbersome, that it was literally impossible that it should endure.

We have purposely forborne to carry to a conclusion the story of the relations of Ferdinand and Isabella with Louis XI of France, because it can be more conveniently finished in connection with the affairs of Aragon and Catalonia, to which we now turn.

We left the old king of Aragon in 1469, at the time of Ferdinand's marriage, in the midst of a military and diplomatic duel with the Angevin suzerains of the rebels in Catalonia. Encouraged by the brilliant success of his Castilian policy, John continued throughout the year 1470 to spin his anti-French intrigues with the Italian states, and to wage desultory warfare with his foes in his own dominions and in Navarre. Finally, on December 16, he had a stroke of good fortune in the sudden death of John of Calabria, the idolized leader of the revolutionists.[1] A triple alliance which John managed to conclude on November 1, 1471, with Ferrante of Naples and Charles the Bold of Burgundy against Louis XI of France, served as an excellent guarantee against the latter's ability to lend aid to the Angevins for a further prosecution of their designs on Catalonia. It also enabled the king of Aragon, who had hitherto been obliged to stand upon the defensive, to take vigorous measures to crush the revolutionists.[2] Throughout the first part of the year 1472 the Catalans continued to hope; but the promises of old René of Anjou availed nothing without the support of the French king, who was by this time convinced that an Angevin occupation of Catalonia would bring him no nearer the realization of his own ends there, and consequently sought rather to oppose it.[3] The refusal of Galeazzo Maria Sforza to permit the Genoese fleet to revictual Barcelona in September, 1472, when the city was besieged by the forces of the king of Aragon, bore witness to the efficiency of the latter's Italian diplomacy, and sealed the fate of the revolutionists. On October 17 John entered his capital in triumph. With a moderation, rare in those days, which does high honor to his political sagacity, the victorious monarch forbore to take vengeance on his rebel subjects; he confirmed all their privileges and assured them of his good will. He thereby obliterated many of the bitter memories of earlier days, and laid the foundations for the restoration of cordial relations between the inhabitants of the county and the throne.[4]

---

[1] Calmette, pp. 300–315; Lecoy de la Marche, *Le Roi René*, i, p. 378.
[2] Calmette, p. 319.
[3] Calmette, pp. 334–337; Lecoy de la Marche, *Le Roi René*, i, pp. 378–383.
[4] Calmette, pp. 337–347.

There remained the difficult problem of the border counties of Cerdagne and Roussillon, which the armies of Louis XI had occupied in 1462, and which the French king had declared, in defiance of the treaty of Bayonne, to be permanently incorporated in his dominions. John was all on fire to reconquer them. The French maladministration of the counties made their inhabitants long for a return to the obedience of the king of Aragon, and constant plots were hatched, with his connivance, for the overthrow of the existing régime. In February, 1473, John was able to enter the town of Perpignan and inspire the inhabitants with his own indomitable courage; and when, two months later, a French army arrived to besiege it, the vigor of its resistance and the fear of the effects of the obviously cordial relations between Charles the Bold and the king of Aragon convinced Louis of the advisability of coming to terms. On September 17, by the peace of Perpignan, John II had the extreme satisfaction of forcing his ancient rival to agree to an arrangement which practically reiterated the provisions of the treaty of Bayonne. One slight modification was this time introduced by the king of Aragon, in the vain hope that it would insure the observance of the pact which Louis had violated ten years before. Pending the payment of his debt — now estimated at 300,000 écus — to the king of France, John insisted that the counties should be administered, not as before by Louis, but by a governor-general selected by the latter from a list of ten proposed by himself. It was as notable a triumph for the diplomacy of the king of Aragon as it was a signal humiliation for the sovereign of France, but it was not destined to be permanent.[1] Notwithstanding all his efforts, John was unable to raise money for the deliverance of the counties; and mean-

[1] Calmette, pp. 358–378.

time a temporary cessation of Louis's difficulties at home enabled the French king to send another army of invasion into the disputed territories, with instructions to "lay waste the land until not a fruit tree remained standing." The inhabitants made a desperate resistance, and Roussillon got the name of the 'graveyard of the French,' but it was all in vain. Perpignan fell on March 10, 1475, and Louis promptly installed his representatives in both counties, with instructions to pillage and plunder indiscriminately, which they were sensible enough to disobey.[1] Had the king of Aragon not been so old and feeble, or had Ferdinand not been so exclusively occupied with the vindication of his rights in Castile, the French king would probably have been expelled at once. As things fell out, the liberation of Cerdagne and Roussillon was bequeathed by King John to his son as a sacred duty, and when at last the opportunity came, we shall see that the latter did not fail to take advantage of it.

Thenceforth the scene of the diplomatic struggle between John and Louis shifts from Aragon to Castile, and Ferdinand begins to replace his father as the protagonist on the Spanish side. Louis's certainty that neither the king of Aragon nor his son would ever permanently acquiesce in the loss of Cerdagne and Roussillon was doubtless an important element in causing him to ally himself with Affonso of Portugal, when that monarch attempted to secure the Castilian succession; and thus the Franco-Aragonese quarrel of the past began to be transformed into the Franco-Spanish struggle of the future. But there was to be one more lull before the final bursting of the storm. The Burgundian troubles, experience of the inefficiency of the Portuguese king, and the traditional friendship of France

[1] Zurita, iv; ff. 205–211, 218–219, 227–229.

and Castile, all combined to persuade Louis XI that, for the time being at least, a policy of peace with the Spanish sovereigns promised better things than a continuation of war. Ferdinand and Isabella, whose hands were more than full with the regulation of affairs in the peninsula, were quite ready to go halfway to meet him.   On October 9, 1478,[1] accordingly, a treaty between the representatives of the two nations was signed at Saint Jean de Luz, in which four previous pacts between France and Castile were formally renewed, and each monarch definitely renounced his alliances with the enemies of the other.   Among the leagues abandoned by Ferdinand and Isabella in this treaty were specially mentioned "all confederations, compacts, and fraternities begun and completed in whatsoever way and with whatsoever signatures, promises, expectations, oaths, and forms of words, either generally or specifically expressed, with Maximilian, duke of Austria, and his wife, or their eldest son."   The "confederations . . . begun and completed" between the Catholic Kings and Maximilian and his wife, to which these words refer, were doubtless the outcome of a series of negotiations which had been in progress between the two courts in 1477 and 1478.   Since Maximilian's wife was Mary, the daughter of Charles the Bold of Burgundy, it was but natural that Ferdinand should seek his alliance, as the obvious way to keep alive the ancient friendship which had previously united his father with that most inveterate of the foes of Louis XI.   The king of England, the duke of Brittany, and the Swiss were also involved in these negotiations, and though we lack precise information in regard to their scope, we may be sure that the shrewd Zurita was not mistaken in thinking that they

---

[1] Not (as Daumet, p. 123, and C. Petit-Dutaillis, in Lavisse, *Histoire de France*, iv, 2, p. 394, have it) on November 9.   The text of the treaty may be found in Jacques Bernard's *Recueil des Traitez*, i, pp. 668, 684.

were based on the fact that 'all these powers were destined
of necessity to be perpetual enemies of the house of
France.' [1] What was meant by the reference to a possible
understanding with Maximilian's "eldest son" is much
more difficult to conjecture. As the Archduke Philip was
only born on July 22, 1478, it seems scarcely possible that
any alliance for him in the family of the Spanish sovereigns
could have been contemplated as early as this, though the
hand of their eldest daughter Isabella (born October, 1470)
was, at this juncture, still free.[2] Still it is certainly worth
noting that the union of the Spanish realms not only was
accomplished in the face of the enmity of the king of
France, but also was apparently in a measure supported
in its earliest years by some sort of an understanding with
the house of Austria. The whole framework of the diplomatic combinations of the succeeding age was fore-
shadowed with startling accuracy at this early date.

The treaty of Saint Jean de Luz wisely left the thorny
question of Cerdagne and Roussillon untouched, and John
of Aragon was included in the general peace. On January
20, 1479, the old king died at Barcelona, in the eighty-
third year of his age; and was succeeded by his son Ferdinand in all his dominions save Navarre, which by the
terms of the treaty of Olite passed to his daughter Eleanor,
the wife of Gaston de Foix. In some of his most cherished
projects he had met defeat; Navarre had escaped him at
the last; at the moment of his death Cerdagne and Roussillon were in the hands of Louis of France; but the mar-

[1] Zurita, iv, ff. 280–281; also J.
Pérez de Guzmán y Gallo, *Dogmas de la
Política de Fernando V el Católico*, p. 21.

[2] Joanna, the second daughter and
third child of Ferdinand and Isabella,
who ultimately married Philip, was
born November 6, 1479; her older

brother John, who became the husband
of Philip's sister Margaret, on June 30,
1478. Is it possible that the negotiations of 1477–78 had contemplated
marriages between children of the two
dynasties as yet unborn?

riage of Ferdinand and Isabella, for which he was primarily responsible, was a triumph beside which his failures shrink into insignificance. The unification of Spain, with all its tremendous consequences, is the contribution of John of Aragon to the history of Europe.

No more fitting celebration of the union of the Spanish kingdoms could have been imagined than that they should jointly proceed to the completion of the great work of the Reconquest, and round out their dominions by the final expulsion of the Moors from the peninsula.

Since the battle on the Salado in the reign of Alfonso XI, the Christians had scored but three important victories against the forces of the kings of Granada. A great battle had been won by the armies of John II at Sierra Elvira, close to Granada, in 1431 ;[1] in 1410 and in 1462 the town of Antequera and the Rock of Gibraltar had been captured.[2] During the latter part of the reign of Henry IV and the first five years of that of Ferdinand and Isabella the internal troubles of the realm effectually prevented any renewal of attacks against the Moorish strongholds. When in 1476 the queen sent to demand payment of the annual tribute due from the king of Granada, the latter evinced his contempt of his Christian overlords by the famous answer, that the mints of his realm "coined no longer gold, but steel."[3] Their Catholic Majesties were still too busy with

[1] Sometimes called the battle of Higueruela: *Crónica de Juan II*, año de 1431, caps. xix–xxi (*B. A. E.*, lxviii, pp. 497–500).

[2] See Vol. I, pp. 130 f. The taking of Gibraltar did not at first promise much advantage to the nation as a whole, for it had been accomplished chiefly through the efforts of the heads of the rival houses of Guzman and Ponce de Leon, whose quarrels were such a pro-

lific source of anarchy during the reign of Henry IV. Moreover the Guzmans, whose ancestor had effected the first capture of the fortress from the infidel in 1309, regarded the Rock as an appanage of their family and could not be induced permanently to surrender it to the Castilian crown till 1502. I. López de Ayala, *Historia de Gibraltar*, pp. 176–210 ; also Palencia, *Crónica*, i, pp. 366–370.

[3] Prescott, i, p. 381.

other cares to heed this insolent reply, and their failure
promptly to chastise their haughty vassal encouraged
him in 1481 to surprise the Christian fortress of Zahara on
the confines of the province of Cadiz. But by this time
the Christians were in better condition to retaliate. The
War of Succession with Portugal had been triumphantly
terminated. John of Aragon was dead, and Ferdinand was
in full possession of his hereditary domains. A report that
the important fortress of Alhama, on a rocky peak in the
vega just southwest of Granada, was inadequately garri-
soned and negligently guarded, led to the despatch of Rodrigo Ponce de Leon, the fiery Marquis of Cadiz,[1] in February, 1482, on a desperate attempt to seize it unawares.
The expedition, which demanded quite as much proficiency
in rock climbing as in fighting, was extremely hazardous
but completely successful; and the subsequent efforts of
the Moors to retake the place were beaten off. From that
moment the campaign against Granada ceased to be a mere
series of forays, and assumed the character of a regular,
methodically conducted war. The sovereigns took it up
vigorously, with the idea of ending once and for all the
Moorish hold on the peninsula. The Emir, reading the
signs of the times, solicited aid from the Merinites across
the Strait, but Isabella checkmated this move by sending
a Castilian fleet to cruise in the adjacent waters, and to
cut off all communication with the African coast.[2]

And now, just at the moment when the Moors of Granada needed all their forces to withstand the Christian attack, they were seriously weakened at home by dynastic

[1] On the career of this man see J.
Durán y Lerchundi, *La Toma de Granada y Caballeros que concurrieron á ella*,
i, pp. 141–205.

[2] Prescott, i, pp. 381–401, and references there to Bernáldez, Pulgar, and
other contemporary writers; W. Irving,
Conquest of Granada (New York, 1852),
chaps. iv–viii; Mercier, ii, p. 410.

quarrels of the typical Mohammedan sort. Jealousies in the harem of the Emir, Abul Hassan, were the source of it; the famous massacre of the Cordovan family of the Abencerrages in the Alhambra and the imprisonment of the queen and her son, Boabdil, were its first results. But the captives contrived to escape from their confinement and to enlist the sympathies of the Granadinos; after a series of bloody feuds the old Emir was expelled, and forced to seek refuge at the court of his brother in Malaga.[1] The latter's energy and bravery had won him the title of *El Zagal* or 'the Valiant,' and his prestige reached its climax in the spring of 1483 by his brilliant victory over an expedition which the indefatigable Marquis of Cadiz had led into the neighboring territories.[2] But the ultimate result of the triumph of El Zagal was distinctly unfavorable to the Moorish cause. It inspired his nephew, Boabdil, to attempt to emulate his exploits; but *El Rey Chico*, as the Spaniards called him, was proverbially unlucky in everything that he undertook, and instead of eclipsing his uncle's victory, as he had hoped, he was speedily defeated and captured by the Castilian Count of Cabra.[3] A vigorous debate ensued among the Christian leaders as to the most profitable way to make use of the prize which fortune had placed in their hands; but the final verdict was that Boabdil should be released and sent back to his own dominions, on terms which bound him hand and foot to the cause of Ferdinand and Isabella, and which consequently insured the vigorous continuance of the internal quarrels in Granada.[4] Boabdil did not refuse these degrading conditions. He sneaked back into his

[1] Irving, chapters iii, ix; Mercier, ii, pp. 410 f.; L. de Egúilaz y Yánguas, *Reseña Histórica de la Conquista de Granada según los Cronistas Árabes*, pp. 1–15.

[2] Prescott, i, pp. 419–430, and references there.
[3] Durán y Lerchundi, i, pp. 343–379.
[4] Prescott, i, pp. 433–439, and references there.

capital,[1] where El Zagal had meantime succeeded in establishing himself; though he failed to gain admittance to the Alhambra and the upper town, he soon gathered his adherents on the banks of the Darro and the Xenil, and waged a murderous war upon his rivals. In the midst of the confusion, the old king, Abul Hassan, disappeared, not improbably a victim of foul play.[2]

While revolt and sedition were thus rife in the Moorish camp, the Christian army presented a spectacle of enthusiastic unity and devotion such as Spain had seldom, if ever, witnessed before. A number of different causes contributed to this happy result. In the first place every effort was used to make men feel that it was a national Spanish enterprise — the first of its kind — made possible by the marriage of Ferdinand and Isabella, and not an affair of merely local import. As the kingdom of Granada nowhere touched the realms of the Crown of Aragon, Castile alone could hope to benefit territorially by its reconquest; nevertheless Ferdinand was fully as active in the prosecution of the war as was the queen, whose services, though undoubtedly extraordinary, have probably been somewhat exaggerated in the gallant phrases of the contemporary chroniclers. And as the best possible method of stimulating the spirit of unity so essential to success, the sovereigns did their utmost to instil into their troops the conviction that the war was rather religious than political in its aims. They strove their hardest to awaken the old crusading ardor, which had been dormant for long periods in the past,

[1] Not, however, in 1483, as the older historians have it: his captivity lasted till 1485 or possibly 1486: cf. M. G. Remiro, *Ultimos Pactos entre los Reyes Católicos y Boabdil* (Granada, 1910), p. 7, and five articles by the same author on "Documentos Árabes de la Corte de Granada," in *R. A.* for 1909 and 1910, 3d ser., xxi, pp. 330–339; xxii, pp. 260–269, 421–431; xxiii, pp. 137–148, 411–423; Eguílaz y Yánguas, *op. cit.*, pp. 18–22.

[2] Prescott, i, p. 461; Mercier, ii, p. 411.

but which, when thoroughly roused, had shown itself capable of working wonders, as in the campaigns of Las Navas and the Salado. During the year 1486, in the very midst of the struggle, the king and queen made a solemn pilgrimage to the shrine of Santiago de Compostela.[1] A huge silver cross, the gift of Pope Sixtus IV, was carried in Ferdinand's tent throughout the campaign; it was invariably raised by the royal standard bearer on the topmost pinnacle of each conquered town and adored with impressive ceremonies by the assembled hosts.[2] Finally, the constant presence of Ferdinand and Isabella in the midst of their advancing armies was a tremendous asset for the cause. It was the surest possible way of keeping the factious nobles from deserting, of maintaining order and discipline in the ranks, of convincing the soldiers that there was no duty they were called upon to perform in which their sovereigns were too proud to bear a part.[3] And the enthusiasm which the enterprise kindled in Spain extended before long to other lands as well. Volunteers and adventurers, many of them of noble birth, flocked to the Christian standards from Germany, France, and England, longing to have a share in the glorious triumph which all felt certain was soon to be won. Prominent among them was a brother-in-law of the Yorkist king Edward IV, by name Sir Edward Woodville, who was apparently not ashamed, as a means of impressing the Spaniards with a sense of his dignity and importance, temporarily to appropriate the title of Lord Scales.[4] These foreigners brought back to their

[1] Galíndez Carbajal, *Anales Breves*, año 1486 (*D. I. E.*, xviii, p. 272).

[2] Prescott, i, p. 459.

[3] Machiavelli, *Il Principe*, cap. xxi; Lea, i, p. 21.

[4] Martyr, *Opus Epistolarum*, lib. i, ep. lxii. There is a brief study of the career of Woodville by the present writer in the *Proceedings of the American Antiquarian Society* for October, 1904. The title of Lord Scales really belonged to Woodville's elder brother Anthony, in right of his wife, Elizabeth, daughter and heiress of Thomas, seventh Baron Scales.

native lands glowing tales of the power of Ferdinand and Isabella; indeed, the reputation which the sovereigns won in Europe through the Granadan war was no small element in accounting for the extraordinarily rapid rise of Spanish prestige in the immediately succeeding years. On the other hand, the Spaniards learned much from their visitors, at the same time that they contrived to impress them. Particularly was this true of a body of Swiss mercenaries who joined the royal standard, and doubtless furnished Gonsalvo de Cordova and Gonzalo de Ayora with many of the ideas which subsequently enabled them to produce the terrible Spanish infantry of the Italian wars.[1]

Two or three outstanding features of the military side of the campaign deserve passing notice; for the Granadan war really forms the introduction to the period of the most brilliant development of the Spanish arms. The forces assembled were apparently very large — according to one doubtless exaggerated contemporary estimate, the grand total reached 80,000 [2] — but the method of their recruitment remained predominantly feudal.[3] The sovereigns saw the difficulty and set themselves to remedy it. Some progress was made toward the formation of a national force by utilizing the troops of the *hermandad*, which had recently been re-created as a royal institution. The above mentioned Swiss mercenaries were also valuable as a nucleus for an army of the modern sort. The mediaeval methods, however, were much too firmly planted to be eradicated at once, and the sovereigns were obliged to wait until after the conclusion of the war for the full completion of their plans of army reorganization. On the other hand, a number of important changes in the methods of fighting were

[1] Clemencin, in *Memorias de la R. A. H.*, vi, pp. 186–191; Prescott, i, pp. 451 f.; Clonard, *Historia Orgánica de las Armas Españolas*, ii, cap. v.
[2] Cited in Prescott, i, p. 447.
[3] Mariéjol, pp. 195–199.

effected before Granada fell. The exceedingly rocky and mountainous character of the greater part of the territory in which the Moorish capital lay rendered it most unfavorable for cavalry. The struggle was bound to be primarily a war of sieges, in which infantry and still more artillery would have to play the principal part. Consequently we find the Christians making strenuous efforts to increase the number and efficiency of their cannon. Engineers and mechanics were summoned from within and without the realm. Numerous pieces of extraordinary weight and still more extraordinary clumsiness were constructed. It was apparently impossible to alter the direction of their aim, either vertically or horizontally, without moving the gun carriages to which they were firmly attached; and infinite labor was necessary to prepare roads for them through the mountain passes. They fired huge balls of stone and iron; the latter were sometimes heated almost to the molten stage, thus producing the effect of a sort of liquid fire. Yet despite their extreme unwieldiness, these rudimentary cannon accomplished their ends. Fortress after fortress which would have defied assault, was battered down by their projectiles.[1] Systematic forays meantime devastated the adjacent vegas, while the Castilian fleet continued to patrol the Mediterranean; and the success of these methods of starvation may be judged by the fact that the Moors soon began to offer to liberate Christian prisoners in return for supplies, until such exchanges were sternly forbidden by Ferdinand and Isabella.[2] Generous terms were usually granted to the inhabitants of conquered towns, but any subsequent infraction of them by either party was sure to be speedily punished — in case of the Christians by vigorous pen-

[1] Clemencin, in *Memorias de la R. A. H.*, vi, pp. 167-176; Prescott, i, pp. 442-444; Mariéjol, pp. 204-209.
[2] Prescott, i, pp. 440-442.

alties, in case of the Moors by sanguinary executions and destruction.[1] The solicitude of the queen for the physical welfare of her troops forms one of the pleasantest chapters of the whole story. She was busily engaged in forwarding provisions from the great base at Cordova. She did her utmost to find surgeons and medical supplies. She even established and equipped at her own expense a large number of special tents for the care of the wounded. It is the earliest recorded case of anything resembling a modern field hospital.[2]

The year 1484 was marked by no important event, but in 1485–86 the Christian lines were drawn considerably tighter around the Moorish capital. The western outpost of Ronda, perched on the summit of a precipitous cliff, succumbed to the artillery of the Marquis of Cadiz. Wedges were driven into the heart of the infidel realm by the capture of Loja and Illora, and the fall of Marbella on the Mediterranean coast afforded an invaluable base of operations for the blockading Castilian fleet.[3] In 1487 everything was concentrated on the siege of Malaga, the largest of the outward defences of the kingdom of Granada, and, with the exception of Almeria, its only remaining seaport of importance. An indispensable preliminary was the capture of Velez, situated on the road from Malaga to Granada ; and in April Ferdinand crossed the Sierras with a large army and finally sat down before its walls. El Zagal sallied forth from Granada in a desperate effort to relieve it, but was unsuccessful ; moreover his treacherous nephew seized the opportunity to make himself supreme within the capital, which shut its gates on El Zagal when he attempted to return thither after his failure, and finally obliged him to seek

[1] Prescott, i, pp. 445 f. [3] Irving, caps. xl, xli ; Prescott, i, pp.
[2] Clonard, ii, p. 86 ; Clemencin, pp.   462 f.
177 f.

refuge in the eastern cities of Guadix, Baza, and Almeria, the only portions of the realm which remained loyal to him.[1] Meantime Velez surrendered, and the blockade of Malaga began. It was a long and arduous undertaking. The garrison was largely composed of African troops, who had more stomach for fighting than the Spanish Moors; the fortifications were very strong, and high hopes were entertained of relief from the Barbary coast. But the vigilance of the Castilian fleet prevented that, while the wretched Boabdil attacked and cut to pieces a rescuing party despatched by his uncle, El Zagal; on the other hand the arrival of Queen Isabella in the camp of the besiegers redoubled their enthusiasm, and imbued them with a chivalrous resolve to do or die for the cause.[2] Sudden assaults by the Christians and sorties by their foes varied the monotony of the blockade; but the crucial event of the entire siege was the effort of a Moorish fanatic, who had gained access to the royal tent on the plea that he was inspired with the gift of prophecy, to assassinate the king and queen. Happily the attempt failed, but the news that the lives of their sovereigns had been imperilled served to rouse the loyalty and ardor of the Christians to the highest pitch.[3] Everything was got ready for a grand assault, which, however, was delayed for a brief period owing to Isabella's desire to save bloodshed; meantime the spectacle of the besiegers' preparations, coupled with the terrible dearth of provisions within the town, convinced the defenders that there was no alternative to an acknowledgment of defeat. After a fruitless effort to extort lenient conditions from Ferdinand by a threat of massacring the five or six hundred Christian captives in the dungeons of Malaga, the inhabitants surrendered at discretion. Whether owing to the fact that the

[1] Prescott, ii, pp. 11–14.   [2] Prescott, ii, pp. 14–21.   [3] Prescott, ii, pp. 23–25.

garrison was largely composed of African troops, or to some other cause, does not appear; but it is certain that the terms which Ferdinand imposed on the conquered town form a most disagreeable contrast to those granted to the places which he had captured before. The whole population was virtually condemned to slavery. One third was transported to North Africa to be exchanged for Christian captives there detained; another was appropriated by the state as payment for the expenses of the campaign; the rest were distributed among the nobles, the Pope, and the sovereigns of friendly lands. One hundred warriors were incorporated into the papal guard and converted, before the year was out, into "very good Christians"; fifty beautiful damsels were presented to the queen of Naples, and thirty to the queen of Portugal. Such was the perhaps not entirely unmerited revenge for the hosts of Christian maidens, seized in Spain during the previous seven centuries and despatched across the dreary wastes of Northern Africa to supply the harems of the Orient.[1]

The fall of Malaga rendered that of Granada ultimately inevitable. But Ferdinand and Isabella were resolved to take no chances, and in order to make assurance doubly sure, directed all their energies during the years 1488 and 1489 to the reduction of that eastern extremity of the Moorish territories which acknowledged the sway of El Zagal. In 1488 Ferdinand advanced along the coast to attack Almeria, only to be beaten off with heavy loss by his crafty opponent. In 1489 the Christians centred their efforts on the siege of Baza with better success. The town finally surrendered, after prolonged resistance, at the very end of the year. As Boabdil did nothing to help his uncle, the latter recognized the necessity of admitting defeat.

---

[1] Prescott, ii, pp. 25–39; Mercier, ii, p. 412.

Negotiations and a personal interview with Ferdinand followed, and finally ended in an arrangement by which the Moorish king surrendered to the Christians all the principal fortresses of the realm, including Guadix and Almeria, and received in return the sovereignty of the small district southwest of Malaga, to be held by him as a vassal of the king of Castile. But El Zagal was much too proud to be permanently satisfied with so shadowy a vestige of royalty. He soon disposed of his new dominions to the king and queen of Castile in return for a money indemnity, and passed over to Africa, where, stripped of everything by the savage Berbers, he ended his days in misery and solitude.[1] He was by far the ablest figure on the Moorish side of this last great contest of Cross and Crescent in the peninsula, and assuredly deserved a better fate.

Meantime the unhappy Boabdil, whose treachery was only equalled by his ineptitude, seized the moment of his uncle's defeat to renounce the obligations to the king and queen of Castile which he had contracted at the time of his capture, and hurled defiance at Ferdinand and Isabella. In the spring of 1490 the Christian armies camped on the broad vega beneath Granada.[2] The troops were in splendid condition; everything combined to make them certain of victory, and yet they did not underestimate the difficulties of the crowning task. With a full realization that time was indispensable to success, and a permanent fortified base on the vega the best guarantee for the maintenance of a rigid blockade, they constructed, during the winter of 1490–91, a new town in the wide plain, six miles to the west of Granada, and significantly named it Santa Fé. It was laid out in the form of a Roman camp, with regular streets crossing each other at right angles — "the only city in

[1] Prescott, ii, pp. 44–66; Mercier, ii, p. 412.   [2] Remiro, *Ultimos Pactos*, p. 15.

Spain that has never been contaminated by the Moslem heresy"; it was destined to be the scene of the capitulation of Granada, and of the signing of the contract with Columbus which led to the discovery of a New World.[1] The sight of such a formidable establishment was profoundly discouraging to the beleaguered Moors. It proved to them that their foes would never cease from their efforts until their object had been triumphantly accomplished; and in October, 1491, negotiations for the surrender of Granada were begun, Hernando de Zafra, the royal secretary, and Gonsalvo de Cordova being entrusted with the conduct of them on the Christian side.[2] After long conferences the terms were finally settled on the twenty-fifth of the following November; they were exceedingly liberal — the sharpest possible contrast to the vengeance that had been visited upon Malaga. The city was to be surrendered within sixty days, and the artillery and fortifications given up. The Moors, however, were to be permitted to retain unmolested their customs, dress, property, laws, and religion; they were to continue to be ruled by their own local magistrates, under the supervision of a governor appointed by the Castilian crown. They were carefully guarded against extortionate taxes, and they were to be furnished transportation to North Africa in case they desired to emigrate. The conditions, indeed, were in general such as did high honor to the magnanimity and generosity of the victors, and rendered the subsequent violation of them the more shameful.[3] The actual surrender took place with impressive ceremonies on January 2, 1492. Pradilla's great painting [4] accurately

[1] Prescott, ii, pp. 82 f.; Balaguer, ii, pp. 349 f.

[2] Pulgar, *Breve Parte de las hazañas del Gran Capitán*, in N.B.A.E., x, p. 577. On the details of these negotiations.

see Remiro, *Ultimos Pactos*, pp. 27 ff.

[3] Text in D. I. E., viii, pp. 411–436; Prescott, ii, pp. 84–86; Lea, *Moriscos of Spain*, pp. 20 f.

[4] Now in the Senado at Madrid.

depicts the scene as the contemporary chroniclers have described it — the stately courtesy of Ferdinand and Isabella, the timorous hesitancy of the vanquished Boabdil.

" Here passed away the Koran; there in the Cross was borne;
And here was heard the Christian bell; and there the Moorish horn." [1]

It was indeed a glorious victory, won at a critical moment, and stained by few acts of treachery and cruelty.   It had evoked all that was best in the character of the Spaniard. It showed that under the inspiration of a Holy War, hallowed by nearly eight centuries of national tradition, he could rise superior to petty local aims and ambitions, and was capable of really great things.   It served, as perhaps nothing else could have done, to win enthusiastic support for the throne of Ferdinand and Isabella, by identifying their rule at the very outset with the advancement of the Faith, and with the successful completion of the national task.   But there is grave danger in regarding the conquest of Granada merely as marking the end of an epoch.   In many ways it was not so much an end as a beginning.   We have already observed that no sharp dividing line can be drawn between reconquest and conquest; the two merge into one another and form a continuous whole.   Attempts had been made to secure a footing in North Africa for centuries before Granada fell; and a year after its surrender Ferdinand and Isabella despatched a certain Lorenzo de Padilla, governor of Alcalá, in disguise to the Barbary coast, to gather information which should be valuable to them in the event of their carrying their arms across the Strait. [2]   Clearly the Catholic Kings had already made up their minds to pursue the Crescent beyond the borders of Spain.   More-

---

[1] Lockhart's *Spanish Ballads*.
[2] Lorenzo de Padilla, *Crónica de Felipe I*, cap. v, in *D. I. E.*, viii, p. 16: clearly the envoy was a relative (possibly the father) of the chronicler, who was born about 1485.   Cf. also C. X. de Sandoval in *Revue Africaine*, quinzième année (1871), p. 177.

over, it so happened that in the midst of all these exciting events a very persistent Italian mariner, whom many men thought to be half mad, but whom the sovereigns believed in and supported, came back from a long voyage of discovery into the West, with marvellous tales of new lands to conquer beyond the seas. Everything combined to beckon the new monarchs forward and onward at this crucial stage in their career. Certainly it was no time for them to rest on their laurels.

But internal reforms of the most drastic and far reaching sort were the indispensable preliminary to foreign conquest. They had indeed been largely accomplished during the period of the Granadan war, and we must study them carefully before turning to the story of Spain's new career of expansion beyond the seas.

BIBLIOGRAPHICAL NOTE

See the bibliographical note at the end of the preceding chapter, and add:

Sources and Contemporary Authorities. — *Lettres de Louis XI*, edd. Joseph Vaesen and Étienne Charavay for the Société de l'Histoire de France (Paris, 1883–1909, 11 vols.). Hernando del Pulgar, *Crónica de los Señores Reyes Católicos* (Saragossa, 1567; Valencia, 1780; also in *B. A. E.*, vol. lxx, pp. 225–511, Madrid, 1878), and Andrés Bernáldez (El Cura de los Palacios), *Historia de los Reyes Católicos* (published by the Sociedad de Bibliófilos Andaluces, Seville, 1870, 2 vols.; also in *B.A. E.*, lxx, pp. 567–773, Madrid, 1878), are the two standard contemporary accounts of the reign of Ferdinand and Isabella. Pulgar unfortunately stops in 1492; Bernáldez goes down to 1513: the latter is especially valuable on the events of Andalusia (e.g., the Granadan war). For further information on these two men cf. Prescott, i, p. 464; ii, pp. 98 f.; Fueter, *Historiographie*, pp. 280–282. Pulgar also wrote, probably about 1526, a *Breve Parte de las hazañas del excelente nombrado Gran Capitán*, which was republished in 1908 by A. Rodríguez Villa in the *N. B. A. E.*, x, pp. 555–589; it deals chiefly with the story of the siege of Granada. Peter Martyr d'Anghiera, *Opus Epistolarum* (Alcalá de Henares, 1530; Amsterdam, 1670), is a history of the years 1488–1525 in the form of letters. Antonio de Lebrija (Nebrissensis), *Rerum a Fernando et Elisabe Regibus gestarum Decades II* (Granada, 1545; Frankfort, 1603, in Schott, vol. i, pp. 789–905), is largely based on Pulgar, but goes only to 1485. Lucius Marineus Siculus, *De Rebus Hispaniae Memorabilibus* (Alcalá, 1532; Frankfurt, 1603, in Schott, vol. i, pp. 291–517), is diffuse and unreliable. Lorenzo Galíndez Carbajal, *Anales Breves* (in *D. I. E.*, vol. xviii, pp. 227–421, Madrid, 1851, and in *B. A. E.*, vol. lxx, pp. 533–565, Madrid, 1878), covers very briefly the years 1468–1518. On these last three authors and their work cf. Antonio, *Bibliotheca Hispana Nova*, vol. ii, pp. 3 f.; Prescott, i, pp. 465 f.; ii, pp. 68–70; and Fueter, pp. 285–288; numerous references to them will be found in the footnotes to Prescott as cited in the text. The most important Portuguese chroniclers of the period are Ruy de Pina, *Chronica d'El-Rei D. Affonso V*, published in vols. xxix–xxxi of the *Biblioteca de Classicos Portuguezes* (Lisbon, 1901–02), and Damião de Goes, *Chronica do Príncipe Dom João* (first edition, 1567, latest, by A. J. Gonçalvez Guimarãis, in 1905), which goes only to the death of Affonso the African. On these cf. Sitges, *Enrique IV y la Excelente Señora*, pp. 28 f.

Later Works. — Víctor Balaguer, *Los Reyes Católicos*, in the *Historia General de España* (Madrid, 1894–98, 2 vols.), goes only to the fall of Granada; it is based almost entirely on Pulgar, and is very prolix. J. Pérez de Guzmán y Gallo, *Dogmas de la Política de Fernando V el Católico* (Madrid, 1906: Discurso de la R. A. H.), is a brief but valuable essay, with a useful bibliographical appendix. On the siege of Granada, see Washington Irving's *Chronicle of the Conquest of Granada* (first edition, London, 1829, 2 vols.), a literary rather than an historical work (the Fray Antonio Agapida, on whose manuscript the author states that it is based, is a totally fictitious personage); Joaquín Durán y Lerchundi, *La Toma de Granada y Caballeros que concurrieron á ella* (Madrid, 1893, 2 vols.), principally a series of biographies, with appendices of printed documents; Leopoldo de Eguílaz y Yánguas, *Reseña Histórica de la Conquista del Reino de Granada según los Cronistas Árabes* (second edition, Granada, 1894), useful; and M. G. Remiro, *Ultimos Pactos y Correspondencia íntima entre los Reyes Católicos y Boabdil* (Granada, 1910), a valuable study, which corrects a number of errors, and emphasizes the importance of the diplomatic negotiations which accompanied the military operations.

CHAPTER XIV

ABSOLUTISM VERSUS SEPARATISM. UNITY OF FAITH AND RACE

STRIKING similarities have often been noted in the internal development of the three great states of Western Europe during the fifteenth century. In each a period of unparalleled anarchy and confusion was followed by the erection of a strong central monarchical government, capable alike of defying the factions at home and of taking the lead in campaigns of aggression and conquest abroad. To the terrible strife of the Armagnacs and Burgundians in France, correspond the Wars of the Roses in England, and the wretched disorders which characterized the reigns of John II and Henry the Impotent of Castile. The efficient royal despotism which emerged in France under Charles VII and Louis XI has its English counterpart in the reign of the first king of the house of Tudor, and its Spanish in the rule of Ferdinand and Isabella. Of the three states, France was on the whole the first in point of time to achieve national consolidation; the Spanish realms came second, and England third. How far the last two profited from the experience of the first; how much actual institutional borrowing occurred between them, is a vastly interesting subject, about which much has been surmised, though little definitely proven; but we cannot enter into it here.[1] All that it is

[1] Useful suggestions on this topic may be gleaned from F. W. Maitland, *English Law and the Renaissance* (Cambridge, 1901), *passim*; W. Busch, *England under the Tudors*, tr. Todd (London, 1895), pp. 266–274, especially pp.

important for us to remember in the present connection is that the great work of national unification which the Catholic Kings performed was thoroughly in harmony with the highest aims and aspirations of the most enlightened statesmen of their day and generation in other European lands. Royal despotism was the form of government best suited to the stage of development which had been attained in the fifteenth century. It offered the sole sure means of escape from the intolerable evils of baronial anarchy. Order had to be reëstablished before constitutional liberties could be observed.

The foregoing paragraph will have made clear that many of the problems with which Ferdinand and Isabella were confronted, when at last they were able to call their thrones their own, were almost precisely identical with those which had already been dealt with by the kings of France, and were subsequently to be attacked by the kings of England. Such, for example, were the domination of the rebel baronage, the reëstablishment of the royal finances, and the reorganization of the administration of justice; and in the solution of each of these problems we shall encounter many resemblances between the methods of the Catholic Kings and those of their French and English contemporaries. But there were at least two special questions with which Ferdinand and Isabella were obliged to deal, which were emphatically *cosas de España* — peculiar to the Iberian Peninsula and absolutely without parallel north of the Pyrenees; in answering these two special questions the Spanish kings had

272 and 274, notes; J. A. Brutails, ed., *Documents des Archives de la Chambre des Comptes de Navarre* (Paris, 1890), *passim*; and H. Pirenne, "The Formation and Constitution of the Burgundian State," in *American Historical Review*, xiv (1909), pp. 477–502. A study, previously noted, by R. Altamira, called "Magna Carta and Spanish Mediaeval Jurisprudence," in *Magna Carta Commemoration Essays*, ed. H. E. Malden (1917), pp. 227–243, deals with the legal side of the same subject in an earlier period.

no foreign precedents to guide them. Both were of such fundamental importance for the future of the Iberian realms and of the Spanish Empire that no apology is needed for a thorough consideration of them at the outset. The first arose out of the fact that Christian Spain contained at least four separate states — Castile, Aragon, Catalonia, and Valencia — each with an independent set of institutions, which it would be difficult, if not impossible, to weld into a single homogeneous whole, even though the dynasties that ruled over them had been united by a fortunate marriage. The second was the direct result of the large measure of racial and religious toleration which had pervaded the Iberian realms during the greater part of the Middle Ages, and which had revealed itself again in the very liberal terms of the capitulation of Granada in 1491 — namely, the existence of numerous and important Jewish and Moorish communities within the realm, whose presence was a most emphatic negation of the fundamental principle of unity on which the rule of the Catholic Kings was to be built up.

One of the surest proofs of real statesmanship is the ability to distinguish what is possible to accomplish from what is not. A completely united Spain, ruled under a single set of institutions and a single crown, would doubtless have been more in consonance with the ideas of political centralization prevalent at the time, than the maintenance of the system of separate and autonomous kingdoms which had been inherited from the Middle Ages. But with all their enthusiasm for strong central government, it is by no means certain that Ferdinand and Isabella really desired to see the process of unification proceed as far as this. They themselves inherited the separatistic traditions of their race, and despite the fact that the current was flowing strongly in the opposite direction, they were not improbably anxious, in some degree at least, to maintain them. In any case, whatever their personal desires and predilections may have been, they must have realized from the very first that any complete fusion of Castile and the realms of the Crown of Aragon was, for the time being, outside the sphere of practical politics. The largely fortuitous union of the thrones through their marriage was no indication that the institutions of their respective realms could be made to follow suit. Dualism, in fact, was inevitable from the very first. The only question was how to work out the details.

The principal source of information in regard to these is the marriage treaty, which was drawn up and signed by the high contracting parties in January, 1469, nine months before the celebration of their wedding.[1] It is principally made up of a series of limitations imposed upon the authority of Ferdinand in Castile; there was no need under the circumstances to emphasize the corresponding restrictions of the rights of Isabella in the realms of the Crown of Aragon. Ferdinand promised to respect all the laws and customs of the western kingdom, both local and national; all the separate institutions of the different realms whose crowns were to be united were thus maintained in their pristine vigor. All appointments in Castile, whether political, ecclesiastical, or military, were to be made in accordance with the queen's desires, and her consent was necessary for the preferment of any foreigner within the realm. No portion of the domain of the Crown of Castile was to be alienated unless Isabella gave her permission; no grant or favor was to be bestowed there save by her. In deference to the greater size and importance of the western kingdon, Ferdinand promised to fix his residence there, and not to depart

---

[1] Printed in Clemencin, pp. 579–583; Balaguer, *Reyes Católicos*, i, pp. 187– 192; and elsewhere. Cf. also Zurita, iv, ff. 162–164.

thence without the queen's consent. He also pledged
himself to the prosecution of the national Castilian task,
the reconquest of the entire peninsula from the Moors. As
a final evidence of his acquiescence in these arrangements,
and also, perhaps, of the completeness of the understanding
between the royal pair in other matters as well, it was
stipulated that all laws, ordinances, treaties, and other
documents of a public character should bear the signatures
of both.

Whether Ferdinand had ever intended loyally to abide
by these arrangements may well be doubted. There is
strong reason to believe that from the very beginning he had
cherished hopes of quietly setting aside the terms of the
marriage treaty, and of demanding independent authority
for himself in the western kingdom. Certainly the words
in which the herald proclaimed the accession of the new
sovereigns in Segovia after the death of Henry IV in 1474
were highly displeasing to him: "Castile, Castile," sounded
the cry, "for King Don Ferdinand and his consort, Doña
Isabella, Queen Proprietress of these realms." [1] With the
idea of making one last effort to assert himself, Ferdinand
now came forward with the claim that as great-grandson
of John I of Castile he was in his own right lawful sovereign
of that kingdom, and that females were excluded from the
succession; but the law of the land was clearly against him
here, and his attempt to override the provisions of the
marriage treaty simply led to a reconfirmation of them

[1] Galíndez Carbajal, in *D. I. E.*,
xviii, p. 255; Lucius Marineus Siculus,
De Rebus Hispaniae Memorabilibus, in
Schott, i, p. 470.

[2] It is said that Ferdinand was so
incensed at the failure of his efforts,
that he threatened to retire to Aragon.
The queen, however, managed to dissuade him at the last moment by pointing out that unless her own independent

rights were fully recognized in Castile
a dangerous precedent would be created
for carrying the sovereignty of Spain
out of the peninsula, in case the Infanta
Isabella — the only child who up to
that time had been born to the royal
pair — should marry a foreign prince.
Lucius Marineus Siculus, in Schott,
pp. 471 f.; Mariéjol, pp. 122–124.

All the terms of the previous instrument were reiterated, though perhaps in some instances less specifically than before; there were also added several new stipulations tending to emphasize the concurrence of both parties in the arrangements that had been made. Of these the most important were that justice should be administered jointly by both monarchs when they were residing in the same place, and by each one separately when they were apart; that the heads of both were to appear upon all coins; and that the united arms of Castile and Aragon (the former being given precedence) were to be borne on a common seal and carried on a common standard.[1] The famous *Tanto Monta* ("One is as good as the other") which the monarchs adopted as their motto, is another evidence to the same effect.[2] But despite all these efforts to accentuate the indivisibility of the interests of the two sovereigns, the fundamental principle of the agreement of 1474–75, as in that of 1469, was the complete independence and autonomy of the realms whose crowns had been united. Save for the foreign policy, in which henceforth all the Spanish kingdoms would naturally move as one;[3] save for the Inquisition, which was to be established in 1481 with a single organization for Castile and the realms of the Crown of Aragon; and save for the abolition in 1480 of the prohibition of the exportation and importation of certain commodities from one kingdom to another (the customs duties, however, being maintained),[4] the union of the crowns made no difference in principle in the government of the states of Christian Spain. Though the fundamental object

[1] Pulgar, *Crónica*, pt. ii, cap. ii (*B. A. E.*, lxx, pp. 255 f.); Zurita, iv, ff. 223–224.

[2] The full sentence was "Tanto monta, monta tanto Isabel como Fernando." Balaguer, i, p. 240.

[3] In theory at least; though there naturally continued to be wide divergences of interest on this topic between Castilians and Aragonese, as the sequel will show.

[4] *Cortes*, iv, pp. 185 f. (Toledo, 1480, orden. 111); Colmeiro, *Introd.*, ii, p. 61; Altamira, § 594.

of the administration of the Catholic Kings had been to secure internal unity, the particularistic traditions of their native land forced them to restrict their efforts to the attainment of that end *within* each of the separate realms which composed their dominions; fusion or amalgamation into a single state was at present out of the question. The absolutism which their government produced was therefore an absolutism of an essentially decentralized nature; and the special problems and difficulties with which the builders of the Spanish Empire were subsequently confronted can never be adequately appreciated unless this fundamental characteristic is constantly borne in mind.

On the other hand, it is important to remember that the measure of decentralization and separatism which was insured by the régime above described was in practice considerably less than might at first sight appear. The principal reason for this was, of course, the fact that Castile comprised by far the larger part of the Iberian Peninsula that she was greatly preponderant, from almost every point of view, over the three realms of the Crown of Aragon put together. It was not as if the crowns of four kingdoms of approximately the same size had been united, with the separate laws and institutions of each maintained in full force; it was rather a most unequal partnership, in which the western realm by the natural course of events was inevitably bound to assume by far the most important rôle. We have already seen that during the Middle Ages the kings of Castile were sometimes loosely spoken of as kings of Spain, thus indicating how completely the western realm overshadowed the eastern ones in the eyes of the world at large; and during the reign of Ferdinand and Isabella its preponderance became more marked than before. Castile alone had reaped the fruits of the conquest of Granada. The discovery of

America, of which it was practically the sole beneficiary, still further increased its power and resources, and transferred the centre of the Spanish Empire from Barcelona to Seville. The court resided in Castile the greater part of the time, and before long it became necessary to appoint viceroys to represent the authority of the crown in each of the Aragonese kingdoms. Naturally this increased preponderance of the western realm was bound to have its effect upon the constitutional arrangements of the time. From the very first the Catholic Kings centred their reforming energies on Castile. This was partly, no doubt, because it was in much worse case than the eastern kingdoms, and because the royal absolutism which it was the sovereigns' chief aim to set up would there be opposed by selfish barons with whom no true patriot could sympathize, rather than, as in Aragon, by a set of democratic institutions firmly grounded in national tradition and good will. But a much more important reason why Ferdinand and Isabella devoted their chief attention to the western kingdom was because they realized that if they gained their ends in Castile, their victory would be far more significant than if they won it in the realms of the Crown of Aragon. With Castile pacified and under control, they could well afford to ignore the probably more difficult and certainly less profitable task afforded by Aragon, Catalonia, and Valencia. They could make the former the real centre of their dominions, and permit the various institutions by which the latter attempted to limit the royal prerogative, and of which Spanish separatism refused to permit the abolition, gradually to wither and decay for lack of material to work upon. Queen Isabella is said to have once remarked to her husband, "Aragon is not ours, we must go and conquer it anew";[1] but the words, if they were ever

[1] Altamira, § 578.

actually spoken, cannot be taken to indicate any settled intention on the part of the Catholic Kings to make over the institutions of the eastern realms with anything like the same thoroughness with which they reformed the institutions of Castile. In our examination of the various constitutional changes which added lustre to their reign, we shall therefore be occupied almost exclusively with the western kingdom; occasionally the eastern realms are the scene of some reform of sufficient importance to deserve special mention, but for the most part they fall into the background. From the time of the union of the crowns, Castile overshadowed the other Spanish kingdoms; and though the latter's separate constitutions were not wholly abrogated until the advent of the Bourbons in the eighteenth century, they were so completely permeated by Castilian principles and methods that their practical importance was very slight.

We pass to the topic of racial and religious divergence. Save for the latter part of the Visigothic period and the great wave of clerically stimulated fanaticism which swept through the Iberian realms in the second part of the fourteenth century, the Spanish tradition, as we have already seen, favored a large measure of liberality to differing creeds and foreign peoples.[1] Intolerance was emphatically not an indigenous national trait. Yet the spectacle presented by the large number of Moors and Jews, converted and unconverted, who resided in their dominions, must have been gall and wormwood to Ferdinand and Isabella, with their ideas of absolute unity and the levelling of all distinctions under the throne. Particularly obnoxious were the *Conversos*, or nominally Christianized Jews, who were justly believed to be secretly loyal to the faith of their fathers. Differences

Cf. Vol. I, pp. 87 ff., 197 ff., 456.

in race alone no one as yet would have dreamed of attempting to obliterate, and frankly avowed and acknowledged differences in religion were not held at the time of the accession of the Catholic Kings to call for drastic action; but that there should be concealed disloyalty within the pale of Holy Church was a thought that the pious Isabella, at least, could not endure. Unity and purity of the Faith were the cornerstone of her policy, and, in her eyes, the first essentials to unity of the state. Open and traditional disbelievers could perhaps be regarded as beyond the scope of Christian inquiry, but those who had been once converted, even against their wills, must not under any circumstance be suffered to relapse.[1] It was to deal with the *Conversos*, or false Christians as they were sometimes called, that Ferdinand and Isabella resolved to apply to Pope Sixtus IV for permission to introduce the Inquisition into the kingdom of Castile, where it had never been known before.

The desired permission was promptly granted in a bull bearing the date November 1, 1478, but it was not till more than two years later that the institution it created really got to work; the long interval simply shows how difficult it was for the sovereigns to overcome the various forces which were hostile to their new departure.[2] But when at last the new tribunal began to sit, its unique and original constitution, differing so sharply from that of the ancient mediaeval ecclesiastical Inquisition, gave it a "peculiar and terrible efficiency." The essence of this was "its combination of the mysterious authority of the Church with the secular power of the crown. The old Inquisition was purely an ecclesiastical institution. . . . In Spain, however, the Inquisition represented not only the pope but the king; it

[1] "Judaei non sunt cogendi ad fidem, quam tamen si invite susceperint, cogendi sunt retinere." Decretal of Pope Gregory IV: cf. Lea, *Inquisition of Spain*, i, p. 41, note 3.

[2] Lea, *op. cit.*, i, pp. 157–161.

practically wielded the two swords — the spiritual and the temporal — and the combination produced a tyranny, similar in character, but far more minute and all-pervading, to that which England suffered during the closing years of Henry VIII as Supreme Head of the Church."[1]

The foundation for this invasion by the state of a realm hitherto exclusively reserved to the church was the initial demand of Ferdinand and Isabella, which Sixtus IV granted without realizing its true significance, that the appointment and dismissal of all the officials of the new institution, from the Inquisitor General down, should be made, or at least controlled, by the monarchs themselves.[2] In common with the other kings of their day and generation, Ferdinand and Isabella were resolved to reduce to the lowest possible terms all papal interference in the management of ecclesiastical affairs within their realms. They had no intention of setting up within their own dominions any institution whose officers should be nominated from Rome. But the right of appointment and dismissal was by no means all. The crown supervised the 'instructions' issued by the inquisitors. It insisted that the Inquisition's confiscations should be paid into the royal treasury. It controlled and regulated salaries. From interference with the spiritual side of the Inquisition's activities, Ferdinand and Isabella for the most part abstained, but in matters temporal their authority was complete and unchallenged. What doubtless combined to fortify and establish the measure of their royal control was the fact that the first crucial years of the existence of the Inquisition in Castile coincided with the period when the most important political and constitutional reforms of the reign were carried into effect. Everything was being directed towards the centralization of authority

[1] Lea, *op. cit.*, i, p. 289.   [2] Lea, *op. cit.*, i, pp. 158 f., 289 f.

in the hands of the crown at the very moment that the new institution first saw the light; small wonder that it yielded to the current of the times. A single example will suffice. One of the principal methods by which Ferdinand and Isabella established their royal power in political affairs was by the increase and development of the powers of the Consejo Real, and the creation of responsible offshoots of it to control the different branches of the government service. The major part of this work was accomplished by the famous Cortes of Toledo of 1480, of which anon; by 1483 the success of the experiment had been proved beyond the possibility of a doubt; and in that year a new council — *Consejo de la Suprema y General Inquisición*, popularly designated as the *Suprema* — was brought into being to secure and maintain the royal authority over the tribunal which had recently been called into existence.[1]

Any detailed examination of the growth, powers, and procedure of the new institution lies entirely beyond the scope of the present work; moreover, it would be supererogatory, if not positively impertinent, to attempt to traverse again so soon the ground that was so thoroughly covered by one of America's most distinguished historians only a decade ago. The Inquisition's privileges and prerogatives gave it 'supereminence' over every other institution in the state from the time of its establishment; and this high position was on the whole maintained and strengthened, despite occasional setbacks, during the two succeeding centuries. Its permanent courts under the Crown of Castile (including the Canaries) reached the total of twelve, while those in the realms of the Crown of Aragon numbered four. It was extended, as we shall later see, to Sardinia, Sicily, and the American

[1] Lea, *op. cit.*, i, pp. 289–294. For the Catholic side, cf. Gams, *Kirchengeschichte von Spanien*, iii, 2, pp. 16–93, *passim*; Ludwig Pastor, *Geschichte der Päpste* (2d ed.), ii, pp. 580–586.

possessions; and numerous temporary tribunals were set up in the course of its development.[1] We have already remarked that, save for the sovereigns themselves, the new institution was the only one common to the eastern and western kingdoms; except for the period 1507–18, when, owing to the death of Isabella and Ferdinand's second marriage to Germaine de Foix, a new separation of Aragon and Castile seemed likely to occur, there was but a single Inquisitor General for all Spain and all the Spanish possessions, and a single organization which embraced them. In more ways than one, then, the Inquisition fostered and advanced all the projects of union and centralization on which the internal policy of the Catholic Kings was founded; and in so far as it accomplished this, it was certainly possible to defend it according to the political theories of that day.

Yet the price which Spain had to pay for this advantage — if advantage it may be called — in the fastening upon herself, beyond all hope of escape, of a detestable spirit of racial and religious intolerance to which she had hitherto been for the most part a stranger, was out of all proportion to what she had gained. At the period of its establishment we find countless evidences, particularly in the eastern kingdoms, of the dread with which the Inquisition was regarded. Its erection was the worst kind of a blow to the aspirations for liberty which have always animated the Spaniards, and thinking men had already perceived that intolerance was ultimately certain to beget economic ruin. But as time wore on, the signs of the Inquisition's unpopularity gradually diminished, and the Spaniards were converted "from the most tolerant to the most intolerant nation in Europe."[2] Their passion for racial and religious

[1] Lea, *op. cit.*, pp. 541–555.

[2] *Ibid.*, i, pp. 35, 244–259. The murder of the inquisitor Pedro Arbués at Saragossa on September 15, 1485, was the turning point of the story in Aragon; "its immediate effect was to

unity had been fired at precisely the moment that they had at last attained the national consolidation for which patriots hitherto had so ardently but fruitlessly longed. It was thus natural that the two things should become inseparably connected in their minds, just as it was natural that the history of Prussia during the last two centuries should serve to imbue the normally peaceable German with the idea that militarism is the inseparable adjunct of imperial greatness and power. And the growth and development of the Inquisition was by no means the sole evidence of this alarming increase of the spirit of racial and religious intolerance.

The Holy Office, as we have already pointed out, had no jurisdiction over the avowed and professed Jews, who were generally held to be beyond the pale of Christian inquiry.[1] The number of these had, of course, greatly diminished owing to the persecutions of the fourteenth century; in 1474 there were only about twelve thousand families of them left in Castile.[2] Down to the foundation of the Inquisition, the wealth and prosperity of the *Conversos* had caused large numbers of orthodox Hebrews to follow their example, and come, nominally at least, within the bosom of the church; but when the Holy Office was finally established and got to work on the 'false Christians' the lot of the latter ceased to be enviable and became distinctly the reverse; everything now combined to cause the professed Jew to cling more steadfastly than ever to the faith of his fathers.[3] There was no longer any hope of his conversion; if complete unity

cause a revulsion of popular feeling, which hitherto had been markedly hostile to the Inquisition."
  [1] Save when a Hebrew rendered himself "subject to it by proselytism, by seducing Christians to embrace his errors." Lea, *Inquisition of Spain*, i, p. 130.

  [2] *Ante*, Vol. I, p. 201.
  [3] The laws valid for the Jews of Castile during the period just previous to their expulsion may be found in Montalvo's *Ordenanzas Reales* (cf. *infra*, p. 225), lib. viii, tit. iii.

of the faith was to be attained in Spain, expulsion was the only possible method of securing it.[1]

But the policy of expulsion was so utterly at variance with the traditions of mediaeval Spain, and the economic consequences of it were so obviously destined to be disastrous, that it was some years before Ferdinand and Isabella, with all their zeal and energy, were able to put it into practice. It appears that the queen made a move towards getting rid of the Andalusian Hebrews in 1480, at the time of the foundation of the Inquisition,[2] but nothing came of it; twelve long years more of deliberate inculcation of racial intolerance and stimulation of anti-Semitic prejudice were necessary before the fatal step could be finally taken. The conquest of Granada furnished the desired opportunity. Some sort of recognition of God's goodness and mercy in delivering over the last stronghold of the infidel in the peninsula was clearly due; and the fact that with the conclusion of the campaign there was no longer the same need of the Jewish contributions which had gone far towards supporting it [3] was a practical consideration which may well have settled the matter. Despite the efforts of prominent Hebrews to bribe their Catholic Majesties to postpone or abandon it,[4] the edict of expulsion was signed at Granada on March 30, 1492; it granted the professed Jews of all the Spanish realms four months — until July 31 — either to accept baptism or else to leave the land.[5] They were given no fair or adequate means of disposing of their property or of collecting the debts justly due them; the time was all too short, and the government took no effective measures to protect them from robbery and fraud; moreover, the

---

[1] Lea, *op. cit.*, i, p. 131.
[2] Pulgar, *Crónica*, pt. ii, cap. lxxvii (in *B. A. E.*, lxx, pp. 331 f.).
[3] Cf. *D. I. E.*, xxxix, pp. 418 ff.
[4] Cf. in this connection the story of Torquemada in Lea, *op. cit.*, i, p. 135.
[5] Amador de los Rios, *Historia de los Judíos*, iii, pp. 387–432.

laws forbidding the export of gold and silver made it difficult, if not impossible, for them to carry away the equivalent of such possessions as they were obliged to sell. The total number of the exiles, of the dead, and of those who submitted to baptism to escape expulsion was probably rather less than more than 200,000; [1] but even if we accept Colmeiro's doubtless exaggerated estimate of the population of Spain in that period as 10,000,000,[2] we shall unquestionably conclude that the loss was far greater than she could afford. And "the sum of human misery" inflicted, as Lea has rightly said, "was incomputable." [3] Most of the exiles passed over to the Italian lands or to the Moorish states of North Africa, where tribulations of various kinds and degrees awaited them. Some of them fled to Portugal, where they were permitted to remain for a time on payment of a heavy impost to the crown. In 1497, however, as we shall see more fully in another connection, Ferdinand and Isabella insisted, as part of the price of the marriage of their daughter Isabella to Emmanuel the Portuguese king, that the latter should follow their example and expel the Jews from his dominions, which he accordingly did. Their most

---

[1] Lea, *Inquisition of Spain*, i, p. 142.

[2] Colmeiro, *E. P.*, ii, p. 13; cf. also Gams (*Kirchengeschichte von Spanien*, iii, 1, pp. 468 f.), who cites Colmeiro's figures and himself arrives, independently, at an estimate of 9,320,691. Of these he gives 7,500,000 to Castile, and 1,100,120 to the realms of the Crown of Aragon — a totally inadmissible proportion, for the eastern kingdoms, though smaller, were much the more thickly populated; moreover, he specifically states that his figures for Castile are uncertain, so that it is obviously necessary to lower them rather than to raise the others. If we accept the estimate of the eastern kingdoms as approximately correct, the sum total for all Spain could scarcely exceed 5,000,000. By another method of computation we get a somewhat larger figure. Alfonso de Quintanilla, *contador mayor* to the Catholic Kings, reported to their Majesties in 1482 that there were 1,500,000 *vecinos* (resident property holders) in Castile, excluding Granada (*Censo de Poblacion de Castilla en el Siglo XVI*, p. 393). Taking the relative proportion of *vecinos* to inhabitants as one to four, this makes 6,000,000 for Castile: adding 1,500,000 or 2,000,000 more for Granada and the eastern kingdoms, we get a grand total of 7,500,000 or 8,000,000. Comparisons with England and France in this period, however, lead one to prefer the lower figure.

[3] Lea, *op. cit.*, i, p. 143.

satisfactory place of refuge was unquestionably the domain of the Sultan of Turkey, who properly estimated their economic value and scoffed at the praises which the bulk of Western Christendom lavished on the mistaken policy of the Catholic Kings. And the horror and loathing of their native land, which the unfortunate Israelites carried with them wherever they went, was not the least ominous feature of the situation. The Jews were perhaps too small a portion of the population to have their enmity count for much; but when in years to come the Moors and the Protestants were added to the victims of Spanish intolerance and exclusiveness, the nation drew down upon itself the bitter hatred of some of its most powerful neighbors, so that the fabric of its empire was shaken to the very foundations.[1]

Racial and religious animosity had certainly made great strides between 1480 and 1492, but the next decade saw it increase more rapidly still; and this time, as the Jews were gone, it was the Moors who bore the brunt of the attack. The terms of the capitulation of Granada, as already remarked, had granted the most generous possible conditions to the vanquished infidels.[2] They were to remain undisturbed in the enjoyment of their own property and customs, laws, and religion. All attempts forcibly to convert them were strictly forbidden, and they were guaranteed the favor and protection of the Castilian crown. For at least five years after the fall of Granada, the main provisions of the capitulation were loyally observed; indeed, in April, 1497, when the king of Portugal expelled all the Moors from his dominions, Ferdinand and Isabella specifically invited the exiles either to come and settle in Spain, or else to pass through it on their way to their final place of refuge.[3] But

[1] Bernáldez, caps. cx–cxiv; Lea, op. cit., i, pp. 137–142.
[2] Ante, p. 73; and Lea, The Moris- cos of Spain, pp. 20 f.
[3] Lea, Moriscos, p. 23.

in the immediately succeeding period there came a change. In 1492 Isabella determined to revive the high episcopal traditions which Granada had enjoyed in Roman and Visigothic times, to erect it into an archbishopric, and to confer it upon her confessor, the saintly Hernando de Talavera.[1] Under his gentle influence numerous Moorish converts to Christianity were made; but the process did not advance with sufficient rapidity to suit their Catholic Majesties, who in November, 1499, took the decisive step of associating with Talavera a man of a very different stamp — the redoubtable Francisco Ximenes [2] de Cisneros, archbishop of Toledo. Inflexible determination and fanatic zeal for the propagation of the Christian faith were the principal traits of this extraordinary prelate; from the moment of his arrival in Granada he dominated everything; the gentle Talavera was simply elbowed aside. Conversion by compulsion and terrorism supplanted conversion by persuasion and instruction; baptism *en masse* — 3000 at a time on one occasion — by the use of the *aspergillum* or baptismal sprinkler, replaced the individual rite.[3] When rebellions ensued as a result of these proceedings, Ximenes insisted that the Moors had thereby forfeited their lives and their property, and that they ought not to be pardoned unless they promised either to accept Christianity or else to leave the realm.[4] The sovereigns lent a willing ear to these representations; and the Holy Office, which had been extended to Granada in the same year that Ximenes had been sent there, urged them still further along the path of persecution. Ferdinand was unquestionably less amenable to clerical argument than was Isabella. He recognized the high value

[1] Lea, *Moriscos*, p. 26.
[2] I have retained the old-fashioned spelling of this name, which is sanctioned by usage: "Jiménez" is strictly speaking more correct.
[3] Lea, *Moriscos*, pp. 29–31.
[4] Lea, *Moriscos*, p. 35.

of the Moorish portions of the population from the economic point of view, and often strove to check the ardor of his more fanatic spouse.[1] But the queen was determined to rid Castile at all costs of the last remnant of its non-Christian population, and on the plea that it was impossible to prevent the avowed and confessed Moors from entering Granada, where they would infallibly contaminate those whom Ximenes had baptized, she finally issued, on February 12, 1502, an edict for their expulsion. This provided that all unconverted adult Moors, except a few slaves with whom it was impossible to interfere, should leave the realms of Leon and Castile before the end of the following April. As a matter of fact, however, the edict really amounted to a sentence of conversion or death, for the conditions under which it provided that the expatriation should be carried out were quite impossible of fulfilment. The prescribed places of embarkation were too remote to be reached within the allotted time, and resort to the adjacent Iberian and North African realms was prohibited. The edict was virtually an order for the forcible conversion of all the non-Christian inhabitants of Leon and Castile and the consequent bringing of them within the jurisdiction of the Holy Office.[2]

The edict against the Moors in 1502, in contrast to that against the Jews of ten years before, did not for the present apply to the realms of the Crown of Aragon. Not until the reign of the Emperor Charles V was it extended to the eastern kingdoms. Isabella, as we have seen, was primarily responsible for it; indeed, after her death in 1504 her husband did what he could to mitigate the severity of its enforcement. Ferdinand's whole career shows him to have been much less intolerant than the queen; in this respect at

[1] Lea, *Moriscos*, p. 47.
[2] Lea, *Moriscos*, pp. 43 f.; for the other side of the question see Fray
Jayme Bleda, *Corónica de los Moros de España, passim*.

least his point of view was far more modern. But even his efforts to stem the tide of persecution were in the end totally fruitless; the movement begun by Isabella and her clerical allies and advisers was to continue practically unchecked until its force was broken by the scepticism of the eighteenth century. How far the effects of this baleful arousing of the demon of persecution and exclusiveness was responsible for the fall of Spain and her empire, it is profitable to inquire, provided we do not expect a definite answer. Certainly it was a cause, and, in all probability, a principal one; but to hold it solely or even almost solely responsible for the disasters that followed, is too much. The Spanish Empire of the sixteenth century was such a vast, unwieldy, and heterogeneous organization that it is idle to attempt to account for its rise or fall on the theory of any single explanation. Many exceedingly complex, and in large measure accidental, elements combined to effect its sudden growth and decay; and if the present work lays less than the usual emphasis on the errors of Spain's racial and religious policy, it is because the writer feels that they were but one of a number of reasons that went to produce the final result.

BIBLIOGRAPHICAL NOTE

See bibliographical notes at the end of the two preceding chapters, and of Chapter IV in Volume I, and add:

J. H. Mariéjol, *L'Espagne sous Ferdinand et Isabelle* (Paris, 1892); a valuable survey of the social, constitutional, economic, and intellectual aspects of the reign. H. C. Lea, *The Moriscos of Spain* (Philadelphia, 1901); a brilliant study, based on the sources, covering the period from the conquest of Granada to the final expulsion in 1609. Fray Jayme Bleda's *Corónica de los Moros de España* (Valencia, 1618) presents the older Spanish Catholic view of the Moorish problem. Useful statistics may be found in a *Censo de Poblacion de las Provincias y Partidos de la Corona de Castilla en el Siglo XVI*, ed. Tomas Gonzalez (De orden del Rey, Madrid, Imprenta Real, 1829).

CHAPTER XV

INTERNAL REORGANIZATION

HAVING disposed of the two distinctively Spanish problems with which Ferdinand and Isabella were confronted, we can take up the story of their principal administrative reforms, which were inspired, one and all, by the idea of giving the nation peace, order, and union under the absolute authority of the crown. Before any positive work towards the upbuilding of a strong central government could be attempted, it was essential to clear the way for it by two negative measures of fundamental importance. An end must be put to the long course of unpunished crime and contempt for authority which made the name of Castile synonymous with anarchy even in that lawless age; and the rebel aristocracy, the principal foe to the omnipotence of the king, must be permanently reduced to subjection.

The quotation from Andrés Bernáldez, with which this volume opens, may well be supplemented by a description from the pen of another contemporary, in order to portray the full horrors of the period in which Ferdinand and Isabella began to reign. "So corrupt and abominable were the customs of these realms, that every one was left free to follow his own devices without fear of reprehension or punishment; and so loosely were the conventions of civilized society observed, that men practically relapsed into savagery, in such fashion that the wise and prudent deemed it next to impossible to bring order out of such chaos, or regulation out of such confusion; for no justice was left in

98

the land. The common people were exterminated, the crown property alienated, the royal revenues reduced to such slight value that it causes me shame to speak of it; whence it resulted that men were robbed not only in the open fields but in the cities and towns, that the regular clergy could not live in safety, and that the seculars were treated with no respect, that sanctuaries were violated, women raped, and all men had full liberty to sin as they pleased." [1]

In times of such agony the Hermandad had proved itself the sole effective remedy in the past, and in the reign of Henry the Impotent "the extension of the malady made the cure more urgent still." [2]   A new Hermandad, far larger and more powerful than any that Castile had seen before, had therefore been inaugurated in 1465 and definitely constituted two years later.   A set of laws and ordinances, which were drawn up for it at a general assembly of its representatives at Castronuño near Valladolid, exhibit the institution at the height of its independent development, and show that the municipalities, disrupted and shaken though they were by the anarchy of the times, were still centres of patriotism and national pride.[3]   These ordinances declare that a Hermandad, comprising the important towns of Leon, Castile, Asturias, and Galicia, is established for the execution of justice, and for the preservation of the well-being of the realm and its royal crown.   They prescribe the forms of its organization, from the alcaldes in the towns, on whom fell the important duty of intervening to prevent crime and disturbance, through the eight deputies who

[1] Diego de Valera, *Forma en que estos reynos quedáron, al tiempo que los serenisimos principes comenzáron á reynar* — quoted in L. Saez, *Demostración del Valor de las Monedas durante el reynado de Enrique IV* (Madrid, 1805), p. 1, note.

[2] Palencia, *Crónica*, i, p. 522.

[3] Printed in Puyol y Alonso, *Las Hermandades de Castilla y León*, pp. 107–125.

headed each provincial subdivision of the institution, to the supreme general assembly or *Junta General*. They lay down the methods of recruiting and utilizing the military forces of the institution, the contribution due from each municipality for their support, the means of forcibly collecting it in case of a refusal, and also the difficult question of conflicts of jurisdiction with the ordinary authorities. They are, in fact, the constitution of a powerful "administrative, judicial, legislative, and military machine," "a state within a state, or, more exactly, the sole state then existent in Castile." [1] The excessive praises of contemporary chroniclers must not lead us into thinking that it succeeded in fully accomplishing its purposes, or "that there was once more safety on the roads in such manner that men could travel anywhere without fear." [2] The evils of the day were far too deep seated for that; but had it not been for this Hermandad of 1465–67 they would probably have been much worse. In any case, the institution had demonstrated its value so signally and so recently, that, in casting about for some means of restoring order at their accession, it was impossible that Ferdinand and Isabella should ignore it.

One of the most striking features of the administration of the Catholic Kings, and also one of the most convincing proofs of their statesmanship, was their careful avoidance of gratuitous innovations. If their purpose could be as well served by the remodelling of an ancient institution as by the creation of a new one, they unhesitatingly chose the former alternative, knowing full well that the permanence of their work would thus be more completely assured. The application of this principle to the Hermandad was

[1] Puyol y Alonso, *Hermandades*, pp. 85 f.

[2] Enríquez del Castillo, *Crónica*, cap. lxxxvii (*B. A. E.*, lxx, p. 155).

obvious and important. The institution was highly esteemed and enjoyed noble traditions. It had stood in the past for objects of which no true patriot could fail to approve. With crown support it would be able to accomplish its purpose far more effectively than ever before, while the monarchy itself would gain prestige from association with it. Finally, under royal control, it could never lend itself to enterprises hostile to the throne. Accordingly, after consultation with the principal personages in the most important cities of the realm, the sovereigns promulgated a plan for the reorganization of the ancient Hermandad under the auspices of the central government, at the Cortes of Madrigal, April 27, 1476.[1] On the basis of this proclamation, a new constitution was drawn up by the representatives of the different municipalities in solemn conclave at Dueñas on July 25, and sanctioned by the sovereigns on August 13 following.[2] Three features of this new constitution deserve special emphasis.[3] First, in order to preserve the authority of the crown over the institution as a whole, a representative of the monarchy, the bishop of Cartagena, was installed as president of the *Junta* or council of the Hermandad, which was composed as formerly of provincial delegates. Before this body all questions of importance were ultimately certain to come, and the sovereigns were thus enabled to keep in touch with every phase of the institution's activities. Second, in addition to preventing crime and maintaining

---

[1] *Cortes*, iv, pp. 3–11.

[2] Galíndez Carbajal, in *D. I. E.*, xviii, p. 259, notes 2 and 5.

[3] For further details see *Novísima Recopilación*, lib. xii, tit. xxxv, containing a *Cuaderno de Leyes de la Hermandad* published by Ferdinand and Isabella at Cordova in 1496, and considerably fuller than the original one, which is exceedingly rare; Pulgar, *Crónica*, pt.

ii, cap. li (*B. A. E.*, lxx, pp. 300–303); Palencia, *Crónica*, iv, pp. 73–76; Lucius Marineus Siculus, in Schott, i, pp. 477–481. Of the more recent works, besides Puyol y Alonso, Clemencin, *Elógio*, pp. 134–141; A. Du Boys, *Histoire du droit criminel de l'Espagne*, pp. 444–457; and Mariéjol, pp. 16–23, are the most valuable.

order, the new Hermandad was given complete jurisdiction over certain classes of crimes, and full power to punish them. Among these may be mentioned robbery and arson in the open country, rape, and all acts of rebellion against the central government; and elaborate rules prevented the ordinary judicial authorities from interfering in such cases. Finally, the amounts of the contributions due from each town for the support of the new institution, the sources and means of collecting them, and the penalties for default were regulated more carefully than ever before, as were also the size and distribution of its military contingents throughout the realm. No rank or class of men, whether nobles or clergy, was exempt from the tribute which the maintenance of the Hermandad required; "for as it was equally useful to all, so it was but fair that all men should pay their share." [1] The new institution may thus be regarded as "the first attempt to establish a system of taxation to which every one should contribute irrespective of his estate and condition, and therefore as the initial step towards the abolition of the ancient privileges" [2] and the levelling of all distinctions under the throne.

The efficiency of this reorganized or Holy (*Santa*) Hermandad is the best possible justification of the wisdom of the sovereigns' treatment of it. The pursuit of criminals was carried relentlessly forward, lap on lap, by the squadrons of archers which were maintained in each locality. When the limits of the territory of one company were reached, it relinquished the chase to a fresh one, which was always on hand to take it up. Death or mutilation were the regular punishments. Whenever possible the malefactor was brought back to the place where he had committed his crime to undergo them; and the death penalty was in-

[1] Pulgar, *Crónica*, in *B. A. E.*, lxx, p. 303.   [2] Puyol, *Hermandades*, pp. 98 f.

variably inflicted by a discharge of arrows at the body of
the victim, bound upright to a wooden post, which, as the
ancient law significantly specified, "should never be permitted to have the form of a cross." [1] Yet despite the
ruthlessness of its procedure, the new institution met with
little resistance or complaint. The nobles alone, who
realized that it was certain ultimately to curtail their excessive powers, were bitterly hostile, but since they were
themselves the fundamental cause of the prevailing anarchy,
we may well believe that Ferdinand and Isabella paid no
attention to their remonstrances. The Hermandad was
vigorously supported by the crown in all its proceedings,
and rendered splendid service in return. We have seen
that, in addition to their regular duties, some of its contingents formed a useful nucleus for the Christian army in
the Granadan war. A similar institution was established
in Aragon in 1488 and endured until 1510.[2] Long before
the latter date, however, the more important Castilian
Hermandad had accomplished the work which it had been
reorganized to do. Crime and rebellion had been suppressed,
peace and order established. That this happy consummation was largely due to other contemporary measures of
the Catholic Kings, which we shall examine in their proper
place, it would be idle to deny; and it is certain that the
character and prestige of the monarchs themselves counted
for much. Still the Hermandad must always be remembered as the entering wedge of the administration of the
Catholic Kings. By the year 1498 there was no longer any
need for its continued existence — at least not in the form
in which it had been reconstituted in 1476. The taxes for
its maintenance were already very high and steadily in-

---

[1] A. Du Boys, *Droit criminel*, p. 455.
[2] Pulgar, *Crónica*, pt. iii, caps. xiv and xcv (in *B. A. E.*, lxx, pp. 379, 473).

creasing, and Ferdinand and Isabella resolved radically to modify and restrict it. By an ordinance of July 29 of that year they suppressed the supreme council or Junta of the Hermandad, its salaried officers, and the imposts which its upkeep demanded. Appeals from its sentences to the ordinary courts of the realm were thenceforth specifically permitted, and the severity of its ancient punishments was moderated by the order that criminals should be hung before being shot.[1] Its archers indeed were to be maintained in the different localities to watch over the security of the roads; but this last was probably little more than a concession to popular conservatism. To all intents and purposes the Hermandad had finished its work and been discontinued.

At the same time that Ferdinand and Isabella were bringing the active agents of crime and rebellion to book, they took measures of repression against the Castilian aristocracy, in whom they rightly recognized the ultimate authors and fomenters of the manifold evils of the times. That many of these measures were ostensibly gentle and pacific must not blind us to their real effectiveness, or lead us to imagine that the sovereigns did not realize the deadly peril to their throne that lurked in the excessive powers of the baronage. It simply shows that they shrank from open collisions, whenever it was possible to avoid them and to attain their ends without provoking civil war. Moreover it is important to notice that most of the steps they took to curb the rebel nobles were specifically sanctioned by the Cortes of Castile, and therefore, nominally at least, bore the stamp of the approval of the representatives of the entire realm. The national assembly furnished valuable aid to the Catho-

---

[1] Ramirez, *Pragmaticas del Reyno*, ff. lxxxiv–lxxxvi; *Novisima Recopilación*, lib. xii, tit. xxxv, ley 18; Du Boys, *op. cit.*, pp. 455 f.

lic Kings in the establishment of their absolutism against
internal anarchy and baronial rebellion. After it had
successfully accomplished that purpose and had itself
begun in turn to constitute a menace to the omnipotence
of the crown, it was destined, as we shall subsequently see,
to be rather cavalierly cast aside.

Systematic destruction of a large number of baronial
castles — strongholds of unlicensed tyranny and rebellion
— was a distinguishing feature of the early years of the
reign, and effectively supplemented the activities of the
Hermandad.[1] The nobles were also formally commanded
to keep the peace among themselves, and heavy punishment was unsparingly meted out to those barons whose
misdeeds rendered them subject to it;[2] for rank and
lineage were no longer to be permitted to shield any malefactor from the consequences of his crime. The Cortes
of Madrigal in 1476 carried the good work considerably
further. In addition to taking the first steps toward the
reform of the royal councils and courts, which we shall
examine in another place, they initiated a thorough reorganization of the royal household; by this the duties
and powers of Chancellor, Mayor domo, Adelantado Mayor,
and the other ancient dignitaries of the crown were so
strictly limited and defined that the great lords and clerics
who held these offices were virtually deprived of all influence
in the government.[3] But the hardest blows were dealt
through the Cortes of Toledo in 1480, which a contemporary
chronicler admiringly characterizes as "a God-given means
of remedy and reformation for the past disorders."[4] Two
petitions, ostensibly emanating from the procuradores,

---

[1] Prescott, i, p. 266.
[2] Días de Montalvo, *Ordenanzas Reales de Castilla*, lib. iv, tit. ii, ley 1; Mariéjol, pp. 29–30.
[3] Cf. Vol. I, pp. 209 ff.; *Cortes*, iv, pp. 15 ff; Mariéjol, pp. 165–171.
[4] Galindez Carbajal, *D. I. E.*, xviii, p 267.

but in all probability inspired by the sovereigns to whom they were addressed, set the ball rolling in the right direction. The first demanded that the royal revenues be restored to their proper proportions, 'since failure to do so would inevitably mean increased taxes'; the second required that the various alienations, whether of lands, cities, or funds, which had been made without sufficient cause during the preceding reign, should be promptly revoked.[1] In pursuance of these requests a great Act of Resumption was passed, by which the nobles lost and the crown gained an annual revenue of 30,000,000 maravedis. The details were worked out by the queen's confessor, Hernando de Talavera, whose high character insured him the confidence of all men, in consultation with the very nobles against whom the measure was aimed. The amount that each one should give up was settled according to the merits of his particular case; if he could prove that he had rendered services commensurate with the grant that he had received, he was permitted to retain it, but most of the beneficiaries lost the whole or a large part of what they had been given. There was some grumbling, of course; but the measure was almost a *sine qua non* of national financial salvation, and the fact that the queen in her final will and testament revoked some of the grants which had been allowed to stand in 1480, as well as certain others which she herself had made, shows that Talavera's verdicts had not been unduly severe.[2] That the nobles themselves had been invited to participate in every stage of the process by which they had been deprived, was the best possible answer to any complaints.

The annexation of the grand masterships of the three

[1] *Cortes*, iv, pp. 164–170; Colmeiro, *Introd.*, ii, pp. 63 f.; Clemencin, *Eló-*   *gio*, pp. 141–167.
[2] Colmeiro, *Introd.*, ii, p. 64.

great orders of military knighthood really forms a part of
the story of the sovereigns' measures against the Castilian
baronage; intrenched as these institutions were, behind
privileges both aristocratic and clerical, it was doubly
essential that they be made to bow before the majesty of
the throne. The first move came in 1476 on the death of
the grand master of Santiago. When the news reached
Isabella at Valladolid she promptly took horse, and after
three days' hard riding, the last part of it in a pouring rain
and at night, she appeared at the convent at Uclés, where
the thirteen dignitaries of the order were discussing the
selection of a successor.[1] The magnates were amazed at
her vigorous insistence that they suspend their proceedings;
they were dumfounded by her announcement that she
desired that the coveted office be conferred on her husband,
and that she had written to Rome to ask for a bull of investiture from the Pope; but the charm and power of her
personality overcame all resistance. The royal ambassador
at the Vatican wrote that "the Pope and cardinals held it
to be a most monstrous thing and contrary to all precedent
that a woman should have any rights over the administration of orders";[2] but his urgency finally triumphed, and
the desired provision of Ferdinand to the grand mastership
of Santiago at the request of the queen was duly granted.
It is true that Ferdinand, whose whole handling of this
problem of the grand masterships was marked with even
more than his usual caution, did not at once avail himself
of the permission that he had received. The candidate
whom the dignitaries had intended to elect was permitted
to assume the office and to hold it until his death in 1499.[3]
But in 1487 the Catholic King utilized the opportunity

[1] Pulgar, *Crónica*, pt. ii, cap. lxiv
(*B. A. E.*, lxx, p. 317).
[2] Uhagon, *Órdenes Militares*, p. 36.
[3] Pulgar, *Crónica*, pt. ii, cap. xcvi
(*B. A. E.*, lxx, p. 355).

afforded by the death of the grand master of Calatrava to give effect to the papal bull and possess himself of that office; in 1494 he took over that of Alcántara in similar fashion; and when five years later the grand mastership of Santiago once more fell vacant, he repeated the process there.[1] As these offices had only been conferred upon Ferdinand for his lifetime, the process of annexation was not complete until in 1523 a bull of Pope Adrian VI definitely incorporated all three military orders into the crown of Castile; but their ultimate fate was inevitable from the moment of Isabella's first dramatic interference in 1476. What had been one of the principal sources of political anarchy and disruption during the two preceding centuries had now been converted into a source of added wealth and power to the monarchy.[2]

A number of other measures, all of which aimed directly or indirectly at the depression of the Castilian baronage, may be briefly mentioned   The Cortes of Toledo of 1480, in addition to passing the great Act of Resumption already described, further indicated their compliance with the royal desires by numerous petitions for the restraint of aristocratic abuses and usurpations. These were for the most part accepted, and converted into laws prohibiting the use of phrases, dignities, or methods of address which were anciently prerogatives of royalty. The grandees, for example, were henceforth forbidden to place crowns above their coats of arms, or to have maces carried before them on state occasions.[3] The erection of new castles — one of the most harmful of baronial privileges — and the practice of duelling

[1] Uhagon, pp. 35–37, and Danvila's *Contestación* printed therewith, pp. 141–143.

[2] A useful note on the amount of revenue gained by the annexations may be found in U. R. Burke's *History of Spain*, ii, p. 52.

[3] Díaz de Montalvo, *Ordenansas Reales*, lib. ii. tit. i, ley 2.

were also explicitly prohibited.[1] At the same time the nobles were one by one deprived of important political offices, save in those rare cases where their loyalty was certain and their ability unquestioned.[2] The advancement to the most important posts in the realm of low-born, subservient, self-made men — preferably legists or clerics — is as notable a feature of the policy of Ferdinand and Isabella as of that of their contemporaries in France and England, and left scant room for the baronage. Yet the sovereigns were keenly alive to the danger that the aristocracy, if removed from the government service, where the monarchy could in a measure superintend them, might retire to their great landed estates and hatch plots against the throne. To guard against this peril they made every possible effort to induce the nobles to dance attendance upon themselves. This process of converting their proud hidalgos into servile courtiers was exceedingly difficult to accomplish. The independent traditions of the Castilian baronage made it almost impossible to change them over at short notice into king's minions, and Ferdinand and Isabella scarcely did more than make a beginning. But their methods of operation were skilful and exceedingly interesting. They flattered the aristocracy by permitting them to retain most of the empty rights and honors to which they were tradi-tionally entitled ; even a few of the significant and impor-tant ones, which it might have been dangerous to attempt to abolish, were permitted to remain. Thus the highly prized privilege of keeping their hats on in the royal presence con-tinued to be the distinguishing badge of the Castilian nobil-ity ; so much so, in fact, that a common form of announcing the grant of a title was a command from the king to the

---

[1] *Novísima Recopilación*, lib. vii, tit. i, ley 6; *Cortes*, iv, pp. 171 f.

[2] Díaz de Montalvo, *Ordenansas Reales*, lib. vii, tit. ii, ley 13.

recipient, in the presence of the full court, to 'be covered.' [1]
It was also judged wise not to meddle with the ancient
aristocratic exemptions from torture, imprisonment for
debt, or even from the payment of regular taxes — much as
the sovereigns must have disliked them.[2] A considerable
increase in the number of titles and of titled persons, moreover, was apparently held to be good policy by the Catholic
Kings : they doubtless hoped in that way to diminish the
importance of the distinction. There were, for example,
but seven dukes in Castile at the time of their accession;
during their reign the number was raised to fifteen.[3] Flat-
tery and cajolery were thus judiciously mixed with vigorous
measures of suppression, in the sovereigns' treatment of
their unruly magnates.

Such were the principal means by which Ferdinand and
Isabella succeeded in vindicating the authority of the
monarchy against the class which more than any other had
contrived during the past two centuries to hold it in tutelage.
By them the preponderance of actual power in the body
politic, which hitherto had been unquestionably possessed
by the aristocracy, was made to pass to the crown, where
it equally unquestionably remained until the days of the
French Revolution and Napoleon Bonaparte. That such
a shifting of the centre of authority at home was the indispensable preliminary to the efficient upbuilding of an empire abroad must be evident to the most casual observer.
And in order to understand the relentless persistency with
which the Spanish kings attempted to safeguard and con-
serve every minutest particle of their royal authority in
the New World, it is essential to keep in mind the tremendous exertions which they had been obliged to put forth to

[1] Mariéjol, pp. 282–284; M. Hume,   Reales, lib. iv, tit. ii, leyes 2–5.
The Court of Philip IV, p. 49.   [3] Mariéjol, p. 284.
    [2] Díaz de Montalvo, Ordenanzas

establish it, at the very moment when they entered into possession of their new dominions.

At the same time that Ferdinand and Isabella contrived to curb and dominate the enemies of strong central government throughout their dominions, they took effective positive measures to upbuild their own power. The first and by far the most important of these — indeed the source and mainspring of the entire administration of Spain and the Spanish Empire down to the very end of the old régime — was their reform and development of the Royal Council.

We have already examined the origin and growth during the fourteenth and early fifteenth centuries of this interesting institution, the various changes in its composition and powers, and finally its subjection in the reign of John II and Henry IV, along with most of the other organs of the central government, to the factious control of the baronage.[1] Obviously, if it were ever again to perform the function for which it had been originally created — namely, to advise and aid the king in the management of the realm — its personnel would have to be completely altered, and it would have to be once more brought back into close and intimate contact with the monarchy. A good beginning was made toward the attainment of these two ends in the Cortes of Madrigal in 1476. In spite of the fact that the original summons to this assembly makes mention of a long list of prelates, nobles, and legists as members of the Royal Council, the third of its enactments specifically provides that that body should in future be composed of but one bishop, two barons, and six *letrados*, with six secretaries;[2] and at another place the monarchs distinctly promise that no new person shall be added to the Council unless there is

---

[1] Cf. Vol. I, pp. 211 ff.   [2] *Cortes*, iv, pp. 13 f.

a vacancy, or without the consent of the existing members.[1] The aristocracy and ecclesiastics were thus in large measure hunted out, and the preponderance was definitely handed over to the legists. Moreover, throughout the portion of the *cuaderno* of these Cortes which deals with the Consejo, there occur various phrases which indicate that the sovereigns and procuradores had made up their minds that all the members of that body ought to be in constant residence at the court, but that the facts did not correspond to their desires.[2] No specific rule was laid down on this matter for the time being; but it is clear that Ferdinand and Isabella had discerned the dangers inherent in the chronic absenteeism of many of the members of the Council in the past, and had determined to put an end to it.

All the progress made at the Cortes of Madrigal in 1476 was consolidated and increased at those of Toledo in 1480. The first thirty-three sections of their *cuaderno* are almost exclusively occupied with the reform of the Royal Council: the first two and the thirty-second of these sections deal with its membership and place of meeting; the rest with its procedure and powers.[3] Its composition was now definitely fixed at one prelate, three nobles, and eight or nine legists, all but the first of whom were named in the *cuaderno*. A sop was thrown to the humbled aristocracy by the permission to those magnates, both lay and clerical, whose dignities anciently entitled them to the position of crown counsellors, to attend the meetings of the Consejo whenever they chose; but as the right to vote and transact business was specifically restricted to the regular members, the privilege was largely illusory.[4] All meetings of the

[1] *Cortes*, iv, p. 73.
[2] Torreánaz, *Consejos del Rey*, i, p. 194.
[3] *Cortes*, iv, pp. 111–120; Díaz de

Montalvo, *Ordenanzas Reales*, lib. ii tit. iii.
[4] *Cortes*, iv, p. 120.

Council were to be held in the royal dwelling, wherever
the monarchs happened to be, "and if there was not room,
then as near to it as possible"; [1] no separation of the crown
from its advisers was to be tolerated in future. It was
clearly the intention of the sovereigns that the reorganized
institution should work, and work hard, to earn the large
salaries which were paid to its members. It was to sit
every day except Sundays and holidays — from six to ten
in the morning between Easter and mid-October, and from
nine to twelve during the rest of the year : if the business
on hand could not be finished within the appointed time,
the sessions were prolonged.[2] Every member was sworn
to inviolable secrecy.[3] Four councillors, of whom two
must be legists, constituted a quorum. Elaborate regulations prescribed the methods by which business should
be conducted. Speed, order, and efficiency were the watch-
words at every turn. It is clear that written records were
kept of all the most important proceedings. In that way
the sovereigns could inform themselves concerning the
doings of their Council much more accurately than through
oral reports; and moreover an enormous body of valuable
experience and administrative and judicial precedents was
thus accumulated and preserved for the guidance of those
to come after. Huge stacks of documents and copies of
documents of every sort and description became in fact a
distinguishing characteristic of Spanish administration from
the days of the Catholic Kings.[4]

The competence and powers of the reorganized Council
were exceedingly extensive; in theory every phase of the
government of Castile fell within its purview. It acted as
an advisory body to the crown in appointments, grants,

[1] *Cortes*, iv, p. 112.
[2] *Cortes*, iv, pp. 112 f,
[3] *Cortes*, iv, p. 116.
[4] *Cortes*, iv, pp. 112–116; Mariéjol, p. 152.

and the bestowal of the royal patronage, as well as in certain
matters of policy; and in such cases the sovereigns alone
signed the document announcing the decision, though some
of the councillors might indorse it.[1] But the Council also
dealt independently with a number of administrative affairs
on its own authority. It doubtless often consulted the
sovereigns in such cases, if doubts arose as to the proper
course to pursue, but the royal signature did not appear
on the paper which announced the verdict; those of the
councillors were held to suffice.[2] It even went so far as to
exercise one of the most distinctive prerogatives of royalty
after the death of Queen Isabella, and summon on its own
authority the Cortes which all men demanded.[3] It was
also the supreme court of justice of the realm, to which appeal lay from the lower tribunals, to which all men without
distinction of rank or lineage were unquestionably subject,
and whose decision was absolutely final; it was thus the
principal means of centralizing the administration of justice in the hands of the crown. "When the liberties of the
nation had perished, it preserved the laws."[4] Fridays
were set apart for the exercise of its judicial functions,
and during the earlier part of the reign the sovereigns lent
all the majesty of their presence to these occasions by presiding whenever possible in person.[5] We shall revert to
this phase of the Council's activities in another place; for
the present we need only remark that contemporaries were
so deeply impressed with it that the old name of *Consejo
Real* began to give way to that of *Consejo de Justicia*
Consejo de Castilla, however, ultimately became the regular
designation of it, though all three titles continued to be used

---

[1] *Cortes*, iv, pp. 117 f.; Torreánaz, i, pp. 234 ff.
[2] *Cortes*, iv, p. 119.
[3] Zurita, vi, f. 89.
[4] *Cortes*, iv, p. 117; Torreánaz, i, pp. 261–274.
[5] *Cortes*, iv, pp. 115, 120; Mariéjol, p. 181.

THE COUNCIL OF CASTILE

indiscriminately for the same body for many years to come.
Finally, in conjunction with the monarch the Council possessed the right to issue orders and proclamations which
had the force of laws; but its legislative powers through the
so-called *autos acordados* were not fully developed until the
days of the Hapsburgs.[1] The ancient notion that valid
laws could only be made in and by the consent of the Cortes
had not been entirely abandoned in the reign of the Catholic
Kings.[2]

It will be readily understood that all the vast powers
above enumerated could not possibly be exercised in full
by a single body with a personnel so limited as that which
we have just described. A large amount of work would
have to be delegated to minor tribunals, and a passage in
Pulgar in reference to the Cortes of 1480 has led many authors to conclude that four other councils, each with a separate function of its own, were already in existence and full
working order at that date. "At the time of these Cortes,"
says the chronicler, "there were five councils in five separate
apartments in the royal palace where the king and queen
were staying;" and he then goes on to a brief description
of their duties and personnel.[3] But to assume that all
these bodies were permanently established in their final
form at this early period, is to antedate by over forty years
the constitutional arrangements of the time of Charles V,
and to ignore indisputable proofs of their subsequent organization. Of the four, outside the Consejo Real, only
one, that of the Hermandad, can be regarded as having attained anything like its final form in this period; and it
only lasted, as we have already seen, until 1498. The
other three bodies which Pulgar describes were merely

[1] Torreánaz, i, p. 235.
[2] Colmeiro, *Curso*, pp. 335 f.

[3] Pulgar, *Crónica*, pt. ii, cap. xcv
(B. A. E., lxx, p. 354).

groups of the chiefs of certain special branches of the administration, nuclei out of which full-fledged councils were afterwards evolved. What the words of the chronicler do show is that there was already a certain set of men — and it was the only one in which the grandees were permitted to play a prominent rôle — in which Ferdinand confided with reference to foreign affairs; this was the origin of the Council of State, which emerged in its final form in 1526.[1] "In another part of the palace," continues the story, "were the *Contadores Mayores* and the officials who kept the accounts of the royal treasury and the crown domain;" from these was ultimately evolved the *Consejo de la Hacienda*, though it did not take final shape till 1593.[2] Finally, a number of nobles and legists resident at the court, but natives of the realms of Aragon, Catalonia, Valencia, and Sicily, and well versed in the laws and customs of those lands, were intrusted, according to Pulgar, with the administration of the affairs of those kingdoms; yet it was not till November 19, 1494, that the *Consejo de Aragon*, of which this body was the origin, was definitely constituted for that purpose. In its final form it was composed of five legists; and it is worth noting that two of them were also members at one time or another of the *Consejo de Castilla*, an arrangement which the continuous presence of both bodies at the royal court rendered possible. This cannot, however, be taken to indicate any effort towards the fusion of the two bodies or of the different realms over which they had jurisdiction. It is explained by the very high ability of the two men in question, Alfonso de Caballeria and Felipe Pons, which made them indispensable. The Councils of Castile and of Aragon continued to deal exclusively with the affairs

[1] Colmeiro, *Curso*, p. 558.
[2] Pulgar, *Crónica*, pt. ii, cap. xcv (*B. A. E.*, lxx, p. 354); *Novísima Reco-* pilación, lib. vi, tit. x, leyes 1 and 2; Gounon-Loubens, *Essais sur l'administration de la Castille*, p. 275.

of the realms to which they respectively belonged; neither one trespassed upon the territory of the other.[1]

In addition to these different committees, there were two regular councils which took definite shape before the close of the reign. These were the *Consejo de la Suprema,* which we have already examined in connection with the Inquisition, and the *Consejo de las Ordenes,* which was certainly in existence in 1515.[2] The *Consejo de Indias,* whose origin and early development may most conveniently be considered in another place, was apparently spoken of as such as early as 1509, though it was not finally established until 1524.[3]

The measure of independent authority possessed by these different bodies, both before and after they emerged from the stage of amorphous committees to that of full-fledged councils, varied widely, as was natural, in every case; but the immense preponderance of the Council of Castile is in general the all-important fact to be borne in mind. It was spoken of by the sovereigns as *Nuestro Consejo* in the *Ordenanzas Reales* as if no other council existed; if others took their places beside it in the succeeding years, it certainly maintained its preëminence. The *Contadores de Hacienda* did little more than carry out in detail the main lines of the financial policy, which were laid down by the superior body. The Councils of the Hermandad, the Suprema, and the Indies doubtless enjoyed a somewhat larger measure of autonomy, but it was impossible for them to initiate a course of action repugnant to the Council of Castile. In the Council of Aragon we have, in theory at least, rather a coördinate than a subordinate jurisdiction during this period; but the fact, already noticed, that two of its members had seats in the

[1] Torreánaz, i, pp. 264–266. p. 157.
[2] Colmeiro, *Curso,* p. 559; Mariéjol, [3] Cf. *infra,* pp. 227 f.

Council of Castile, was an excellent safeguard against the two bodies falling to loggerheads with one another; and in case of difference of opinion on any isolated point, there could be no question which would prevail. The Council of State, on the other hand, was a purely advisory body with no real authority at all. Though it was usually placed at the head of the list of all the *consejos* in official descriptions of the government of Spain, the precedence accorded it was merely a sop to the grandees who had seats there, and for practical purposes amounted to nothing. The Consejo de Castilla continued to vindicate its position at the head of the great conciliar system whose ramification is the salient feature of Spanish constitutional development during the next three centuries; under the king it was the supreme power in the Spanish Empire, of which, as time went by, Castile became more and more unquestionably the centre.[1]

It is not easy to state what measure of authority was possessed by each of these different bodies apart from the sovereign. In this matter, as in the relation of the different councils to one another, the facts doubtless varied in every case. With the Hacienda, the Suprema, and the Hermandad, the sovereigns had probably little to do, save through the Council of Castile. With the Consejo de Indias they were doubtless somewhat closer in touch, and still more so with the Council of Aragon. The Council of State, on the other hand, was almost wholly dependent upon the presence of the crown, since foreign affairs, with which it dealt, were always directly guided from the throne. The powers of the all-important Council of Castile, as we have already seen, were

---

[1] On all this, cf. Mariéjol, pp. 150–164, and Gounon-Loubens, *Essais*, pp. 127–200; a "Discurso sobre los Consejos" by a certain Agustin Álvares de Toledo exists in manuscript, in the Biblioteca Nacional at Madrid (E 31 (Mss. 904), pp. 99–138), and contains a number of additional items of importance. I expect to print the whole or part of this document in a later volume.

partly exercised independently of the sovereigns, and partly in conjunction with them; but the tendency, as time wore on, was towards a marked increase of its own authority apart from the crown. During the early part of their reign, the monarchs were in constant attendance. They feared that in their absence it might get out of hand; and we have already seen that they made a special point of presiding in person on Fridays, when it dealt with judicial affairs. After the forces of anarchy and rebellion had been definitely overthrown, however, they felt safe in leaving it more and more to its own devices. This is doubtless the significance of the first definite emergence in 1489 of an office of which there had previously been only vague hints — that of the President of the Council of Castile, or, as he soon came to be called, the President of Castile. It was conferred in that year on Don Álvaro de Portugal — "a very upright and most prudent man" — and again ten years later on Juan Daza, bishop of Oviedo and later of Cartagena.[1] Its occupant soon came to be by far the most important person in the realm after the monarch · but the days of its greatest independent power and prestige did not come until the seventeenth century, when lazy, pleasure-loving 'picture kings' succeeded to the throne of the indefatigable Ferdinand and Isabella. Their Catholic Majesties were far too active and omniscient to permit any subordinate person to usurp their functions.

Such were the foundations of that great system of councils which formed the framework of the administration of the Spanish Empire, and which we shall encounter again and again in our examination of the different branches of the service of the crown. Through them the sovereigns carried their absolutism into every department and subdivision

[1] Torreánaz, i, pp. 220–233.

of the conduct of the government. Every single member of each of these different councils was appointed by the monarchy and could be dismissed at its pleasure. We have already pointed out that the overwhelming majority of these appointees, save in the Council of State, were *letrados*, whose origin and training rendered them fit instruments for the erection of a system of royal despotism; yet it is important to observe that Ferdinand and Isabella, in sharp contrast to many of their Hapsburg successors, were glad to advance men of originality and independent power to these important posts. The kind of councillor that Charles V, and still more Philip II, preferred, was the man who would obediently nay almost slavishly, follow orders and precedents and never strike out into a line of policy of his own; and this characteristic was not the least important of a number of elements that combined to paralyze the efficiency of Spanish administration in the end of the sixteenth century and give it that reputation for extreme slowness, heaviness, and inadaptability which has clung to it ever since. But these defects did not appear, or at least they are not at all prominent — save perhaps in connection with the government of remote colonies and dependencies — under the Catholic Kings Partly no doubt because the Spanish Empire had not yet attained its ultimate unwieldy proportions, but also because the sovereigns were not afraid to trust the management of it to men of ability, provided their loyalty was beyond question, the government of Ferdinand and Isabella forms an agreeable contrast to that of their successors in the comparative speed and efficiency of its operations.

Next in importance after Ferdinand and Isabella's reorganization of the Royal Council and its satellites come unquestionably their reforms in the administration of justice. To these the establishment of the Hermandad was an indispensable preliminary; for so terrible was the situation at the time of their accession that emergency measures were imperatively necessary before the ordinary courts of the realm could be expected to discharge their functions. At the same time, however, the sovereigns did their best to restore the badly shaken prestige of the regular tribunals; and they began, as we have already seen, at the top of the ladder by regularly lending the majesty of their presence to the Council of Castile on the days which it devoted to judicial affairs. The penalties meted out by that body in the early years of the reign were extremely severe. Villalobos, the medical adviser of Ferdinand and also of Charles V, characterizes the mutilations and beheadings that it inflicted as "terrifying and horrible vivisections";[1] but it is doubtful if any less drastic methods would have served the purpose. Certainly they enjoyed the warm approval of contemporaries, and Isabella in particular received, as was probably her due, the lion's share of the credit for the restoration of respect for the law. Fernández de Oviedo, writing in 1556, describes the early years of the reign as "an age of gold and of justice, when he who was in the right obtained his due. Since God has taken away the saintly queen, it is far harder to get an audience of a secretary's valet than it used to be of her and her Council, and a great deal more expensive."[2]

The reorganization of the Council of Castile and the emphasis laid upon its judicial functions effected all the reform that was necessary at the fountain head; the next problem was how to deal with the royal *Audiencia* or *Chancillería* below it. During the troublous times of the preceding reign

---

[1] *Los Problemas de Villalobos*, in B. A. E., xxxvi, *Curiosidades Bibliográficas*, p. 429.

[2] Oviedo's *Quinquagenas*, cited by J. Amador de los Rios, *Historia de Madrid*, ii, pp. 165 f.

the functions of this tribunal had been continually inter-
rupted, and its place of abode constantly changed, despite
the pragmatica of 1405 which had established it at Valladolid; in 1480 the sovereigns definitely ordered it back to
that city, where it henceforth remained.[1] This, however,
was only a beginning. It soon became evident that there
was far too much work on hand for a single royal court to
perform — especially as Ferdinand and Isabella, with the
growing security of their thrones and the increased complexity of their administration, tended more and more to
hand over to it many of the cases hitherto reserved to the
Council of Castile, in order to leave the latter body more
time for the discharge of its governmental functions.[2] They
therefore set up a second tribunal, first at Ciudad Real in
1494, and subsequently at Granada in 1505, for the southern
part of the realm; this body and that at Valladolid were
always known after 1494 as Chancillerías, a name which
emphasized their proximity to the throne.[3] The Tagus
marked the boundary between their jurisdictions.[4] A subsidiary tribunal also made its appearance in Galicia in
1486,[5] and others were created in subsequent reigns with
the gradual extension of the dominions of the crown;[6]
these lesser bodies were all called Audiencias, and we shall
later encounter that term, though with a somewhat different and extended significance, in the Spanish possessions
in the New World. But the two original courts enjoyed

[1] *Cortes*, iv, p. 121, note 3; Días de
Montalvo, *Ordenansas Reales*, lib. ii, tit.
iv, ley 4.
[2] Gounon-Loubens, *Essais*, pp. 203 f.
[3] Cf. Vol. I, p. 230, note 3; and *Novísima Recopilación*, lib. v, tit. i, leyes 1
and 2.
[4] *Novísima Recopilación*, lib. v, tit.
i, leyes 1 and 2; Antequera, *Historia de
la Legislación Española* (4th ed., Madrid, 1895), p. 394; F. Mendizábal,

"Origen, Historia, y Organización de la
Real Chancillería de Valladolid," in
R. A., 3d ser., xxx, pp. 61–72, 243–264,
437–452; xxxi, pp. 95–112, 459–467.
[5] *Novísima Recopilación*, lib. v, tit.
ii; Pulgar, *Crónica*, pt. iii, cap. lxvi
(*B. A. E.*, lxx, p. 443); Antequera, p.
394, dates the establishment of this
Audiencia in 1504.
[6] *Novísima Recopilación*, lib. v, tits.
iii–x.

for a long time by far the greatest measure of prestige.
Especially was this true of that of Valladolid. The number of its judges steadily rose as the reign progressed,
owing to the enormous accumulation of suits that were
brought before it. The four *oidores*, mentioned in the Cortes
of Toledo of 1480, were increased to eight and later to sixteen; so that at the end of the reign there were four *salas
de lo civil* in place of one. The *sala de lo criminal*, composed
of three alcaldes, remained unchanged, as did also the *sala
de los hijosdalgo*; but there was also added a special *sala*
and *juez* for natives of the province of Vizcaya.[1] One-year
terms were prescribed for most of the judges. Apparently
the sovereigns dreaded lest with a longer tenure they might be
in danger of getting out of hand;[2] and their fear of aristocratic intrusion is once more revealed by their stern prohibition of all such claims to "the enjoyment of any judicial
or governmental office by virtue of any hereditary right or
title" as had been made in the two previous reigns.[3] The
increase and development of the duties laid upon the *pro-
curador fiscal*, or prosecutor on behalf of the crown, form
one of the most striking features of Ferdinand and Isabella's
judicial reforms. He was constantly urged to display the
greatest energy and activity in order that the prerogatives
and revenues of the monarchs should in no wise be diminished
or impaired.[4] The sovereigns also zealously guarded the
judicial rights and privileges of the poor. In the larger tribunals they maintained special counsel for those who could not
afford to pay for it at their own expense; and in the minor

---

[1] *Cortes*, iv, p. 121; Ramirez, *Pragmaticas*, ff. xxiv–xxx; *Novísima Recopilación*, lib. v, tits. i and xi–xxxiv, passim; Mendizábal, in *R. A.*, 3d ser.,
xxx, pp. 256–258.
[2] In 1491 the President and oidores
of Valladolid were deprived of their
offices for permitting a case which they
should have settled themselves to be
appealed to Rome. Galíndez Carbajal,
Anales (in *D. I. E.*, xviii, p. 278).
[3] *Cortes*, iv, pp. 161 f.
[4] *Cortes*, iv, pp. 133 f.; Días de
Montalvo, *Ordenanzas Reales*, lib. ii,
tit. xii; Mariéjol, p. 183; Mendizábal,
in *R. A.*, 3d ser., xxx, p. 258.

ones they commanded that all the lawyers in attendance should give freely of their services to the destitute "without payment and for the love of God."[1]   The audiencias, the chancillerías, and the Council of Castile were protected against petty and vexatious suits by the provision that no case of less than 3000 maravedis' value could be brought before them; but various interesting precautions were taken to prevent the miscarriage of justice in the lower courts.   One of these provided that cases which could not be appealed might be tried over again at the request of either of the parties, before the same judge with two or three other persons of known integrity associated with him.[2]   A number of other elaborate regulations prescribed the methods of procedure of the Castilian audiencias and the nature of the cases that could come before them.[3]   Such details in regard to the minor and municipal tribunals as are relevant will be described under the head of local administration.[4]

In Aragon, Ferdinand evinced his enthusiasm for *letrados*, and also his distrust for such measure of independent authority as had been preserved to the Justicia, by insisting, in 1493, that when dealing with certain cases that magistrate should be obliged to take counsel with five legists appointed by the crown.[5]   It was a long step towards get-

---

[1] *Novísima Recopilación*, lib. v, tit. xxii, leyes 13, 14; Mariéjol, pp. 183 f.

[2] *Cortes*, iv, pp. 122–128, *passim*; Mariéjol, pp. 184 f.

[3] Most of these may be found in an ordinance "por la brevedad y orden de los pleytos" put forth by the sovereigns at Madrid in 1499. A copy of this may be found in the British Museum, Add. Mss. 9929, ff. 38–47, and there is a photograph of it in the Harvard College Library.

[4] The practice of maintaining, in constant residence at the Royal Court, eight provincial alcaldes (two from each of the four quarters of the realm) and

two special *alcaldes de corte y de su rastro* had been inherited from earlier days. Ferdinand and Isabella retained and amplified it, raised the number of *alcaldes de corte* to four, and carefully defined the limits of their jurisdiction. This institution was further developed under the Hapsburgs after the capital had been fixed at Madrid. Cf. *Cortes*, iv, pp. 124–127; *Novísima Recopilación*, lib. iv, tit. xxvii, leyes 8, 9; tit. xxviii, leyes 1, 2; Altamira, §§ 445, 582.

[5] *Fueros y Observancias*, ii, *Fori qui modo non sunt in usu*, ff. 43 ff.; Toreánaz, i, p. 263.

ting rid of the older associates of the Justicia, over whom the Cortes had managed to retain a considerable measure of control; and the process was completed in the succeeding reigns.

A necessary supplement to the reform of the tribunals was the codification and standardizing of the laws they administered. We have already seen that some progress had been made towards this end from the reign of Alfonso the Learned onward, and that the Roman elements in Spanish law had gained steadily at the expense of the native ones.[1] The process, however, had not gone nearly far enough to satisfy the sovereigns; diversification and contradiction were still far less frequently the exception than the rule. The first step taken to remedy the existing state of affairs was to intrust a certain jurist named Díaz de Montalvo with the task of collecting all the ordinances and pragmaticas put forth subsequently to the Fuero Real, the Partidas, and the Ordenamiento de Alcalá: he began his work in 1480, and finished it on November 11, 1484.[2] Despite the doubts of certain earlier writers, there can be no question of the legal validity of this collection,[3] which is popularly known as the Ordenanzas Reales, and of which no less than five editions were printed before 1500. On the other hand, it did nothing towards diminishing the discrepancies of the already existing codes; nay more, it even failed to reconcile its own provisions with those of the earlier collections; so that, if possible, it rendered confusion worse confounded. Petitions were presented by the procuradores of the Cortes of Toledo in 1502 that measures be taken to cure this crying evil, and to explain the many ambiguities in the existing laws;[4] for this purpose eighty-three enactments were put forth by the

---

[1] Cf. Vol. I, pp. 235 ff.
[2] Ladreda, *Estudios sobre los Códigos de Castilla*, p. 152.
[3] Ladreda, *op. cit.*, pp. 153 f.; Antequera, p. 422.
[4] Colmeiro, *Introd.*, ii, p. 69.

Cortes of Toro in 1505, which are usually known as the *Leyes de Toro*.[1] The remedy was good as far as it went, but it was totally inadequate. Nothing short of a complete fusion of all of the valid laws of the realm into a single code would do the work, and that was not accomplished until the *Nueva Recopilación* in the reign of Philip II. A striking passage in Isabella's will[2] reveals her dissatisfaction with the existing state of affairs in this particular, and her deep solicitude for improvement; but events moved so fast, and there was so much new legislation during her reign, that it was perhaps just as well that the task of codification was postponed to a more static period. The collection known as Ramirez's *Pragmaticas* (1503), to which reference has been several times made in the preceding pages, was a supplementary compilation of a less official character;[3] those of its provisions which attained recognized validity were subsequently embodied in the *Nueva Recopilación*.

The absolutist theories of Ferdinand and Isabella made them chafe under the restrictions of their royal authority which were imposed by the powers of the Castilian Cortes. At first, while their attention was centred on breaking the power of the baronage, they concealed their dread of the national assembly, and skilfully utilized it as an ally against the nobles. It will be remembered that the Cortes of Madrigal in 1476 and of Toledo in 1480 lent them valuable aid in this particular. But with the aristocracy reduced to impotence, the sovereigns' fears of democratic opposition not unnaturally revived.[4] They saw that the indispensable ally of the past might easily develop into the menacing rival of the future, unless it was carefully restrained; they therefore

[1] Ladreda, pp. 161–166; *Cortes*, iv, pp. 194–219.
    in Dormer, *Discursos Varios*
[2] *de Historia*, pp. 314–388 (378–380).
[3] Clemencin, *Elógio*, pp. 214–220.
[4] Zurita, vi, f. 96.

took pains to summon the national assembly as infrequently as possible, and, whenever they were obliged to have recourse to it for financial purposes, to make the most of those germs of decadence which had already begun to appear in its constitution and procedure. The result was that the history of the Castilian Cortes under the Catholic Kings shows a decline quite as marked as the development of the powers of the Council. The salutary victory of the monarchy over the aristocracy — an indispensable condition of continued national existence — was dearly bought by the stifling of those aspirations for liberty which formed the brightest feature of mediaeval Castilian life. At the most critical stage of its existence the realm was transformed from a turbulent oligarchy, whose lawlessness was partially redeemed by a somewhat undisciplined passion for freedom, into a monarchy so omnipotent that nothing, save the national tendency towards separatism, could hold out against it.

The chronology of the Castilian Cortes under the Catholic Kings forms a significant commentary on these developments. According to the official reckoning[1] they were summoned sixteen times between the death of Henry IV (1474) and that of Ferdinand (1516): of these meetings four took place before 1483 and the other twelve after 1497.[2] The explanation of this curious distribution is not far to seek. The first four sessions represent the period when the monarchs needed the alliance of the Cortes against the aristocracy. The gap between 1482 and 1498 indicates that the sovereigns had won their battle and dismissed their ally; and the hiatus would inevitably have been prolonged, had

[1] *Catálogo de las Cortes de los reinos de España* (ed. R. A. H., Madrid, 1855), pp. 63–69.
[2] Only six of these assemblies have left *cuadernos*; the others were summoned solely for the recognition of heirs to the throne or for grants of funds. Cf. *Cortes*, iv, pp. 1–259.

it not been for the necessity of obtaining national recognition of new heirs to the throne, and still more of gaining extra funds for the prosecution of the Italian wars. Careful comparison of the dates of most of the last twelve meetings with the ebbs and flows of the foreign conflict will reveal close interrelation between them.[1]

Besides their refusal to call the national assembly together, except when absolutely necessary, the sovereigns utilized every quiet and inconspicuous means to accelerate the deterioration of its powers. Most important was their omission to summon the two privileged orders. Both nobles and clergy came in 1476 and in 1480,[2] but afterwards we hear little or nothing of them; and by the end of the reign the Castilian Cortes had become to all intents and purposes a meeting of thirty-six procuradores from eighteen cities — "a number" which, as has been well said, "was too large for a council, but not enough for a national assembly." [3] In strict legality there can be little doubt that the sovereigns were fully justified in leaving the privileged orders out, since their presence was entirely dependent on the will of the crown.[4] On the other hand the tradition of their attendance was so strong that it is almost inconceivable that Ferdinand and Isabella could have succeeded in breaking it, if the persons concerned had made a stand for their rights. It is at their own door that the blame for the gradual elimination of the nobles and clergy from the national assembly is chiefly to be laid; but it is not difficult to see how they came to lose interest in the meetings of a body, whose functions, as time went on, came to be more and more exclusively restricted to the voting of taxes from which they were exempt.

[1] Mariéjol, p. 139.   Mariéjol, p. 138.
[2] Colmeiro, *Introd.*, ii, pp. 40, 51.   [4] Cf. Vol. I, pp. 219 ff.
[3] *Ibid.*, i, pp. 23 ff.; ii, p. 52;

At the same time that the two privileged orders ceased to attend, the independence and ability of the procuradores of the cities declined.[1] The humble, indeed almost abject tone of their petitions to Ferdinand and Isabella forms a striking contrast to the haughty claims which their predecessors had addressed to previous sovereigns.[2] The remodelling of the municipal constitutions and fueros, which we shall subsequently describe, placed their selection more than ever in the hands of the crown and of its representatives; and the degradation of the Cortes was still further accelerated by the initiation, in 1501, of the practice of voting salaries to their own members.[3] Most of their various rights and powers, save the control over the *servicio*, rested rather on custom than on written law, and were exercised only in consonance with the wishes of the crown; all this made it the easier for Ferdinand and Isabella to override them. In legislation, for instance, the increased activity of the sovereigns and of the Consejo left the Cortes little to do. They continued, of course, to frame petitions on a wide variety of topics, but as they possessed no real hold over the crown, the monarchs could afford coolly to disregard such requests as were not to their liking. Even in financial affairs the powers of the Cortes were really very slight. The list of revenues which came to the crown independent of their vote was so long that in times of peace the government managed to subsist without their aid,[4] as is shown by the long period from 1482 to 1498, in which the

[1] Despite all the wise laws about them, which had been passed in previous reigns, and were incorporated in the *Ordenanzas Reales*, lib. ii, tit. xi.

[2] Mariéjol, p. 144.

[3] Colmeiro, *Introd.*, ii, p. 69.

[4] Bernáldez (cap. xciv), however, tells us that, in order to do this, the sovereigns were obliged, at the height of the Granadan war, to levy on the inhabitants of the towns and cities every twenty days. On an earlier occasion the queen appropriated some of the plate in the churches (Pulgar, pt. ii, cap. xxv, in *B. A. E.*, lxx, p. 274) and also pawned her own jewels (Clemencin, *Elógio*, pp. 310 f.).

national assembly was not summoned once. Isabella, it is true, had grave misgivings as to whether the *alcabala* could be lawfully levied without the Cortes' consent; but her dying request that the matter be carefully investigated was disregarded.[1] Over the *servicio* the Cortes did retain undisputed control; but their extraordinarily ineffective procedure, and their failure to make the most of their authority in other respects, enabled the sovereigns in the long run almost invariably to extort what they wished from them. The baleful effect of this state of affairs on the financial development of a nation which possessed unusually little comprehension of economic principles, and the external demands of whose government increased by leaps and bounds in the succeeding period, requires no additional emphasis.

The Cortes of the realms of the Crown of Aragon were of course in far better condition to resist the invasion of their ancient prerogatives by the monarchy. Realizing the difficulties of the situation there, Ferdinand followed his usual policy of leaving them as far as possible alone. The Aragonese Cortes, the most obstinate of all, met but seven times during his reign, those of Valencia once, and those of Catalonia six times, while the General Cortes of the three realms were convoked only thrice.[2] Money came far harder from the assemblies of the eastern kingdoms when they did meet than from those of Castile, with the natural result that a totally unfair proportion of the financial burden of the Spanish Empire was thrown upon the western kingdom.

All in all, the Catholic Kings had managed to drive the Cortes of their various realms a long way on the road to destruction; but with all their efforts they were unable

---

[1] Cf. *infra*, p. 135.
[2] *Catálogo de las Corte* (ed R A. H.) pp. 120–122, 156–158, 179.

entirely to exterminate the ancient Spanish love of freedom and democracy, as the revolt of the *comuneros* in the succeeding reign was to prove in dramatic fashion. The Emperor, who was considerably less hostile to popular assemblies than his predecessors, gave the Castilian Cortes one last and very advantageous opportunity to vindicate their ancient position; but that body, when the chance came, showed itself lamentably unable to take advantage of it.

Consideration of the national assembly naturally leads on to that of the national finances, whose reëstablishment was rendered doubly essential by Spain's active foreign policy and brilliant imperial prospects. To this the great acts of retrenchment and resumption in the Cortes of Madrigal and Toledo were the indispensable preliminaries; and at the same time a solemn prohibition forbade the further levying of any extra or special imposts by individuals or corporations, in virtue of any grants or favors of the preceding reign.[1] Vigorous efforts were also made to reduce to the smallest possible dimensions the measure of exemption from taxation enjoyed by the two privileged orders. Especially noteworthy is a law providing that when any church, university, or notable person enjoyed the right of extending such exemption to any one else, it should be exercised only in favor of poorer men, and not in the case of the rich.[2]

These early measures really give the keynote to the whole financial policy of the Catholic Kings, who with their usual conservatism strove rather to correct the defects and abuses of the system they had inherited, than to augment

[1] *Cortes*, iv, pp. 106 f.; Altamira, § 585.

[2] *Cortes*, iv, pp. 179, 181; Altamira, § 585; Colmeiro, *Introd.*, ii, pp. 59 f.

their income by inventing new sources of revenue. According to the figures usually given, the total annual yield of the Castilian imposts amounted to only 885,000 reals in 1474, while thirty years later it had increased to 26,283,334; [1] but during this long period only two new types of revenue were added. The first of these was the product of the mines of the Indies, which we shall take up in another place; for the present we need only observe that the amount of it, during the early years of discovery and exploration, was not large. The second was the so-called Bulla de la Cruzada, or system of indulgences conceded by the Pope, through which those who contributed to the Moorish wars could purchase immunity from the penalties of Purgatory. As actually administered, it was an intolerable exaction. It was continued after the expulsion of the infidel from Granada, and the revenues derived from it were used for all sorts of purposes which had never been intended; what had been originally granted temporarily and for a specific end, became in fact a regular and permanent crown revenue. Subsequently it was even collected in the American possessions.[2] The Cortes of 1512 complained vigorously against these abuses. "The preachers of the Bull," they protested, "keep men two and three days in the churches from morning to evening to listen to their sermons, and thus prevent them from earning their daily bread; and when they find that they cannot thus induce them to take the said Bull, they parade through the streets, asking every one they meet if they know their Pater Noster and Ave Maria; and if perchance they find any one who does not, they force him to take the said Bull as a penance; and if any one does not take it they drag him around with them in shackles to hear their preachments, and thus force him at

[1] Clemencin, *Elógio*, p. 154.   [2] Bourne, *Spain in America*, p. 303, note 3.

last by compulsion and intimidation to do their will." [1]
Yet the sums derived from the Bull of Crusade formed,
after all, an insignificant portion of the grand total; the
bulk of the income of the Catholic Kings was obtained from
the older sources. Of these, as we have already seen, there
were a very large variety, in theory at least, over and above
the *servicio*,[2] but the disrupted state of the realm and the
inefficiency and corruption of the royal taxgatherers prevented all but a very small portion of the sums that should
have been collected from ever reaching the royal treasury.
The first aim of the financial policy of the Catholic Kings was
to secure some sort of an approximation between the amounts
due to the crown and those which were actually received.

The group of men, or Council, as Pulgar somewhat pre-
maturely describes it, which constantly resided at the court
and busied itself with the royal revenues, was of course the
head and centre of the new system. It was composed, so
the chronicler tells us, of "the contadores mayores and the
officials of the books of the treasury and royal domain, who
managed the king's taxes and the salaries and grants that
were paid by the crown, and settled everything that concerned the royal property and patrimony." [3] This body
was divided, early in the reign, into two separate offices
or *contadurías* — one for the treasury itself (*contaduría de
hacienda*), and one for the royal accounts (*contaduría de
cuentas*) : each was directed by two *contadores mayores*,
who had at their disposal a large secretarial force.[4] And

[1] *Cortes*, iv, pp. 236 f.

[2] Cf. Vol. I, p. 248.

[3] Pulgar, *Crónica*, pt. ii, cap. xcv
(*B. A. E.*, lxx, p. 354).

[4] *Colección de leyes, ordenanzas, etc.,
para la contaduría mayor de Cuentas*
(Madrid, Imprenta Real, 1829), pp.
16–20; Díaz de Montalvo, *Ordenanzas
Reales*, lib. vi, tits. i–iv, *passim*; *Cortes*,
iv, pp. 19–109 *passim*; Gallardo Fernández, *Origen de las rentas de la Corona*,
i, pp. 25–29; Piernas Hurtado, *Tratado
de Hacienda Publica*, ii, pp. 60–69; C.
Espejo, "Organización de la Hacienda,"
in *Cultura Española* (1907), número vi,
pp. 403–408; R. Fuente Arias, *Alfonso
de Quintanilla, Contador Mayor de los
Reyes Católicos* (Oviedo, 1909, 2 vols.).

the increased efficiency of the central financial council
which resulted from this reorganization was equalled, if
not surpassed, by that of the subordinate officials whom it
sent out to do its bidding throughout the length and breadth
of the realm.[1] The royal taxgatherers seemed to be every-
where. The corregidores, whose activity, as we shall later
see, was one of the most striking features of the administration of Ferdinand and Isabella, were always on hand to
protect and support them in exacting the uttermost far-
thing. Backed up by the authority of the powerful monarchy, they could no longer be intimidated by local magnates
into shirking their duty.

Under such a system as this the ancient revenues of the
crown took on a new lease of life. The *diezmos de aduanas*
mounted fast and high, partly no doubt because of the
permission to deal with Aragon in certain commodities
hitherto forbidden, which paid the ordinary duties in crossing the line; more because of the general increase of the
commerce of the whole realm which accompanied the restoration of order, and because the customs officials were able
to perform their functions.[2] A new and elaborate schedule
of rates for the *derechos de sello* or *chancillería* in the *cuaderno*
of the Cortes of Madrigal shows that the sovereigns were
determined to make men pay liberally for any grant or
favor from the crown.[3] Most notable of all was the reform
in the collection of the *alcabala*. In 1491, before Granada,
the sovereigns put forth a long series of regulations concerning its incidence and collection, and the prevention
of the frauds that had hitherto occurred in connection with
it.[4] A great increase in the yield resulted from this measure,

[1] Díaz de Montalvo, *Ordenanzas Reales*, lib. vi, tit. iv.
[2] Altamira, §§ 585, 594.
[3] *Cortes*, iv, pp. 33–45.
[4] Most of these many be found in *Novísima Recopilación*, lib. x, tit. xii, leyes 11–15, 17–19.

despite the queen's insistence that the clergy, who had hitherto like the nobles been subjected to the *alcabala*, should henceforth be exempted from it.[1] Its collection was at first let out to farmers for a certain fixed sum; but this method aroused such bitter protests that at a suggestion from Ximenes it was finally turned over to the municipalities themselves, which were allowed to use their own methods in gathering it in, but were expected in return to hand over annually to the royal treasury sums proportionate to their size and importance.[2] Even this reform did not entirely silence complaint, and the matter was a constant source of worry to Isabella down to the day of her death. The rate remained at ten per cent throughout the reign; and despite the clerical exemption it was the most important of all the revenues of the crown.[3]

A thorough reform and standardization of the value of the coinage accompanied these measures. Most of the work was carried through in 1497; and though the debased or 'vellon' currency was permitted to remain in circulation, its relation to the gold and silver money was more strictly defined than before, so that the confusion in values, though still extreme, was by no means so bad as in previous reigns.[4]

None of these financial reforms, however, could have effected their ends had they not been accompanied by a general revival of the economic life of the realm as a whole. Had the wealth of the nation remained where it was in the reign of Henry IV, the government could have done nothing but 'borrow from beggars.' The solicitude of Ferdinand

[1] *Novísima Recopilación*, lib. i, tit. ix, ley 8. A few specially privileged cities and towns and certain persons about the court shared this exemption. Gounon-Loubens, p. 282.

[2] Mariéjol, pp. 218 f.

[3] Some additional information on the *alcabala* as well as on other phases of the financial history of the period may still be found in H. Schäfer's article, mentioned on p. 168, *infra*.

[4] L. Saez, *Demostración del valor de las monedas durante el Reynado de Enrique IV* (Madrid, 1805); Clemencin, *Elógio*, pp. 507–556; Lea, *Inquisition of Spain*, i, pp. 560–566.

and Isabella for the prosperity and wellbeing of their people in this respect is highly creditable. The economic progress of Castile under their administration is not one of their most conspicuous triumphs, and it is idle to deny that they made a number of serious mistakes. But when we consider that they inherited a people with little or no talent for affairs, and a traditional aversion to agricultural labor, and when we remember that their religious policy committed them to the expulsion of the portions of the population most valuable from an economic point of view, we shall certainly admit that their successes outweighed their failures. Their Hapsburg heirs did not do nearly so well in this respect, though it is fair to say that the problems with which they were confronted were harder. Indeed, if the Spanish empire in the New World had not been launched on the crest of a temporary wave of prosperity at home, it is doubtful whether it could have survived its earliest trials.[1]

The inevitable clash of the agricultural and pastoral interests was one of the foremost subjects to engage the monarchs' attention. At first sight their policy appears to indicate a willingness consistently to sacrifice the former to the latter. Certainly their favor and protection gave the Mesta at the end of their reign a far stronger position than it had occupied at the beginning. Yet on the other hand it is only fair to point out that they also strove to do their best by the proverbially thorny problem of Castilian agriculture. Though the *labrador* — or laborer in the fields — still remained a social outcast and a political nonentity, his estate and condition were ameliorated in a number of different ways. A pragmatica of 1480 granted the

---

[1] On this and the succeeding paragraphs, cf. A. Lope Orriols, *Política Económica de los Reyes Católicos* (Barcelona, 1894), *passim*.

solariego the right to remove from one place of abode and settle in another, and permitted him to take with him such possessions as he desired, and to sell the rest, irrespective of distinctions of *tierras de señorio, de abadengo,* or *de realengo,* or *behetría.*[1] This law was by no means rigidly observed, even by the monarchs themselves, but it marked a considerable advance over the conditions that had obtained before. It may in fact be justly regarded as dealing the death blow to serfdom in Castile. Earlier legislation forbidding the seizure for debt of cattle for the plough and of agricultural implements, and exempting one pair of oxen on each farm from taxation, was revived at the Cortes of Madrigal; and a new regulation was passed in 1496 commending laborers and their property to the special protection of the Hermandad.[2] An important **pragmatica** was also issued in the latter year at Burgos, insisting on the preservation of the forests, gardens, and vineyards of the cities.[3] The sovereigns' encouragement of great fairs at the chief centres of the realm naturally helped the circulation of agricultural products.[4] On the other hand, the sale of grain was subject to heavy taxation[5] down at least to the year 1504, when a series of bad harvests caused the impost to be suppressed.[6] One gains the impression that in good years, such as came with gratifying frequency in the last decade of the fifteenth century, Castilian agriculture could just manage to hold its own; but that it was in no condition to resist bad ones, of which there was a long succession after 1503. Of course there was the

---

[1] *Novísima Recopilación,* lib: vii, tit. xxvi, ley 6; Colmeiro, *E. P.,* ii, p. 78; Altamira, § 568.

[2] *Cortes,* iv, pp. 95 f.; Días de Montalvo, *Ordenanzas Reales,* lib. xii, tit. v, leyes 7, 8; *Novísima Recopilación,* lib. xi, tit. xxxi, ley 14; Altamira, § 593.

[3] Ramirez, *Pragmaticas,* ff. lxii–lxiii.

[4] Díaz de Montalvo, *Ordenanzas Reales,* lib. iii, tit. vii.

[5] Ramirez, *Pragmaticas,* f. cxlii.

[6] Altamira, § 593.

greatest difference in the situation in the different parts of the realm. Portions of Murcia and Andalusia were so fertile that they could take care of themselves in any season, while some of the barren stretches of the meseta defied the most favorable possible conjunction of climatic conditions and human effort.

In the realms of the crown of Aragon Ferdinand also strove to better the lot of the peasants and serfs, largely no doubt as a blow to the nobles and on broad humanitarian grounds, but partly in order to serve economic ends. In Aragon, indeed, where the condition of the rural poor was far worse than in Castile, he had to admit defeat, and permit the continuation of certain ancient abuses which he had hoped to eradicate. In Catalonia, however, where the *payeses de remensa* had risen in revolt under the turbulent rule of John II and continued their rebellion during the first years of his own reign, he finished the noble work which had been begun by his predecessors by definitely abolishing the six *malos usos* in the so-called *Sentencia arbitral de Guadalupe* in 1486.[1] Various measures of precaution were naturally maintained to guard against any fresh outbreak, and some of the ancient financial exactions were suffered to continue, in order to satisfy the claims of the baronage; but the process of liberation had by this time advanced too far to be ever permanently checked; and an important rôle in the history of his native land was assured to the Catalan peasant in the succeeding generations.

Meantime the Castilian Mesta made rapid and consistent progress. It had a long start on its agricultural rivals in the western kingdom when the reign began, and a combination of court favor, and of the general prosperity which

[1] Hinojosa, *Cuestión Agraria en Cataluña*, pp. 311–318; Altamira, §§ 568 f.; J. Coroleu, in *Estado de la Cultura Española en el Siglo XV* (Conferencias leídas en el Ateneo Barcelonés), p. 32.

accompanied the restoration of internal order, placed it in an almost impregnable position before Ferdinand's death. Hitherto the crown's control over this great sheep owners' gild — the dominant force in the principal national occupation — had been preserved by the king's appointment of the *alcalde entregador*, or principal judicial protector of the Mesta, who kept open the *cañadas* and regulated the interminable quarrels arising out of the encroachments of the pastoral on the agricultural lands and vice versa. In 1454 this important office had been conferred on Pedro de Acuña, a member of the Royal Council, in order that the monarchy might be kept the closer in touch with the Mesta's affairs. This, however, was not enough to suit the Catholic Kings, who were determined still further to strengthen their hold over the Castilian sheep owners, and to derive the largest possible revenue from their profits. In the year 1500, accordingly, they created a new position, the Presidency of the Mesta, to be held *in perpetuo* by the senior member of the Council of Castile, with the duty of supervising all the inferior officers of the institution, and of directing its internal organization and external relations. The President naturally superseded the *alcalde entregador* as the principal link between the Mesta and the crown; in 1568 the alcalde's office was finally taken over by the Mesta itself for the sum of 750,000 maravedis. In 1492 and 1511, moreover, the Catholic Kings caused a new set of ordinances to be drawn up for the regulation of the Mesta's internal constitution: the bulk of the work was done by Doctor Palacios Rubios, one of the famous *letrados* of the day, who was also prominent in the early history of the administration of the Indies.

But if the creation of the office of President of the Mesta and the promulgation of new laws for its observance brought the institution more closely than ever under crown control, they also insured to it a great increase of crown protection and support. The first part of the sixteenth century unquestionably witnessed the climax of its development. Its extraordinary power and prosperity in this period are the outward emblems of the victory of the pastoral over the agricultural interests in Castile, in a conflict which presents many interesting analogies to the contemporaneous English struggle over enclosures. The Mesta was now not only a highly organized and specially privileged corporation, securely intrenched behind the favor and protection of the crown and amply capable of defending itself against the hostility of municipal officers and local magnates. It was rapidly becoming a considerable political force, which could lend valuable aid to the monarchy in its struggle to dominate the Cortes, the municipalities, and the courts. It is needless to add that the crown took good care to secure to itself a liberal recompense for its patronage of the Mesta in money as well as in reciprocal political support. The revenues it derived from *servicio y montazgo*[1] were multiplied many times over in the reign of the Catholic Kings; moreover the latter appointed special judges of their own — *jueces pesquisidores* — to hear suits between the Mesta and the local tax collectors, so that a good many of the imposts which had previously been levied by the municipal authorities gradually found their way into the royal hacienda. It was also in this reign that the Mesta began the practice of occasionally voting special contributions to the crown, over and above the taxes it ordinarily paid; under Charles V the sums yielded by this custom were substantially increased[2]

---

[1] The phrase *servicio y montazgo* came in during this reign to replace *pontazgo y montazgo*, as the designation of the taxes paid by the Mesta to the central government. *Pontazgo y montazgo* continued to be used for the local imposts.

[2] My chief authority for this paragraph is Dr. J. Klein's doctoral disser-

The industrial and commercial policy of the Catholic Kings was dictated, like that of their contemporaries in other European lands, by the strictest principles of state regulation and protection. Standardization of weights and measures, minute regulations concerning the manufacture and production of different commodities, sumptuary laws of infinite variety and scope, and stern prohibition of the export of certain commodities and of the import of others occupied a large share of the attention of Ferdinand and Isabella.[1] Much pains was spent on the revival of manufacturing, for which the sovereigns discerned the country's exceptional advantages. Hitherto Castile had exported chiefly raw material and bought most of its manufactured commodities abroad. Now, with the idea of righting the balance in one of the most important staples of Castilian trade, the sovereigns ordained that no more than two thirds of the raw wool produced in the realm should be sent out of it, and forbade the importation of manufactured cloths.[2] For the time being the result was highly gratifying. The woollen industries of Toledo and Seville became famous throughout Western Europe, while in the south the manufacture of silk, which had flourished so notably under the Moors, was maintained at such a point that in 1504 the factories of eight cities in Andalusia paid about 9,000,000 maravedis a year in taxes to the royal treasury.[3] All the internal tolls and economic barriers which had been established within Castile with the connivance of Henry IV since 1464, and from which the nobles drew the greatest profit, were abolished[4]; the sovereigns also showed the most

tation on the Mesta; cf. *ante*, Vol. I, pp. 263, 270.
[1] Ramirez, *Pragmaticas*, ff. cxii, cxvii-cxx, cxxiii, cxxv, cxxvi, cxxxiii, clxxvii-clxxxiv; Clemencin, *Elógio*, pp. 243-258.

[2] *Cortes*, iv, p. 254.
[3] Altamira, § 591.
[4] Excepting, of course, the municipal *portazgo* and *montazgo*: *Cortes*, iv, pp. 172 ff.

persistent energy in improving the public roads and highways.[1] Though the high tariffs at the custom houses on
the frontiers of the realm were maintained, its foreign commerce flourished as never before. The list of consuls maintained in other countries to look after the interests of
Castilian trade in this period reminds one of the palmier
days of Barcelona.[2] As in other lands, the export of
gold and silver was strictly prohibited. A law was passed
in the Cortes of Toledo to that effect,[3] and elaborate
precautions were adopted to give effect to it. When
any Spaniard left the realm, he was to inform the corregidor of the place where he resided what sum of money
he carried with him. At the frontier the same formality
had to be gone through before an *alcalde de las sacas*
and three other witnesses. The destination and the probable length of the traveller's stay had also to be revealed,
and all the details were written down, so as to be available
as testimony against him in case it was found that he had
lied. Foreigners were forbidden, by a pragmatica of 1491,
to take any money out of the realm; if they came as merchants they were obliged to exchange their goods for the
products of the land.[4] Of all the features of the monarchs'
commercial policy, that which bore most directly on the
fortunes of the Spanish Empire was their zeal for the increase of shipping. The ramifications of the subject are
very wide. Even the course of foreign affairs was at times
affected by it; for rival navigation acts were one of the chief
causes of the bickerings of Ferdinand and Henry VII of
England, which formed such an unedifying feature of both
monarchs' declining years.[5] But, whatever its results, the
origin of the policy was primarily economic. The discovery

[1] Colmeiro, *E. P.*, ii, pp. 288 f.
[2] *Ibid.*, ii, pp. 319 f.
[3] *Cortes*, iv, p. 157.
[4] Clemencin, *Elógio*, p. 247.
[5] Busch, *England under the Tudors*, tr. Todd, pp. 158–164, 206–228, *passim.*

of America furnished the needed impetus, and in 1495 the sovereigns offered a large premium for the construction of ships of six hundred tons and upwards. In 1500 they forbade the loading of any foreign vessels in their harbors if a Castilian one was available. In 1501 a fresh pragmatica forbade the sale of any Spanish vessel in a foreign land without the express authorization of the crown.[1] Such measures as these produced the desired results. In 1481 their Majesties were able to despatch but seventy ships to aid Ferrante of Naples in putting the Turks out of Otranto;[2] in 1496, before the full effects of their policy could have been felt, we are told that they sent 130 vessels, carrying 20,000 men, to convey their daughter to Flanders, at the same time that another squadron was blockading the coasts of Cerdagne and Roussillon.[3] All in all, it is clear that the Catholic Kings succeeded in arousing the economic energies of Castile in a variety of directions, and to an extent previously unknown.

In Catalonia and in Majorca, on the other hand, the reign of Ferdinand and Isabella witnessed a marked economic decline. A number of causes contributed to this result. In the first place, the devastating civil wars and internal uprisings which occurred under the rule of John II dislocated the commercial activities of Barcelona and of Palma. In the second, the constitution of the former city was thoroughly remodelled by Ferdinand for the benefit of the monarchy in such a way as to sap the vitality of its ancient democratic institutions, and also seriously to injure its trade. The ancient practice of electing the members of the Concell and of the Concell de Cent was exchanged for a system of *insaculación*, and the representatives

[1] Ramirez, *Pragmaticas*, ff. cxxxv–cxxxvii; Colmeiro, *E. P.*, i, pp. 398 f.
[2] Pulgar, *Crónica*, pt. ii, cap. xcix (in *B. A. E.*, lxx, pp. 358 f.).
[3] Fernández de Navarrete, *Viajes*, i, pp. l–li.

of the mercantile and artisan classes were gradually elbowed aside.[1] Thirdly, it seems perfectly clear that the economic effect of the Inquisition and of the expulsion of the Jews was felt much more quickly and acutely in the eastern kingdoms than in Castile. A larger proportion of their trade was managed by Hebrews, and the complaints of the citizens of both capitals to Ferdinand plainly show that, in their estimation at least, the evil results of religious intolerance were chiefly responsible for their misfortunes. The advance of the Turks in the eastern Mediterranean deprived both Catalonia and Majorca of some of their most valuable markets in the Levant, and at the same time the discovery of America diverted the economic energies of Spain as a whole in a new direction. Castile suddenly became the centre of interest, and the eastern kingdoms were eclipsed. Barcelona lost a fifth of its population during the last third of the fifteenth century; in the early part of the sixteenth it revived somewhat, owing probably to the Italian wars, which necessarily focussed men's attention on the Mediterranean shores; but it never regained its former prestige. In 1491 the *consules* of the Lonja memorialized Ferdinand in a truly pitiful strain. "The commerce of this your city," they declared, "is entirely prostrated and abandoned . . . and the workmen and the artisans, who can no longer gain a livelihood or ply their trades, depart and transfer themselves to other kingdoms. "[2]

The principles of centralization and monarchical supremacy on which the internal policy of Ferdinand and Isabella was founded left scant room for the maintenance of the high

Cf. Bové, *Institucions de Catalunya*, pp. 119 f.; Altamira, § 580.

[2] Capmany, *Memorias*, ii, p. 299; Altamira, §§ 580, 595: Lea, *Inquisition* of *Spain*, i, pp. 260 ff.; J. Arias y Miranda, *Examen del influjo que tuvo en el comercio etc. de España su dominacion en América, passim.*

traditions of municipal self-government which had been inherited from the days of the Reconquest. The decline of the Castilian cities had begun more than a century before the accession of the Catholic Kings.[1] Many of the ancient fueros had been shamefully transgressed, and royal appointees had begun to supersede the locally elected officials under the earliest sovereigns of the house of Trastamara; but hitherto the effect of these changes had been rather to convert the municipalities into centres of corruption and violence, than to render them amenable to the control of the crown. The monarchy had not yet attained a position sufficiently strong to enable it to reap the benefit of the abrogation of the local liberties; it had not succeeded in acquiring for itself the powers of which the concejos had been deprived. Dissipation of authority, rather than its concentration in royal hands, had thus far resulted from the crown's premature attempts at municipal regulation. The town of Caceres in Estremadura was a case in point. In the reign of Henry IV it was apparently divided into two hostile factions, which fought so bitterly over the possession of the city offices that "deaths and other improprieties," as Pulgar significantly expresses it, were the usual result.[2] But Ferdinand and Isabella did not propose to tolerate the continuance of such conditions as this. The queen visited Caceres in person, in the year 1477, and ordained that the municipal magistrates, who had hitherto been elected annually, should now be chosen by lot and hold office for the rest of their lives; but that when, through deaths, future vacancies should occur, she and her successors would appoint to the same in such manner as would best conduce to the service of the crown. "And this she

---

[1] Cf. *ante*, Vol. I, pp. 194 ff.
[2] Pulgar, *Crónica*, pt. ii, cap. lxix (*B. A. E.*, lxx, p. 323).

established as the regular law and custom of this place, and all the inhabitants thereof rejoiced in it, because it put a stop to their quarrels and the evils that followed in their train, which had resulted from the elections of earlier days." [1] Apparently the cities were perfectly ready to renounce their ancient liberties, now that at last they had got a monarch sufficiently powerful to give them peace and order in return.

The prevalence of such sentiments as these afforded the Catholic Kings an admirable opportunity to subvert the foundations of local autonomy in Castile without the sacrifice of popularity which such a measure would naturally be supposed to entail; and Ferdinand and Isabella took full advantage of the situation to carry their absolutism into every corner of the land. A number of ordinances were put forth in the Cortes of Toledo of 1480 to strengthen their control over the municipal magistrates. Hereditary grants of offices were revoked, and deathbed resignations in favor of kinsmen or friends forbidden. If a *regidor* was found to have leased his position to some other person he was to forfeit it as penalty for his offence; though, on the other hand, the crown not seldom put up the local magistracies for sale.[2] All cities which did not possess a *casa de ayuntamiento* or town hall were directed to build one within two years, in order that municipal affairs might be conducted with dignity and decorum; they were also commanded to keep written records of all their special laws and privileges.[3] Certain local institutions were judged to be so dangerous that, instead of attempting to modify them, the Catholic Kings determined to abrogate them entirely.

[1] Pulgar, *loc. cit.*; *Privilegios de Caceres*, ed. P. de Ulloa y Golfín (1679?), pp. 277 ff.

[2] *Cortes*, iv, pp. 139 f., 151, 176, 179 f., 182 f.; Colmeiro, *Curso*, pp. 505 f.; Altamira, § 579.

[3] *Cortes*, iv, pp. 186 f.; Colmeiro, *Curso*, p. 505.

Such was the case with the *Hermandad de las Marismas*, which, by a pragmatica of 1490, was forbidden to hold further meetings, save under the supervision of the corregidor of Vizcaya — a mortal blow to its independent existence.[1] Still, for the most part, Ferdinand and Isabella proceeded cautiously in this as well as in the other phases of their internal policy. Indeed, many of the municipal reforms which they initiated seemed to be quite as much inspired with the idea of improving conditions in the cities as with that of augmenting their own power at the expense of the concejo or ayuntamiento.

Yet it was not on the remodelling of the city governments themselves that Ferdinand and Isabella chiefly relied to effect their ends; but rather on a great increase of the authority of the representatives of the central government whom they sent out to inspect and override them. It was in this reign that the *pesquisdores, veedores,* and *corregidores* for the first time really came into their own. The first named continued as before to play a primarily judicial role; they were usually dispatched to settle cases which the municipal alcaldes could not manage by themselves, and to see that other royal officials did their duty.[2] The second, as their name implies, were supposed to exercise general oversight of the public affairs of the locality to which they were assigned, and report to the crown. The *corregidores* were by far the most important of all. Beginning in the year 1480, they were sent, for the first time, to all the Castilian cities without exception, so that the institution was henceforth definitely extended over the entire realm.[3] At the same time,

[1] Altamira, § 579.

[2] Pulgar, *Crónica*, pt. iii, cap. c (*B. A. E.*, lxx, p. 478).

[3] Pulgar, *Crónica*, pt. ii, cap. xcv (in *B. A. E.*, lxx, p. 354). According to Castillo de Bovadilla, *Politica para Corregidores*, bk. v, cap. xi, there were 66 *corregimientos* in Castile (in addition to two others in the Canaries) in the latter part of the sixteenth century.

the sovereigns were careful to keep these important offices out of the hands of the aristocracy, and especially of the knights of the three military orders.[1] In 1500 the corregidores had attained to such importance that an elaborate pragmatica was put forth on June 9 at Seville, describing their functions and responsibilities. This pragmatica remained valid throughout the sixteenth century, and gives the best existing description of the institution at the height of its power.[2] As soon as he had been appointed, the corregidor, if present at the court, was obliged to take his oath of office [3] before the Council of Castile, which delivered to him his special instructions. Arrived in his *corregimiento*, he must refrain from imposing any illegal taxes, from mingling in local factions, from the purchase of real property, or from building himself a house without the royal license, from selecting his subordinates from the inhabitants of the region over which he had been set, and from farming out any of the privileges or offices in his control. He was specially recommended to guard against any encroachments of ecclesiastical and seigniorial jurisdiction, to prevent the construction of castles or fortified houses in the cities, and to see to it that no new impost of any kind was established on any pretext whatsoever. He must learn the special laws and customs of his *corregimiento*,

---

Cf. also *Novísima Recopilación*, lib. iv, tit. xv, ley 1. Of these 46 were individual cities, and the lands immediately adjacent to them; the other 20 were geographical areas, or groups of smaller towns. I have been unable to find any similar list for the time of Ferdinand and Isabella; probably the number of *corregimientos* was somewhat smaller than when Bovadilla wrote, but there is no reason to think that the difference was very great. I find no evidence that the corregidores were extended to Aragon before the eighteenth century.

[1] Díaz de Montalvo, *Ordenanzas Reales*, lib. ii, tit. xvi, especially ley 12.
[2] This pragmatica is printed in Ramirez, ff. lii ff. There are two separate copies of it in the British Museum (Add. Mss. 9926, ff. 504–534, and 9929, ff. 258–264) and a reprint (dated Burgos, 1527) is to be found in the Harvard College Library. It is well summarized in Gounon-Loubens, *Essais*, pp. 222 ff.
[3] Cf. Pulgar, *Crónica*, pt. iii, cap. xxxix (*B. A. E.*, lxx, pp. 409 f.).

in order, if he deemed it expedient, that he might reform them in collaboration with the local *regidor*; he was to keep a close watch on the local finances, and inform himself in regard to the wealth and extent of the public lands of the municipality and the best methods of increasing their yield. Inspection and regulation of the relations of Moors and Christians, oversight of gambling houses and prevention of forbidden games, superintendence of local customs dues, general police and executive authority, and above all the securing of the impartial administration of justice to all men, both in civil and criminal affairs — these and many other things besides were included in his official functions. The corregidores were, in fact, omnicompetent servants of an absolute king. Nothing less than this would suffice if they were to make head against the tremendous current of Spanish separatism which had rolled on unchecked for centuries. Even as it was they were unable completely to arrest it or to make it possible for the sovereigns to effect a national unity in any way comparable to that of France. Decentralization, as we have already observed, continued to be the salient feature of the life of the peninsula, even after the advent of despotism had crushed the nobles and sapped the vitality of the concejos. The ancient forms remained, though the animating spirit had fled. But without the corregidores it is certain that Ferdinand and Isabella would have been able to accomplish far less than they did. By them every man in the realm, no matter how obscure or remote, was brought into direct and immediate contact with the central power. They were as indispensable to the crown in local affairs as was the Council of Castile in national ones.[1]

---

[1] Cf. also, on this paragraph, Castillo de Bovadilla, *Politica para Corregidores, passim*, and Danvila, *Poder Civil en España*, i, pp. 470–475.

This vast accumulation of power in the hands of the corregidor explains why the Catholic Kings took such unlimited pains to get the best men in the realm for the office. Bovadilla describes, with interminable prolixity, the qualifications and characteristics of the ideal corregidor, and the way in which he should make use of the authority confided to him. Though his book was not published till 1597, it seems certain that the author was thinking, when he wrote, rather of the appointments of the Catholic Kings than of those of their successors, for the average was distinctly lower under the Hapsburgs.[1] And it was not merely by exercising great care in their selection that Ferdinand and Isabella maintained the highest standard for their corregidores. At the close of their term of office these magistrates were subjected to a most searching test through the development in this reign of the institution of the *residencia*. We have already seen that it had come to be the practice in Castile, at least as early as the reign of John II, that the corregidores should remain at their posts for a period of fifty days after the expiration of their appointment, in order that any complaints against them might be heard and justice done accordingly;[2] and we may remark in passing that this seems to dispose of the well known statement of Herrera, that King Ferdinand imported the residencia from Aragon. On the other hand, it is quite possible that some of the fresh developments and improvements of the institution which marked this reign may have been suggested by the Catholic monarch.[3] Of these the following are the most important. The length of the period of the residencia was shortened from fifty to thirty days; but evasion of it, which had not seldom occurred

---

[1] Gounon-Loubens, *Essais*, pp. 223 f.
[2] Cf. Vol. I, pp. 234 f.
[3] Cf. Helps, *Spanish Conquest in*

America, iii, p. 103, referring to Herrera, *Historia General*, dec. v, lib. v, cap. 5.

in the past, was henceforth prevented by an elaborate system of oaths and forfeits.[1] Many new precautions, moreover, were taken to render the residencia fair and effective. Hitherto the hearing of the complaints against the outgoing official had apparently been a somewhat haphazard affair. Usually it had been intrusted to pesquisidores, who not seldom made dishonest use of their authority, in order to win for themselves the place of the man on whom they were sitting in judgment.[2] To remedy these evils, the conduct of the affair was now turned over to a *juez de residencia* with elaborate instructions in regard to the performance of his duties.[3] He was to be held during the period of the inquiry to the observance of all the rules which had been framed for the corregidor; he was to take care that the residencia be duly published and proclaimed, in order that the remotest portions of the *corregimiento* might be heard from; he was not, however, to be satisfied with general accusations, but was to get specific facts and spare no pains to learn the truth. He was to inform himself concerning the conduct of the local officials and the general state of the *corregimiento*, and to report to the central government. There were, furthermore, numerous regulations defining the limits of his independent authority, and the matters to be referred to the Council of Castile, to which, when the residencia was completed, a full report of it in writing must always be rendered.[4] All this shows that the institution was now regularly and permanently established as an integral part of the administrative system of Castile; moreover, it was utilized henceforth in connection with other officials than the corregidores. "Asistentes, Çorregidores, Gobernadores, Alcades mayores y Tenientes, Alguaciles y

---

[1] Díaz de Montalvo, *Ordenanzas Reales*, lib. ii, tit. xvi, ley 6.
[2] *Cortes*, iii, pp. 37 f.; iv, pp. 136 f.
[3] *Novísima Recopilación*, lib. vii, tit. xiii, leyes 4–14.
[4] Ramirez, *Pragmaticas*, ff. lv–lvii.

Merinos y sus Tenientes" are described in laws of the first
part of the next reign as magistrates whose residencias must
be reported to the Royal Council;[1] and besides, as we shall
later see, the institution made its appearance in the Indies
during the period of Ferdinand and Isabella. Whether it
was primarily intended, as seemed to be the case, to secure
the highest possible standard of honor and efficiency among
the government appointees, or whether the crown was merely
attempting, under the guise of preventing abuses, to gain
for itself a further hold over the officials who represented
it at a distance from the seat of the royal power, it is difficult to say; but it is probable that the first of these alternatives came nearer realization, in the reign of Ferdinand
and Isabella, than it did under their successors. With all
their enthusiasm for centralization, the Catholic Kings
never forgot their zeal for the impartial administration of
justice.

The ecclesiastical policy of the Catholic Kings, in so far
as it is not concerned with the Inquisition and the expulsion of the Jews and the Moors, may be summed up in a
single sentence. The sovereigns would gladly promise
unswerving loyalty to Rome, and enthusiastic devotion
to the advancement of the interests of the church in all
their dominions; but in return they demanded from the
Pope wellnigh complete control of the clergy of Spain and
all her dependencies. The idea of national churches, independent of papal control, which had already manifested
itself in England, France, and the Empire in a variety of
different ways, was firmly upheld by the Catholic Kings.
It tallied closely with their schemes of political centralization; and they put it in practice, as we have already seen,

[1] *Novísima Recopilación*, lib. vii, tit. xii, ley 3.

in connection with the foundation of the Inquisition, whose officials they insisted on nominating themselves. But the measure of the authority which they exercised over the regular ecclesiastical appointments of the realm at the time of their accession did not correspond at all to their desires. During the confusion of the preceding reigns papal provisions to the Spanish sees had increased apace, in defiance of more ancient precedents to the contrary; and they were the more obnoxious in that the nominees in such cases were almost invariably foreigners. A vacancy in the see of Cuenca in 1482 gave the sovereigns a chance to make a stand for their own prerogatives in this respect. After a vigorous dispute they elicited from Sixtus IV an acknowledgment of their right to 'supplicate' in favor of the worthiest candidate for any of the more important ecclesiastical offices of the realm; it was of course understood that in such cases their supplication would not be refused.[1] Practical control of the smaller benefices, which the Pope had reserved for himself in the agreement of 1482, was also subsequently acquired by the sovereigns, through various indirect methods. Moreover, in the conquered realm of Granada, and in the Indies, they were given outright the privilege of appointment to all ecclesiastical posts, as a reward for the services which they had rendered to Christendom in these lands.[2] In 1501 they were also granted all the tithes in the American possessions, to be used for the building and support of the churches there, so that their ecclesiastical authority in the New World was even more securely established and fortified than at home.[3]

Doubtless the Popes. were chiefly inspired by ulterior

[1] Pulgar, *Crónica*, pt. ii, cap. civ (*B. A. E.*, lxx, pp. 362 f.) ; Mariéjol, pp. 27 f.; Altamira, § 590.
[2] Bourne, *Spain in America*, pp.

302 f., notes; Lannoy and vander Linden, *L'Expansion coloniale de Portugal et d'Espagne*, p. 408.
[3] Altamira, § 590.

motives in making these concessions. They recognized the sovereigns' power and prestige; they needed their alliance for political purposes; and they wisely determined to grant with a good grace what they were not strong enough to refuse. Indeed, they gave more than was demanded. At the close of the year 1494, Alexander VI formally conferred on the Spanish monarchs their proudest title, 'the Catholic Kings,' ostensibly as a reward for their great services to the faith — really because he needed their help in expelling the forces of Charles VIII from Italy.[1] And Ferdinand, in turn, took pleasure in exalting the authority of the papacy on a subsequent occasion, when he thought that its assertion might prove politically useful to him. The ancient claim of the Holy See to dispose of the temporal kingdoms of the earth was dramatically upheld by the Spanish monarch in 1515, when he justified his claim to the realm of Navarre before the Cortes of Burgos on the ground that it had been granted to him by Pope Julius II.[2]

But though external political considerations were unquestionably the principal reason for the cordial relations of the papacy with the Spanish sovereigns, it would be grossly unjust to the latter to depreciate the immense services that they rendered to the church within their own domains. The monasteries were reformed and the vices of regulars and seculars punished. The scandalous immorality of the clerics was checked. Their usurpations were restrained and absenteeism was sternly prohibited. Activity and zeal replaced idleness and corruption, for the time being at least, as the distinguishing marks of the Spanish priest.[3] In all this beneficent work the monarchs' right-hand man was Cardinal Ximenes, whose admirable

[1] Prescott, ii, pp 261 f., and references there.

[2] *Cortes*, iv, pp. 249 ff.

[3] Altamira, § 576.

devotion and fervor went far to palliate his unbending intolerance. And no better comment on the position which he desired the church to occupy on earth could possibly be imagined than the memorable words in which he justified the arrangement of the text in the famous Complutensian Polyglot Bible — the fruit of his energy and enthusiasm, and perhaps the most notable triumph of scholarship in the Spain in which he lived. The Old Testament is printed in three parallel columns — the Septuagint on the left, the original Hebrew on the right, and the Vulgate in the centre. "Midway between the Greek of the Church of the East and the Hebrew of the synagogue," runs the Cardinal's sonorous preface, "we have placed Saint Jerome's Latin translation of the Church of Rome, even as Christ was crucified between two thieves." [1]

The needs of the Spanish Empire demanded powerful military resources. One of the most important reforms of the Catholic Kings was their transformation of the scattered and undisciplined feudal levies which had effected the Reconquest, into a modern, organized, efficient, well equipped army, unquestionably superior to any other in Europe down to the time of Gustavus Adolphus.

We have already seen that the recruiting of the troops for the Granadan war was for the most part of the old-fashioned sort. The contingents of the Hermandad afforded a nucleus, it is true, but the bulk of the levies were furnished and commanded by the great nobles, who marshalled them

---

[1] There is an interesting description of this edition in Burke's *History of Spain*, ii, pp. 214–218. It is worth noting that the Complutensian was the first edition of the New Testament to be *printed* in the original Greek (1514); though its publication, which was delayed by papal command till 1520, was preceded by that of the edition of Erasmus, which came out in 1516. James P. R. Lyell, *Cardinal Ximenes* (London, 1917), pp. 24–52, 91–115, gives a wealth of bibliographical information concerning the Complutensian.

under their own special standards.[1] But at the same time
traces of a different type of military organization began to
appear. Pulgar speaks of a body of regular troops, paid
by the crown, which was maintained in Galicia in the early
part of the reign for the repression of disturbance there.
In another place the chronicler tells us of a royal bodyguard
of one thousand men (its numbers were soon to be trebled),
all servants of the king and queen. He also waxes enthusiastic about the body of Swiss mercenaries which had been
sent to the peninsula for the Granada campaign — "warlike men, who fight on foot and never turn their backs on
their foes, and therefore wear all their defensive armor in
front. They go to earn their livelihood in foreign lands and
aid in wars which they consider just. They are good and
devout Christians and hold it a great sin to take anything
by force." [2] This very rosy description shows that Spain
was keenly observant and appreciative of the military progress that was being made in other lands. The sovereigns
had begun to hire foreign soldiers in order to learn from
them new methods of waging war ; they had thus shown that
they realized the necessity of taking the control of military
affairs out of the hands of the baronage. The results of
their experience were evident in a **pragmatica**, dated February 22, 1496, at Valladolid, which announced that thenceforth the state would take one man out of every twelve
between the ages of twenty and forty-five to serve in the
royal armies.[3] It was not intended that the soldiers thus
recruited should be permanently under arms. They were
mobilized only when there was an immediate prospect of
war, but they were paid by the crown from the day on which
they entered active service, and their employment may

[1] Mariéjol, pp. 196–198.
[2] Pulgar, *Crónica*, pt. iii, caps. xiv,
xvi, xxi, lxvi (in *B. A. E.*, lxx, pp. 379,
381, 387, 443 f.) ; Altamira, § 586.
[3] Clemencin, *Elógio*, pp. 603–605.

be justly regarded as a long step towards the formation of a standing army. The Italian wars showed that the measure was inadequate to the needs of Spain's expanding power, and Cardinal Ximenes and Charles V were obliged to develop and augment it; but the days of the old feudal levies were gone forever. The new army was wholly controlled by the central government, and, as long as its pay was forthcoming, generally firm in its allegiance. If funds ran short its behavior was indeed unutterable, as countless episodes in the wars of the sixteenth century were abundantly to prove;[1] the case could scarcely have been otherwise, in view of the fact that rascals and cutthroats as well as patriots and gentlemen found places in its ranks; but it was no worse than the other mercenary armies of the time, and was a vast improvement on the military system which it supplanted.

At the same time that the sovereigns altered the methods of recruitment, a brilliant young officer named Gonsalvo de Cordova, who had fought through the Granadan campaign and reflected on what he had learned there, began to introduce equally radical changes in armament and tactics. He was ably seconded in this important task by Gonzalo de Ayora, who had studied the art of war in Italy.[2] The mediaeval Spanish infantryman, equipped for guerilla warfare in a mountainous country, was far too lightly armed to withstand the shock of contact with the powerful squadrons that had been developed north of the Pyrenees during the preceding hundred years; nor was he adequately protected against firearms or discharges of arrows. On the

[1] Mariéjol, p. 214.

[2] There is no good modern life of Gonsalvo. The most important contemporary accounts of him have been collected and published by A. Rodríguez Villa in the *Nueva Biblioteca de Autores* *Españoles*, x (Madrid, 1908), under the title of *Crónicas del Gran Capitan*. On Ayora cf. E. Cat's *Essai sur la vie et les ouvrages de Gonzalo de Ayora* (Paris, 1890), and C. Fernández Duro in *Boletín de la R. A. H.*, xvii, pp. 433–475.

other hand, the speed and suppleness of the Spanish formation were precious assets which could not be lightly cast
aside; the problem was to preserve them and gain needed
stability at the same time. The ultimate solution was
reached in two different ways. In the first place, the
defensive arms of all the Spanish infantrymen were augmented by the addition of a light helmet with a brim, a
cuirass, gorget, and brassarts. For offensive weapons,
one half of them received long pikes, while one third retained
the short sword and javelin of earlier days, with a small
round shield for additional protection, and the remaining
sixth were given arquebuses of the best and most portable
type. Almost any sixteenth-century battle scene will give
a good idea of this formidable equipment. Then, in the
second place, the organization, grouping, and subdivisions
of the forces were completely made over. The ancient unit
was the company (*capitanía* or *batallata*) of five hundred
men, far too small to be effective in modern warfare. After
much experiment a regiment (*coronelía* or *escuadrón*), under
the command of a colonel and composed of twelve companies,
was gradually evolved, numbering thus, in theory at least,
six thousand men. The proportions of the different sorts
of armament above described were retained by dividing ten
of the twelve companies into two hundred pikemen, two
hundred short-sword-and-javelin men, and one hundred
arquebusiers apiece, and by filling the two remaining ones
with pikemen alone. Six hundred cavalrymen, half light,
half heavy, accompanied each regiment of infantry; their
comparatively insignificant numbers are the best possible
evidence of the great change that had been effected in the
art of waging war. But if the cavalry counted for little,
the artillery was vastly more considerable than ever before.
The Granadan war had taught the sovereigns its value and

importance, and their secretary and counselor, Francisco Ramirez, spent an infinity of time and pains in developing it. The guns were of all sorts, of different sizes and calibers, but the greatest difficulty was that of transportation; for hitherto cannon had been utilized almost entirely as stationary pieces for siege work, and the idea of carrying them about as an inseparable adjunct of an army in the field was relatively new.[1] Before the end of the reign, however, this had all been changed, though it seems that Gonsalvo de Cordova set no great store by his artillery. The normal contingent accompanying each brigade (that is, two *coronelías*) was now sixty-four pieces of different types. In 1505 the entire Spanish army was divided into twenty *coronelías* under the command of a colonel-general. The ancient mediaeval hierarchy of military officers had in the meantime practically disappeared. The office of *condestable* was henceforth merely an honorary distinction, and after the Granadan war we hear no more of his lieutenants or *mariscales*.[2]

The battle tactics of this renovated army made it the terror of Europe for a century to come. The pikemen and short-sword-and-javelin men were usually formed in squares, the latter in the centre, and the pikemen, several rows deep, with their spears advanced, outside. The arquebusiers and artillery were separately disposed, where they could shoot to good advantage, and the cavalry was chiefly utilized for scouting and for the pursuit of fleeing foes. Few charges of hostile horsemen could make any impression on the phalanx of pikes, especially as their ranks were invari-

[1] Cf. *ante*, p. 68.
[2] On this paragraph cf. Clemencin, *Elógio*, pp. 167–191; Clonard, *Historia Orgánica*, vol. ii, *passim*; Mariéjol, pp. 195–214; A. Blázquez y Delgado Aguilera, *Bosquejo de la Administración Militar* (Madrid, 1891), pp. 20–24. Further references may be found in J. Almirante's *Bibliografía Militar de España* (Madrid, 1876).

ably thinned by the Spanish artillerymen and arquebusiers before they reached the point of contact. On those rare occasions when the outer lines of the square were broken, the light-armed troops in the centre were on hand to finish off such riders as had got through. When a phalanx of Landsknechts was encountered, the Spanish formation had two important advantages, besides its above mentioned superiority in firearms. In the first place, the light-armed troops in the centre gave it greater flexibility, so that it was not broken by bad ground to the same extent as were its opponents. Second, when the front ranks closed in combat, and the opposing pikemen began thrusting at one another a spear's length apart, the short-sword-and-javelin men would creep underneath and slash and stab indiscriminately at their opponents, who were too fully occupied in front to defend themselves. Time after time was this manoeuvre repeated with deadly effect, but no one was able to devise means of stopping it until the time of the Thirty Years' War. When we consider the stupendous progress in military implements and science which has been accomplished during the last half century, we cannot help wondering that methods so rudimentary as these should have remained virtually unchallenged for so long.[1]

The efforts of the Catholic Kings to increase the Castilian merchant marine, which have been already described in another place, served also to strengthen the Castilian navy. The line between ships of commerce and ships of war was not yet so clearly drawn but that practically all were available for both purposes, though Ferdinand made some effort to distinguish between them. The development of artillery furnished a splendid opportunity for improvement in efficiency, but was not utilized to the full; the ancient tac-

[1] Clonard, *Historia Orgánica*, ii, cap. xxvi; Mariéjol, p. 213.

tics of ramming and boarding were retained for a long time to come, and were one of the main causes of the defeat of the Spanish Armada in 1588. The *almirante*, like the *condestable*, lost most of his ancient authority; in 1479 a *capitan mayor* was given effective control of the national fleets. — The naval resources of Catalonia diminished, on the whole, in this period, as those of Castile increased. In this matter, as in so many others, the western kingdom asserted its preponderance.[1]

The intellectual life of the Spain of Ferdinand and Isabella gives evidence of the increased cosmopolitanism and contact with the outside world which form one of the principal features of the reign. The Italian influence in art and letters, of which we observed the beginnings in the previous century, is now far more predominant than before; the rule of Alfonso the Magnanimous had made the eastern kingdoms more Italianate than ever, and their union with Castile transplanted the new tendencies to the west. The education of the royal Infantes was intrusted to Italians.[2] Peter Martyr de Anghiera, humanist and historian of the New World, set up a school at the court, in which he taught Latin and history to the children of the greatest families in the land;[3] in fact, if one encountered a learned man in Spain during the early part of the reign of the Catholic Kings, it was usually safe to assume either that he was a foreigner, or else that, if Spanish, he had received a prolonged Italian training. In later years there was a change. Spain saw that she could not afford to remain aloof from the great movement of the Renaissance and send abroad for all her knowledge; and the foundation of the University of Alcalá,

[1] Altamira, § 595; Fernández Duro, *Armada Española*, i, pp. 1–122, *passim*.
[2] Mariéjol, p. 326.
[3] For further references on Peter Martyr and his works cf. Fueter, *Historiographie*, pp. 285 f.

through the efforts of Cardinal Ximenes, at once gave her a standing in the world of scholars which she had not enjoyed since the days of the caliphate of Cordova.[1] But for many years more, inspiration continued to come from without. Antonio del Rincon the sovereigns' favorite painter, was a pupil of Domenico Ghirlandajo. In architecture and sculpture we encounter a strange jumble of ancient Moorish and modern Renaissance styles; profusion of elaborate detail was the not entirely satisfactory result. Ferdinand de Rojas's *Celestina*, a Rabelaisian novel in dramatic form, and perhaps the literary masterpiece of the reign, cuts loose from all the ancient traditions of Castilian prose, and in its accurate delineation of human life under the widest possible variety of circumstances closely resembles the models of Italy and of France. It heralded the approach of the day of Cervantes and of Lope de Vega. New fashions in the writing of history, likewise of foreign origin, begin to make their appearance. The old annalistic forms survive, but men like Hernando del Pulgar and Andrés Bernáldez no longer limit themselves to the narration of battles, uprisings, and royal ceremonies; they give precious details concerning the development of national institutions and customs, and show that they have reflected upon underlying causes and results.[2]

A few last words remain to be added concerning the administration of the Mediterranean territories under the Catholic Kings; but as we shall have a more convenient opportunity to deal with Naples in connection with its re-

[1] V. de la Fuente, *Historia de las Universidades*, ii, pp. 48–54, 66–85; A. de la Torre y del Cerro, "La Universidad de Alcalá," in *R. A.*, 3d ser., xx, pp. 412–423; xxi, pp. 48–71, 261–285, 405–433. This university was moved to Madrid in 1836, and received the title of Universidad Central.

[2] Mariéjol, pp. 309–350; Fueter, *op. cit.*, pp. 280–288.

conquest by Ferdinand in 1503–04, we may restrict ourselves for the present to the affairs of Sardinia and of Sicily.
In brief, the aim of the sovereigns' policy in these islands
was cautiously and gradually to Castilianize them, to abrogate little by little the independent rights and privileges
which they had inherited from the past, or received at the
hands of the sovereigns of Aragon, and to reduce them to
a condition of subservience to the monarch comparable to
that which had been created in the western kingdom. Yet
so anxious were Ferdinand and Isabella to avoid collisions,
whenever possible, with the inhabitants of these *tierras de
allá mar*, that most of the changes which they introduced
were effected quietly, and indeed almost stealthily. It
was not until the end of the sixteenth century that the full
effects of the policy they had initiated were evident, and
that the Sardinians and Sicilians realized how completely
their ancient liberties had been undermined.

The only matter in which the sovereigns ventured to fly
squarely in the face of popular opinion was in the establishment of racial and religious unity. When the interests of
the Faith as they conceived them were at stake, they were
restrained by no considerations of political expediency.
The Spanish Inquisition was extended to Sicily in 1487
and to Sardinia in 1492; in spite of popular disaffection and
complaint, and even bloody revolts, it was maintained without interruption to the close of the reign.[1] In Sardinia,
it is true, the tribunal was in a somewhat decadent condition at the time of the death of Ferdinand, owing chiefly
to the exhaustion of the confiscable property of its victims,
and strenuous efforts were necessary to revive it under
Charles V; but in Sicily we have ample evidence that the
institution was exceedingly active. The edict for the ex-

[1] Lea, *Inquisition in the Spanish Dependencies*, pp. 1–16, 109–115.

pulsion of the Jews was also extended to both islands in 1492. In Sardinia there was apparently no great outcry against it;[1] in Sicily, however, where the Hebrews had perhaps enjoyed greater privileges than anywhere else in Europe, there was considerable resentment, which was greatly increased by the cruel and unjust manner of its enforcement by the viceroy, Ferdinand de Acuña.[2] As elsewhere, its economic effects were disastrous, while polit- ically it formed an admirable basis, as did the Inquisition, for a further introduction of the principles and practices of monarchical centralization at the expense of the national liberties.

In constitutional affairs one of the most important inno- vations introduced by the Catholic Kings was the practice of conferring the office of viceroy on Castilians in place of Catalans and Aragonese. This evoked numerous com- plaints, and demands on the part of the local parliaments that only subjects of the realms of the Crown of Aragon be recognized as eligible for this dignity,[3] but Ferdinand quietly ignored them, as an inspection of the lists of the successive representatives of the crown in both islands will plainly show.[4] The powers of the viceroy were so great that the whole complexion of the administration varied with the character of the appointee. With men at the helm who had been trained in the now thoroughly monarchical at- mosphere of Castile, Ferdinand could rest fairly confident that his Mediterranean domains would be kept well in hand ; Castilians, moreover, were also appointed to some of the subordinate posts. In Sardinia the practice of placing legists, instead of soldiers, in the viceregal office was also

---

[1] Manno, *Storia di Sardegna*, ii, pp. 126 f.

[2] I. La Lumia, *Studi di Storia Sici- liana*, ii, pp. 1–55, *passim*.

[3] Manno, *op. cit.*, ii, pp. 124 f. ; Dexart, *Capitula Regni Sardiniae*, lib. ii, tit. vi, cap. i.

[4] Stokvis, *Manuel*, iii, pp. 708 f., 745.

occasionally adopted in the period; this, again, smacks strongly of the methods of the western kingdom.[1] In 1496, we hear of the appointment there of the first *abogado del fisco*, to conduct financial suits on behalf of the crown, and lend aid in the management of the royal treasury.[2]

The attitude of the sovereigns towards the parliaments of Sardinia and Sicily reflects the conditions which obtained in those islands. Certainly Ferdinand and Isabella rather favored than opposed their meetings. In Sardinia the national assembly was summoned in 1483 and in 1511, after an interruption which had lasted the entire length of the reign of John II. Whether the cause of its convocation was that Ferdinand saw in it the best means of breaking down the old barriers that had divided the island in ancient times, or that he needed the funds which it alone could grant, it is impossible to say; but we know that when it did meet, it used the opportunity to present numerous petitions to the crown. In general one gains the impression that Sardinia enjoyed, under the Catholic Kings, a measure of internal peace and tranquillity to which she had hitherto been a stranger; and that such was her delight in the establishment of order that she raised little objection to such invasion of her autonomous privileges as accompanied it.[3] In Sicily, there was much more vigorous opposition to monarchical encroachments. Nowhere else in the widely scattered dominions of the Spanish sovereigns was the passion for freedom more deeply implanted, and the national assembly was regarded as the emblem and personification of national liberty. Yet Ferdinand made no effort to prevent or curtail its sessions. This was chiefly, no doubt,

---

[1] Juan Dusay, appointed in 1492, was the first legist to hold this office in Sardinia. Manno, ii, p. 126, note 4.

[2] Manno, ii, p. 195, note.

[3] Manno, ii, p. 123.

because he recognized that he was not strong enough openly to defy it, and partly because of financial necessity. On the other hand, he consistently strove to sap its vitality in a number of indirect ways. He played off the two upper orders against the third estate, and refused to accede to a request that the barons and clergy be forbidden to send deputies to represent them in their absence — an abuse which had seriously weakened the efficiency of the Parliament as a whole.[1] He strenuously defended the right of the viceroy to summon the assembly to whatever place he wished, and thus made it possible to hold its sessions in remote or unhealthy spots, where opponents would find it difficult to attend, and if present might easily be bullied into submission.[2] By slight changes of phraseology he managed to extinguish the ancient contractual theory that the granting of the *donativo* was dependent on the royal assent to the petitions of the Parliament and the observance of the national privileges; he also invariably tried to get the financial business of each session concluded first, and to his own satisfaction, before the desires of the representatives were heard.[3] The Sicilian Parliament was undoubtedly far weaker at the end of the reign than at the beginning.

Such were the main features of the great work of monarchical unification and consolidation accomplished by the Catholic Kings. When we consider that the chief aim of their policy ran counter to the most dominant of Spanish characteristics — separatism — and when we remember how widely scattered and differentiated were their various domains, we cannot fail to be deeply impressed with the importance of the results they achieved, even though we

---

[1] Calisse, *Storia del Parlamento in Sicilia*, p. 117.

[2] Calisse, p. 110, note 3.

[3] Calisse, p. 184.

may not always sympathize with the ends they had in view. Perhaps the most remarkable feature of their work was the skill with which they adapted their methods to the widely varying problems with which they were confronted; it was their great versatility that enabled them to handle all sorts of different questions at one and the same time. Wisely recognizing the impossibility of welding all their dominions into a single state, they had concentrated their efforts on the principal one of them — Castile — with the aim of subjecting it completely to their control and making it the pivot of their empire. They had endeavored to imbue the lesser portions of their possessions with some of the principles of Castilian polity, but they did not deprive them of their native laws or institutions, or attempt to absorb them in the greater kingdom; and as new territories were successively acquired in later years, they were treated in similar fashion. The result was a congeries of separate states, differing from one another in race, in traditions, in language, and in government, and bound together solely by the fact that they possessed a common kingship — a loose-jointed, heterogeneous empire, the fundamental principle of whose administration was that of decentralized despotism.

BIBLIOGRAPHICAL NOTE

See bibliographical notes at the end of Chapters IV, V, and XI in Volume I, and of chapters XII, XIII and XIV in this volume, and add: Sources and Contemporary Authorities. — Alonso Díaz de Montalvo, ed., *Ordenanzas Reales de Castilla* (Madrid, 1779–80, 3 vols.); cf. *ante*, p. 125; Prescott, iii, p. 425, note. Juan Ramirez, ed., *Las Pragmaticas del Reyno* (1520); rare, but indispensable for the study of this reign; Ramirez was secretary to the Council of Castile. For further information see Prescott, iii, p. 425, note, and Clemencin, *Elógio*, pp. 214–220. Gonzalo Fernández de Oviedo, *Las Quinquagenas de la Nobleza de España*, ed. V. de la Fuente for the R. A. H. (Madrid, 1880). On this curious compilation see Prescott, i, p. 194, and Clemencin, *Elógio*, ilus. x. *Compilación de Privilegios de Caceres y documentos relativos á la ciudad de Caceres*, ed. Pedro de Ulloa y Golfín (1679 [?]); very rare. A more extensive manuscript copy of it may be found in the Biblioteca Nacional at Madrid (D. 49); cf. Vicente Barrantes, *Aparato bibliográfico para la Historia de Estremadura*, i, pp. 383 ff., and Ureña and Bonilla, *Fuero de Usagre*, p. x.

Later Works. — Heinrich Schäfer, "Geschichtliche Darstellung des Finanz- und Steuerwesens in Spanien vor und während der Regierung der katholischen Könige," in F. C. Schlosser and G. A. Bercht's *Archiv für Geschichte und Literatur*, vol. iv, pp. 68–132 (Frankfort, 1833), contains much that is not to be found elsewhere; Cristóbal Espejo's "Sobre organización de la Hacienda Española en el Siglo XVI," in *Cultura Española*, vol. vi, pp. 403–428; vol. vii, pp. 687–704, though principally concerned with the period of Charles V, is also useful for the time of Ferdinand and Isabella. Liciniano Saez, *Demostración Histórica del verdadero Valor de todas las Monedas que corrian en Castilla durante el Reynado de Enrique IV* (Madrid, 1796), is more valuable for its citations of contemporary authorities than for its own conclusions. Antonio Blázquez y Delgado Aguilera, *Bosquejo histórico de la Administración Militar Española* (Madrid, 1891), and Antonio de la Torre y del Cerro, " La Universidad de Alcalá," in *R. A.*, 3d ser., vol. xx, pp. 412–423, and vol. xxi, pp. 48–71, 261–285, 405–433, are useful monographs on the subjects with which they deal.

BOOK IV

EXPANSION

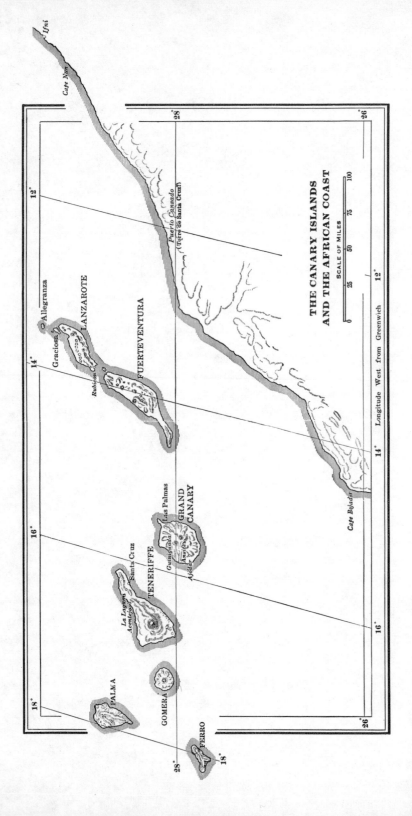

THE CANARY ISLANDS
AND THE AFRICAN COAST

SCALE OF MILES

0   25   50   75   100

Longitude West from Greenwich

Ifni

Cape Nun

Puerto Cansado
(Torre de Santa Cruz)

Cape Bojador

Allegranza

Graciosa

LANZAROTE

Rubicon

FUERTEVENTURA

Las Palmas

GRAND CANARY

Guanarteme

Anaga
Abona

Santa Cruz

TENERIFFE

La Laguna
Acentejo

PALMA

GOMERA

FERRO

12°

14°

16°

18°

28°

26°

12°

14°

16°

18°

28°

26°

CHAPTER XVI

THE CANARIES

WE have already emphasized the continuity of the reconquest of Spain from the Moors, and her conquest of an imperial domain beyond the seas. We have seen that Castile had gained her first outpost in the Atlantic, and that Aragon had won an empire in the western Mediterranean, before Granada fell. The reign of Ferdinand and Isabella, during which the infidel was finally expelled from the peninsula, witnessed the completion of the winning of the Canaries, the discovery and earliest explorations of America, and the acquisition of several important cities on the North African coast; it also saw Spain gain new lands for herself in Europe, and take her place in the front rank among the nations of the earth. For the sake of clearness we shall take up the different phases of this mighty process of expansion one by one, beginning with the conquest of new lands across the water and closing with the relations of Spain to her European neighbors; but we must constantly bear in mind that they were all, roughly speaking, contemporaneous, and that at certain critical moments they exercised an important influence upon one another.

In the course of the war of succession between the Catholic Kings and Affonso the African, the difficult question of the respective rights of Castile and of Portugal in the Canary Islands and the adjacent coasts had kept constantly coming

171

up.   In November, 1476, eight months after the battle of
Toro, Ferdinand and Isabella ordered an inquiry to be opened
in regard to the possession of the island of Lanzarote and to
the right of conquest of the rest of the Canaries; in 1477
a verdict was rendered favorable to the claims of Diego de
Herrera and his wife Inez (Peraza), whose previous history
has been related in another place.[1]   It will also be remembered that in October of that year the Herreras were confirmed in their tenure of the conquered islands of Lanzarote,
Fuerteventura, Ferro, and Gomera, but yielded to Ferdinand and Isabella all claims to the three remaining and
larger ones in return for an indemnity of 5,000,000 maravedis.[2]   The Catholic Kings lost no time in attempting to substantiate their rights.   An expedition of six hundred infantry and thirty horse set sail from Seville in the spring of
1478, under the leadership of an intrepid soldier named Juan
Rejón, with instructions to avoid interference with the Herreras in the four islands that acknowledged their sway,
but to effect a landing in the Grand Canary and to make
preparations for its conquest.   But the Portuguese had no
idea of permitting Ferdinand and Isabella thus to establish
unopposed their sovereignty over the archipelago.   By
way of serving notice that their own claims to the Canaries
were not to be regarded as extinct, they despatched seven
caravels to attack Rejón and his men.   This episode naturally led to a reopening of the old discussion between the two
realms as to priority of occupation and conflicting rights in
the islands and the opposite coasts, with the result that in
one of the treaties signed in 1479, at the termination of the

[1] *Ante*, Vol. I, pp. 156–158; R. Torres Campos, *Carácter de la Conquista y
Colonización de las Islas Canarias* (Discurso de la R. A. H., Madrid, 1901), pp.
24, 121–206.

[2] Cf. *ante*, Vol. I, p. 158; the Spanish
phrase which I have translated 'tenure' is 'dominio útil.'   Cf. Fernández
Duro, *Marina de Castilla*, pp. 253 f.

War of Succession, the Portuguese renounced all title to the
Canaries, but received in return exclusive privileges of conquest and possession on the adjacent African shore, including
the kingdom of Fez and the lands of Guinea, and also in the
Azores, Madeira, and the Cape Verde Islands.   Moreover
the Castilian sovereigns promised that they would not permit their subjects to trade in the territories assigned to Portugal without the express permission of the Portuguese king.[1]
Probably the treaty was not regarded at that time as being
any too favorable to the king of Castile.   Possession of the
Canaries was then held to be important chiefly as facilitat-
ing acquisitions in Africa, on which the eyes of both nations
were at that time directed; and in the neighboring African
territories the Portuguese were recognized as supreme.   No
one then realized that the greatest value of the archipelago
was ultimately to be found in the fact that it furnished a
most convenient stopping place and harbor of refuge on the
way to the Spanish possessions in the New World.

Meantime Rejón and his followers had landed, on June 24,
1478,[2] at the Grand Canary, and were received in friendly
fashion by the natives.   Serious difficulties, however, were
soon to come.   The Canarians were split into two factions,
of which the first, under an upstart military chieftain called
Doramas, was attempting to oust from power Thenesor
Semidan,[3] the brother of the late king, who had been ap-

[1] This treaty, to which reference has
been made on p. 54, was confirmed by
Queen Isabella at Truxillo on September 27, 1479; it was also ratified and
amplified, together with the contemporaneous settlement of the dynastic
questions at issue between Portugal and
Castile (usually known as the treaty of
Alcaçovas) on March 6, 1480, at
Toledo.   The original is in the Torre
do Tombo at Lisbon, and the best edition of it, with full notes and references
and an English translation, is to be

found in Miss F. G. Davenport's recent
volume entitled *European Treaties
bearing on the History of the United
States and its Dependencies to 1648*,
pp. 33-48; cf. *infra*, p. 238.
[2] Millares, *Historia de las Islas
Canarias*, iii, p. 257.
[3] Or Egonaiga, as Löher, *Kanarier-
buch*, p. 195, calls him, probably on the
authority of the eighteenth-century historian of the Canaries, P. A. de Castillo,
whose book I have been unable to see.
Cf. Löher, pp. 60, 582.

pointed regent during the minority of his nephew. Doramas wished to fight the Spaniards, while Thenesor was for
a policy of peace; but the mass of the islanders supported
the former, and before the end of the summer two encounters occurred at Guiniguada, in which the Spaniards,
despite their vastly inferior numbers, were brilliantly victorious.[1] After these battles the Canarians retired inland,
hoping that the invaders would remain content with the
shores; but spasmodic Portuguese interference served to keep
up the fighting spirit of the natives, and led in turn to constant raids and devastations by the troops of Rejón. Meantime the effectiveness of the Spanish operations was greatly
lessened by a dissension of the characteristic sort between
Rejón and Juan Bermudez, dean of Rubicon, who had
been associated with him for the purpose of converting the
natives, but who was chiefly interested in prosecuting his
own schemes. News of their quarrels finally reached the
Spanish court, and in the summer of 1479 Ferdinand and
Isabella sent out a *juez pesquisidor* named Pedro Fernández
de Algaba, and a certain Alfonso Fernández de Lugo, a
soldier of the Granadan war, to find the facts and render a
verdict. Rejón was falsely accused, seized, and shipped
off to Spain. There, however, he soon succeeded in reha-
bilitating himself, and was promptly sent back with fresh
troops to continue the conquest. Meanwhile Algaba had
mismanaged everything in the Grand Canary. His attempt
to win military prestige by a victory over the natives resulted in a disgraceful defeat; and the final upshot of the
matter was that he was accused of treacherous dealings with
the king of Portugal and executed, at Whitsuntide, 1480, by
the order of the very man he had previously been sent out to

---

[1] J. de Viera y Clavijo, *Historia*   36 ff.; Millares, iii, pp. 258 ff.; Löher,
general de las Islas de Canaria, ii, pp.   pp. 196–202.

report upon. Bermudez had meanwhile been banished to the Herreras in Lanzarote, where he soon died of chagrin, and Rejón for the time being was left supreme. The whole story gives a startlingly accurate forecast of the adventures of many of the American conquistadores at a later date.[1] All these quarrels in the Canaries naturally retarded the progress of the conquest of the archipelago, and convinced Ferdinand and Isabella that other means must speedily be employed. The person whom they selected for the difficult task was Pedro de Vera, of ancient Castilian lineage, a renowned fighter in the Moorish wars, whose energy, ambition, and revengefulness made him an uncomfortable neighbor in Spain, but promised well for his success in the rôle of conquistador. His extensive possessions, which enabled him to fit out an expedition largely at his own expense, were of course an added recommendation.[2] Vera was warmly received by Rejón on his arrival in the Canaries in August, 1480, and carefully made the most of the latter's friendship until overwhelming reënforcements arrived to support him; then he lured Rejón on board ship, clapped him into irons, and sent him off a prisoner to the Spanish court to answer to the charge of unjustly executing Algaba, whose widow was clamoring for vengeance. But Rejón had powerful relatives in high places; soon after his arrival in Spain he not only procured his release, but obtained command of new ships and forces; in June, 1481, he reappeared in the Canaries with two caravels and three hundred and twenty men.[3] Meantime Vera had been guilty of dastardly treachery in his dealings with the natives. In order to entice a number of them on board ship, so that they might be sent off and

---

[1] Viera y Clavijo, ii, pp. 43–61; J. de Abreu de Galindo, *History of the Discovery and Conquest of the Canary Islands*, tr. Glas, pp. 100 f.; Millares, iii, pp. 275–300; Löher, pp. 211–223.

[2] Löher, p. 225.

[3] Abreu de Galindo, tr. Glas, pp. 104 f.; Löher, p. 239.

sold as slaves in Spain, he swore to them before a Host, whose consecration by the priest he had secretly forestalled, that they were to be employed to conquer Teneriffe. Most of the islanders jumped off the boat when it touched at Lanzarote, and the complete execution of Vera's plans was thereby prevented; but the impression made by the attempt was of the very worst, and it led to a number of conflicts with the natives, in one of which their gallant leader Doramas met his death.[1] When Rejón finally arrived in the midst of all these exciting events he was not permitted to land. He accordingly weighed anchor, with the intention of passing over to Palma, but stress of weather forced him ashore at Gomera, which was one of the islands still controlled by the Herreras. Diego de Herrera's son Ferdinand, who was usually called Peraza after his mother's family, was in command there at the time; bearing no special good will to the representatives of the monarchs whom he regarded as usurpers of his family domains, he sent a force to capture Rejón on his arrival. In his attempt to resist it, Rejón was killed.[2] His noble widow, Elvira de Sotomayor, departed for Spain in search of revenge, and finally succeeded in having Peraza sent home and tried for his offence. Peraza, however, escaped the penalty which the wife of his foe demanded by a marriage which won him the favor of the queen. King Ferdinand's attentions to a fair maid of honor, by name Eleanor de Bobadilla, had recently aroused the jealousy of Isabella; as the easiest way out of the difficulty, a match was arranged between the lady and Peraza, which served to remove the former from the court, and secured pardon for the latter on his promise to return to the Canaries and bear aid to the king's soldiers in conquering the Grand

---

[1] Abreu de Galindo, tr. Glas, p. 105; Millares, iii, p. 314; Löher, pp. 228 f.   [2] Millares, iv, pp. 12–19; Löher, pp. 238–241.

Canary, Palma, and Teneriffe.[1] The personal note is distinctly dominant during this phase of Spanish progress
toward the attainment of imperial domain.

Meantime in the Canaries the conquest was gradually
progressing. With the death of Doramas, the natives'
spirit of resistance was temporarily broken, and in the early
months of 1482 an expedition under Algaba's companion,
Alfonso de Lugo, resulted in the capture of the *Guanarteme*
or regent, Thenesor Semidan.[2] The latter was by this time
thoroughly reconciled to the prospect of Spanish domination,
and his captors accordingly made haste to utilize him for
that end. He was sent over to Spain, presented to the
king and queen, and was apparently so immensely impressed by their majesty and power that he at once consented to receive baptism and return to his native land in
order to bear aid in the completion of its conquest. So
anxious were Ferdinand and Isabella to make the most of
the favorable opportunity afforded by the submission of the
Canarian chief, that they sent five shiploads of fresh soldiers
— among them some of the contingents of the Hermandad
— to accompany him on his homeward journey.[3] But
even with all these reënforcements (the Spanish soldiers in
the islands cannot at this juncture have numbered much
less than two thousand) the final subjugation of the Grand
Canary was not destined to be accomplished without one
more desperate struggle. A large portion of the natives

[1] Abreu de Galindo, tr. Glas, p. 112;
Viera y Clavijo, ii, p. 82; Löher, p. 243.
The first two of these authors are
clearly mistaken in stating that it was
Beatrice de Bobadilla whom Peraza
married. Beatrice de Bobadilla was
the queen's most intimate friend and
camarera mayor, and was married to
Andrés de Cabrera, Marquis of Moya
(Prescott, i, pp. 206, 233; iii, p. 168);

Peraza's bride was her sister Eleanor,
as Löher has it.

[2] Millares, iv, pp. 29 ff.; Viera y
Clavijo, ii, pp. 83 ff. Löher (p. 246),
places this in 1483, and consequently
postdates a number of subsequent
events. I can find no authority to support him.

[3] Abreu de Galindo, tr. Glas, pp.
114–116; Löher, pp. 245–251.

still favored resistance, and elected the youthful Bentejuí, nephew of the converted Guanarteme, to lead them in a final war against the intruder. Vera at first attempted to utilize the Guanarteme to persuade them to surrender without fighting. Failing in this, he prepared in the spring of 1483 for a vigorous campaign in the mountains. Guerilla warfare was waged for some weeks with varying success. Finally a detachment of Spaniards was lured into a difficult rocky country, honeycombed with caverns and secret hiding places known only to their enemies, and there defeated with severe slaughter, chiefly owing to the great stones which were rolled down on them from above. This reverse at Ajódar (for so the place was then called)[1] was by far the heaviest that the Spaniards had ever suffered in the Canaries, and it would have been worse still had not the Guanarteme been on hand to persuade the victors to spare the lives of many of their vanquished foes. But the invaders were by no means daunted. Vera reorganized and increased his forces and in April was again in the field. Moreover, profiting by his defeats, he avoided his previous mistakes. Instead of sending small detachments recklessly forward into places where they could be captured one by one, he cautiously drove the natives from one stronghold to another, until he had them virtually surrounded in their final place of refuge at Ansite.[2] A brief parley with the Guanarteme, who accompanied Vera wherever he went, convinced the bulk of the natives of the futility of further resistance, and induced them to surrender on promise of good treatment; but the heroic Bentejuí and his most intimate friend refused to endure the humiliation of admitting themselves vanquished, and, after embracing each other on the brow of a high preci-

[1] Viera y Clavijo, ii, p. 93. The modern name is Veneguera: Millares, iv, p. 49.

[2] Millares, iv, pp. 55 ff.

pice, committed suicide by jumping over the brink. The formal capitulation took place on April 29, 1483, with appropriate ceremonies, which were afterwards repeated at the Spanish headquarters on the seashore, already known as Las Palmas. Acceptance of Christianity and of the sovereignty of the king of Castile were, for the time being, the only conditions imposed by the victors, and Vera made haste to report the successful termination of the conquest to the king and queen in Spain.[1]

We must pass on rapidly now to the story of the conquest of Palma and Teneriffe. For six years after effecting the subjugation of the Grand Canary, Vera was chiefly occupied in setting up the framework of the Spanish administration of the island. He was also called upon during this period, however, to bear aid in subjugating a revolt of the natives of Gomera, in which Ferdinand Peraza was killed (1487). In this affair, Vera showed such dastardly treachery and unmitigated cruelty towards the islanders that he drew down on himself the condemnation of the bishop of the Canaries, whose ancient see at Rubicon had been transferred on November 20, 1485, to Las Palmas.[2] Finally, after a series of futile protests against Vera's atrocities, the bishop went home to complain of him, with the result that Ferdinand and Isabella sent out Francisco Maldonado as *juez pesquisidor* to investigate. The charges were impossible to deny, and in December, 1489, Vera was sent back to Spain in irons. Thenceforth he disappears from the history of the Canaries.[3] Maldonado, who succeeded him, inaugurated his term of office with a wretchedly unsuccessful attempt to take Teneriffe; but his failure brought forward the man who was des-

[1] Viera y Clavijo, ii, pp. 93–98; J. Abreu de Galindo, tr. Glas, pp. 117–123; Löher, pp. 252–270.
[2] Millares, iv, pp. 82–89; Torres Campos, pp. 61 ff.
[3] Millares, iv, pp. 128 ff.; Löher, pp. 287–292.

tined to carry the conquest of the archipelago to a triumphant conclusion. Alfonso de Lugo, Vera's old companion in arms, had by this time enjoyed a wide experience of Canarian campaigns. That Palma and Teneriffe remained unsubdued had long been a thorn in his side; and soon after Maldonado's repulse, he returned to Spain to get aid from Ferdinand and Isabella for a final expedition against them. His reputation at the court stood high on account of his previous military successes; he had a large private fortune, which he had substantially increased by his careful management of his estates on the Grand Canary, and consequently was able to offer to fit out the expedition at his own expense. All he demanded was supreme military command for the time, and a promise of the office of *adelantado* and the political authority that went with it in the future; and these Ferdinand and Isabella were glad to grant him. They also apparently invested him with some measure of authority over the adjacent West African coast, despite the fact that by the treaty of 1479 that region had been handed over exclusively to the Portuguese.[1] Armed with these offices and powers, Lugo recruited his forces, and returned to the Canaries in the spring of 1491. On September 29 of that year he landed on the island of Palma. By gentle and conciliatory means, and by skilful utilization of tribal divisions, he managed to win the allegiance of the majority of the natives before the following spring. One clan only, under the chieftain Tanausu, defied him; the latter's headquarters, established in a sort of mountain crater, were so strong that Lugo was unable to storm them. When force did not avail, however, the Spaniard was quite ready to use fraud. Tanausu and his followers were invited to a parley on May 3, 1492, and there treacherously set upon and most of them

[1] Löher, pp. 292–304.

slaughtered; the chief himself was captured alive, but subsequently starved himself to death on board the vessel by which he was being sent to Spain. This barbarous affair marked the end of the natives' resistance. In the summer of 1492, when Lugo sailed back to the Grand Canary, Palma had been virtually incorporated in the domains of the realm of Castile, though there were sporadic revolts by the islanders for many years to come.[1]

Teneriffe alone remained, but Teneriffe was destined to give more trouble than all the rest. Lugo did not underestimate the difficulties of the task. When, in April, 1493, he finally set forth to conquer the island, he took with him no fewer than a thousand foot and one hundred and twenty horse — all picked men, whom his own fame and the cessation of the Granadan war had enabled him to collect.[2] It was by far the largest single force that had yet appeared in the Canaries, and only slightly smaller than that which accompanied Columbus on his second American voyage. Lugo's landing was unopposed, and he made haste to construct a fortified camp, the nucleus of the future city of Santa Cruz. Meanwhile an embassy, accompanied by the invaluable Guanarteme of the Grand Canary as interpreter, was despatched into the interior to parley with the natives.[3] The latter were, as usual, divided among themselves. Benchomo, the ablest and most powerful of the chieftains,

[1] There is the widest discrepancy between the various authors in regard to the date of the conquest of Palma. The statements of Viera y Clavijo, ii, pp. 158 f. (cf. also Bory de Saint-Vincent, *Essais sur les Isles Fortunées*, p. 172) seem fairly conclusive in favor of the dates as given here. Löher (pp. 318, 320) accepts May 3, 1492, as the date of the capture of Tanausu, but he places Lugo's arrival in Palma on September 29, 1490 (p. 308), thus adding a year to the period of conquest, which all the other authors give as seven months. Abreu de Galindo (tr. Glas, p. 145) puts the capture of Tanausu on May 3, 1491, and Millares (iv, p. 180) on May 3, 1493.

[2] Löher, p. 329. Millares (iv, p. 189) places this first expedition against Teneriffe in April, 1494, and makes it stay only two months, instead of a year and two months; but this is clearly wrong.

[3] Viera y Clavijo, ii, pp. 199 ff.; Löher, p. 337.

aspired to lord it over the rest; but his ambitions roused the enmity of various rivals, who were inclined from the first to seek the alliance of the Spaniards against him, while Benchomo himself naturally became the representative of the principle of resistance to foreign encroachment.[1] For a whole year after their arrival the Spaniards strove to utilize these discords of the Teneriffians for their own advantage, and with considerable success, for several of the most powerful of the local chieftains accepted baptism and the suzerainty of the king of Spain; but the mighty Benchomo, with five minor princes who had promised from the first to stand by him, determined to resist until the end. His first blow for the preservation of his country's freedom was certainly highly successful. He drew a large detachment of Spaniards who had ventured to invade his territories into a deep mountain defile at Acentejo, and there suddenly fell upon them unawares.[2] So terrific was the discharge of stones from above that both sides of the gorge seemed to roll down together upon the unfortunate invaders. The horrors of the ensuing rout were vastly increased by the panic among the great herds of cattle which the Spaniards had attempted to bring away with them. Six hundred of their number were slain, and three hundred more of their island auxiliaries. Even Lugo himself was wounded and beaten from his horse; and only a few escaped unhurt. Had Benchomo desired, he could easily have taken the life of every Spaniard in the island, but he was moderate and merciful in victory, and on receiving a promise from a number of the invaders who had fallen into his hands that they would not repeat the attempt, he caused them all to be escorted to the coast. Nevertheless the reverse was so serious that speedy recuperation was obviously impossible, and on June 8, 1494, Lugo left Teneriffe

[1] Viera y Clavijo, ii, pp. 204 ff.   [2] Löher, pp. 342–356.

with all his remaining men and returned to the Grand Canary to collect fresh forces.[1] The ensuing summer was filled with preparations for a fresh campaign. New detachments were brought from Spain and Lanzarote, and loyal Canarians were mustered into service. In November, 1494, Lugo was able to land another large force at Santa Cruz. Wisely refusing again to venture into the mountain regions, he finally enticed Benchomo down to a pitched battle in the plain at La Laguna in early December, and there defeated him with great slaughter. There seems to be some doubt as to whether Benchomo or his brother Tinguaro was slain in this fight, for the face of the corpse was so badly disfigured by sword cuts as to be virtually unrecognizable; the probabilities, however, point to Benchomo, though most of the authorities take the other view.[2] In any case the battle of La Laguna was decisive. Though guerilla warfare continued until September, 1496, ultimate surrender to the invaders was inevitable. Famine and the ravages of the local fever, called the *modorra*, hastened the end. Numerous picturesque episodes and adventures occurred during the final stages of the conflict; of these the most notable was perhaps the love match between the captive Spanish officer, Fernando García del Castillo, and Dazila, the fair daughter of one of the Teneriffian chiefs.[3] But the final result of the struggle was never in doubt. On September 29, 1496, the last of the native rulers recognized the authority of Ferdinand and Isabella, and when Lugo finally returned to Spain in 1497, he carried a number of them with him; one, whom Zurita asserts to have been Benchomo, was subsequently

[1] Viera y Clavijo, ii, pp. 208–222; Löher, pp. 356–367.
[2] Juan Núñez de la Peña, *Conquista y Antiguedades de las Islas Canarias*, p. 146; Viera y Clavijo, ii, pp. 222–228; Millares, iv, pp. 218 ff.; Löher, pp. 379–387, 593.
[3] Löher, pp. 391–396, 405 f.

exhibited in Venice.[1] Lugo was of course the hero of the hour. Not only was the governorship of Palma and Teneriffe conferred upon him, but the title of adelantado of all the Canaries was made hereditary in his family, and his authority over the four smaller Herrera islands was further augmented, at least temporarily, by his marriage with Eleanor de Bobadilla, the fiery widow of Ferdinand Peraza.[2] He even attempted to realize some measure of the rights over the adjacent West African coast, which Ferdinand and Isabella had conferred on him when he first embarked on the conquest of Palma, by the erection of a fort there which should dispute the exclusive claims of the Portuguese; but his efforts in this direction were not particularly successful, and they cost him the life of his favorite son.[3] The rest of his days were chiefly spent in Teneriffe, where he died and was buried early in the year 1525 — one of the most interesting of the Spanish conquistadores, and one of the least known.[4]

Thus by the opening of the sixteenth century the entire Canarian archipelago acknowledged the sovereignty of the crown of Castile. Of the seven islands that composed it, however, the four smaller ones which had been conquered first continued to be administered as family holdings by the descendants of the Herreras down to the end of the eighteenth century;[5] only Grand Canary, Palma, and Teneriffe were completely incorporated in the Castilian realm.[6] The systems of government set up in the two portions of the archipelago naturally differed accordingly. In the lesser Herrera islands the different descendants of the origi-

---

[1] Viera y Clavijo, ii, pp. 267 ff.; Millares, iv, p. 249; Zurita, v, f. 78.

[2] Abreu de Galindo, tr. Glas, pp. 161–165; Viera y Clavijo, ii, pp. 273; 278 f.; Löher, pp. 292–295. 426 f.

[3] Millares, iv. pp. 260 ff.

[4] Viera y Clavijo, ii, pp. 298 f.

[5] On Herrera's descendants cf. Löher, p. 275; Viera y Clavijo, bks. x, xi, xii.

[6] Abreu de Galindo, tr. Glas. pp. 344 ff.; Millares, vii, pp. 57 ff

nal grantees maintained, each one in the district that fell to his share, a considerable measure of political power; but every possible opportunity was utilized to effect a gradual diminution of their authority, and to subject them more and more, as time went on, to the control of officers sent out by the crown. The transference of the episcopal see from Rubicon to Las Palmas deprived Lanzarote of many privileges, and Lugo's office of adelantado gave him numerous opportunities to interfere, as the crown's representative, in the lesser islands, particularly in Gomera and Ferro, where he acted for some time as regent for his wife's children by her first husband, Ferdinand Peraza.[1] Nevertheless, the political rights of the Herreras were by no means extinguished; and the *útil dominio* conferred on them by the arrangement of 1477 continued to be recognized, in theory at least, down to the period of the Napoleonic wars.[2] In Grand Canary, Palma, and Teneriffe, on the other hand, the regular machinery of Castilian government was gradually set up. The office of adelantado remained hereditary, as the original grant had provided, in the family of Lugo and the collateral lines, though it was stripped of all political authority as the result of a residencia in the year 1536–37, so that the administration of the three principal islands was thenceforth directly in the hands of representatives of the crown.[3] But since it was during the earlier period, while the adelantados were still supreme, that the foundations of the permanent system of government were securely laid, the change effected by the above mentioned residencia was only a change in the source of authority; the crown of Castile had merely substituted itself for the local magnate who had previously represented

[1] The marriage of Lugo's son with another of the Herreras further increased the measure of the dependence of the smaller islands on the principal ones.

Viera y Clavijo, ii, p. 304.
[2] Abreu de Galindo, tr. Glas, pp. 218 ff.; Millares, vii, pp. 57 ff.
[3] Viera y Clavijo, ii, pp. 304–322.

it.[1]   Each island was organized as a municipality, the limits of the capital town being held in each case to extend to the shores. A fuero of the most liberal and democratic sort was granted by Ferdinand and Isabella on December 20, 1494, to Las Palmas in the Grand Canary, which soon became the recognized centre of the archipelago ; an *ayuntamiento*, whose membership was variously constituted, makes its appearance, together with *alguaciles, alcaldes, almotacenes,* and all the other familiar concomitants of Castilian municipal life.[2]   A number of special privileges, including notable exemptions from taxation and the coveted distinction of a coat of arms, were also conferred upon it. The islands of Palma and Teneriffe were administered on similar lines. To give unity and cohesion to these three different organizations a supreme tribunal of appeal, or audiencia, was set up in the Grand Canary in 1526–27 ; it was largely owing to the reports which it sent home that the Emperor ten years later took away the political powers of the adelantado.[3]

The treatment of the native Canarians by the Spaniards has been represented in various lights by different authors, and it is by no means easy to determine the facts. The propagation of the faith was of course a primary object of the conquest, and acceptance of Christianity consequently obligatory on the islanders from the very first.[4]   Dominicans and Franciscans established themselves in the archipelago with the first conquistadores, and followed the Castilian banners wherever they went. Two of them, indeed, were hurled from a precipice by those whom they were attempting to convert ; but the proselytizing energy of the government was not to be denied, and before long all the Canarians

[1] Abreu de Galindo, tr. Glas, pp. 344 ff. ; Viera y Clavijo, iii, pp. 105 ff. ; Millares, iv, pp. 69 ff.

[2] Viera y Clavijo, iii, p. 107 ; Milla-res, iv, pp. 97 f.

[3] Viera y Clavijo, iii, pp. 111, 125 ff., 130 f. ; Millares, iv, pp. 106–108.

[4] Torres Campos, p. 26.

adopted the religion of their conquerors.[1] Doubts naturally soon arose as to the genuineness of some of the conversions, and furnished an excuse for the extension of the Inquisition to the archipelago in 1504;[2] but officially the Canarians are to be regarded as Christians from the time of the completion of the Spanish conquest. There can be little doubt that it was the intention of the home government that the natives should be humanely and generously dealt with in other respects, and that they should not be deprived of their right to hold land; but it also seems equally clear that these intentions were not fully carried out in practice.[3] An enormous number of those who had served in the conquering armies, or contributed to their support, had to be rewarded by extensive grants of land; the distribution of *repartimientos*, or allotments of territory among their followers, was one of the most difficult duties of the early adelantados, and one in which much jealousy and ill will were unavoidably stirred up. Under a system such as this it was inevitable that the natives should suffer. Some few of them — especially those who had aided the Spaniards in the conquest — were permitted to retain small and generally undesirable portions of land. Others remained as tenants on the territories that had been handed over to the invaders.[4] Marriages between the natives and their conquerors were also of frequent occurrence.[5] But in general we may be certain that the lot of the indigenous Canarians grew steadily worse during the first two centuries of Spanish rule. More and more were they elbowed aside to make room for the newcomers. There were ample facilities for emigration, owing to the large number

[1] Millares, iv, pp. 93 f.; Löher, pp. 431–433.

[2] L. de Alberti and A. B. W. Chapman, *English Merchants and the Spanish Inquisition in the Canaries*, p. v; Lea, *Inquisition in the Spanish Dependencies*, p. 140, dates its establishment in 1505.

[3] Viera y Clavijo, ii, p. 274; Torres Campos, pp. 42–52, and authorities there cited.

[4] Löher, pp. 429–431.

[5] Torres Campos, p. 66.

of ships that touched at the islands, and the population rapidly declined ;[1] it is, however, but fair to add that Canarians figure very prominently at certain stages of the conquest and colonization of the Americas, and also in Flanders and in Italy.[2]

The question of slavery and the slave trade in the archipelago is perhaps the most difficult of all. During the first three-quarters of the fifteenth century there was certainly a great deal of both, attributable probably rather to the Portuguese than to the Spaniards ; but after the completion of the conquest in the period of Ferdinand and Isabella efforts were unquestionably made to restrict them.[3] The enslaving of the native Canarians, the Catholic Kings did their best to terminate entirely. It continued to be employed as the regular penalty for an insurrection, and occasionally Portuguese raiders succeeded in carrying off small groups of the islanders into captivity ; but if Canarian slaves were brought over to Spain to be sold the crown usually gave orders that they be granted their liberty. On the other hand, the practice of organizing elaborate slave hunts among the natives of the adjacent Barbary coast, across the so-called Mar Pequeña, had been popular in the Canaries for so many years that Ferdinand and Isabella wisely recognized the impossibility of putting an end to it. They therefore strove instead to regulate it in a way favorable to themselves, and to ameliorate the conditions under which it was carried on. Apparently the sovereigns were at first scrupulously careful to observe the arrangements, made in the treaty of 1479, giving the Portuguese exclusive rights on the African coast opposite the archipelago. In 1495 they forbade any expedition by any of their subjects into that

[1] Löher, pp. 433–435.
[2] Torres Campos, pp. 70–81.

[3] Fernández Duro, *Marina de Castilla*, pp. 255–263.

region, unless the formal consent of the Portuguese monarch had been previously obtained.[1] A few years later, however, they altered their policy in this respect, and became much more aggressive, probably as a result of the demands of their subjects in the Canaries, to whom the congenial occupation of slave hunting on the opposite coasts had become a principal means of livelihood. A prolonged dispute with the Portuguese authorities ensued, and finally ended, on September 18, 1509, with an agreement by which the latter acknowledged Castile as the lawful possessor of the Torre de Santa Cruz [2] on the West African coast, and recognized the authority over it of the adelantado of the Canaries.[3]

"A veritable half way house between Europe, Africa, and America" — such are the words in which a recent historian of the Canaries significantly describes them.[4] The Catholic Kings doubtless regarded their conquest as a logical sequel to the War of Succession with Portugal, an assertion that they did not propose to permit that state to monopolize the fascinating occupation of discovery and colonization in unknown lands. The importance of the archipelago was primarily evident in connection with Africa, where the Portuguese had already established themselves. It formed a Spanish outpost on the confines of the Dark Continent, occupying in relation to it a position closely analogous to that of Cyprus to the Holy Land in the days of the Crusades.[5] But in the end the relation of the Canaries to the Spanish conquests in the Western Hemisphere was to prove more intimate and significant still. They became a

[1] Torres Campos, pp. 52–57.
[2] Possibly near the modern town of Ifni, though more probably at Puerto Cansado, farther south.
[3] Millares, iv, pp. 120–127, 261 ff.; cf. also infra, p. 249. This settlement may fairly claim to be the ancestor of the present Spanish colony of Rio de Oro, which lies mostly to the south of it and was given its present boundaries in 1912. Cf. R. Donoso-Cortes, Zonas Españolas de Marruecos, pp. 42–64, 297–309.
[4] Torres Campos, p. 83.
[5] Löher, p. 441.

regular stopping place for outgoing and returning ships. Columbus put in there on each of his four voyages; the *Pinta* was provisioned and repaired in the harbor of Las Palmas in the Grand Canary in the last three weeks of August, 1492; and the island of Gomera was the last bit of land in the Eastern Hemisphere which the great explorer trod before he first set foot in the West Indies. Still more striking were the effects of the conquering, colonizing, and proselytizing experiences of the Spaniards in the Canaries upon their conduct and policy in the New World. The archipelago furnished them with the material for their first colonial experiment, and their methods there were reproduced with remarkably few variations in the Indies.[1] The Canaries in the sixteenth century may, in fact, be justly described as a microcosm of the Spanish dominions across the Atlantic. In some ways the Spanish policy in the archipelago was more liberal than in America. There were not, for instance, the same restrictions on immigration; some foreigners, especially Italians, were allowed to come, and until the establishment of the Inquisition in the archipelago in 1504 a number of Jews sought refuge there. Moreover, owing doubtless to the fact that they held all the islands, and consequently had no reason to fear, as in America, the acquisition of land by hostile powers in disagreeable proximity to themselves, the Spaniards welcomed traders and merchants from other countries, and did their best to establish relations with them.[2] The mineral and agricultural products of the archipelago were both numerous and valuable, and furnished plenty of commodities for commerce; and the government, which rigorously exacted its fifth (*quinta*)

---

[1] Millares, iv, pp. 142–150; R. R. Schuller, *La Posición de las Canarias en el Siglo del Descubrimiento de América* (Montevideo, 1904).

[2] Millares, iv, pp. 80 f.; Torres Campos, p. 52: Alberti and Chapman, p. v.

on every cargo shipped in Canarian ports, did its utmost, though not always in the wisest ways, to promote their material prosperity.[1] Altogether, the archipelago may be said to have occupied a pivotal position in the Spanish Empire from the end of the fifteenth century.

[1] Löher, p. 442. The most impor-   the orchil were dragon's-blood, wine, tant products of the archipelago besides   grain, tallow, and hides.

BIBLIOGRAPHICAL NOTE

See bibliographical note at the end of Chapter III in Volume I, and add:

Sources. — *Alguns Documentos do Archivo Nacional da Torre do Tombo, ácerca das navegações e conquistas Portuguezas*, ed. José Ramos-Coelho (Lisbon, 1892); the most important collection of documents on early Portuguese discoveries; it covers the period 1416 to 1529.

Later Works.—Rafael Torres Campos, *Carácter de la Conquista y Colonización de las Islas Canarias* (Discurso de la R. A. H., Madrid, 1901). J. B. G. M. Bory de Saint-Vincent, *Essais sur les Isles Fortunées* (Paris, 1803). Ricardo Donoso-Cortés, *Estudio geográfico político-militar sobre las Zonas Españolas del Norte y Sur de Marruecos* (Madrid, 1913)• R. R. Schuller, *La Posición de las Islas Canarias en el Siglo del Descubrimiento de América* (Montevideo, 1904).

CHAPTER XVII

THE INDIES

THE story of the discovery of America, like that of the conquest of the Canaries, is intimately bound up with the relations of Castile to Portugal. The latter had been active in foreign exploration and conquest long before the accession of the Catholic Kings. The efforts of Prince Henry the Navigator had made her a Mecca of fifteenth-century mariners. Traditionally she had a far better right to the honor of finding the Western Hemisphere than had her eastern neighbor, and it was largely the result of accident, and possibly of the issue of the War of Succession, that Castile stepped in at the last moment to deprive her of it.

It was probably in the latter part of the year 1476 that Christopher Columbus first appeared in Portugal, and seven years later, towards the end of 1483, that he laid certain propositions for a voyage of discovery into the western ocean before King John II, the son and successor of Affonso the African. Whether these propositions contemplated merely the finding of a shorter and easier way to the eastern shores of Asia, or the discovery of new lands which the explorer had reason to believe lay hidden in the western ocean, or both, we are fortunately not called upon to decide; a group of scientists gave its verdict against the feasibility of his schemes, and in 1484 he left Portugal for Spain.[1]   After despatching his brother Bartholomew to

[1] Vignaud, *Histoire de la grande entre-prise de Christophe Colomb*, i; Channing, *History of the United States*, i, pp. 14–19; Bourne, *Spain in America*. pp. 11–16.

press his suit at the courts of England and of France, he took his own measures for furthering his projects in Castile.[1] The Duke of Medina Sidonia, to whom he first applied, did nothing for him. The Count of Medina Celi,[2] whom he visited next, was more encouraging, but powerless to help him alone; at the end of 1485 he sent Columbus on to the court of Ferdinand and Isabella at Cordova. In April and May of the following year their Catholic Majesties gave audience to the explorer, and charged Hernando de Talavera with the formation of a committee to examine the validity of his claims. This committee held its sittings at Salamanca, where Columbus in all probability appeared before it.[3] With characteristic Spanish deliberation it failed to render its decision before 1490; and during the long interval the explorer, despite the protection of Ferdinand and Isabella, was often hard put to it to get a living. When the sentence of the commission was finally rendered, it was adverse, and the Catholic Kings bade Columbus a courteously worded adieu.[4] Though profoundly discouraged, he soon determined to go and seek better fortune in France. On the way thither, after a visit to his former friend and patron, the Count of Medina Celi, he passed by the monastery of La Rabida, near Palos, where he greatly interested Fray Juan Perez, a former confessor of the queen, in his schemes of discovery and exploration.[5] It also seems highly probable that he succeeded in obtaining at this critical juncture the effective support of the famous pilot Martin Pinzon, who was to be his right-hand man in his momentous voyage.[6] In any case it is certain that Perez was able to make representations to Isabella concerning Columbus's plans and prospects, which resulted in the

[1] Vignaud, *op. cit.*, i, pp. 425–479.
[2] He was created Duke in 1491.
[3] Vignaud, i, pp. 547–599.
[4] Vignaud, i, pp. 702–706.
[5] Vignaud, ii, p. 15 ff.
[6] Vignaud, ii, pp. 25–41.

explorer's recall to the Castilian court before Granada in
the summer of 1491, in order that he might be given another
hearing. Conferences ensued, but the conditions which
Columbus demanded, in respect both to the funds for his
expedition and to the rights and dignities to be conferred
upon himself, were such that all who were consulted regarded
them as inacceptable, and in January, 1492, the explorer
was again dismissed.[1] He had no sooner departed, however,
than a number of persons intervened to demand that he be
brought back once more. Prominent among these was a
wealthy member of the Royal Council,[2] of Aragonese
Jewish extraction, by name Luis de Santangel, and also
Beatrice de Bobadilla, Marchioness de Moya, Isabella's
most intimate friend, and elder sister to the lady who figured
so prominently in the history of the Canaries.[3] The final
result was that before Columbus, on his sorrowful journey
northward, had reached the Puerta de Pinos, two leagues
from Granada, he was overtaken by a royal *alguacil* with
orders to return at once.[4]

Three months more elapsed, however, before terms of
agreement could be reached. The final arrangements were
concluded on the seventeenth of April at Santa Fé. Columbus was granted the rank of Admiral, with all the dignities and privileges thereto pertaining, in such territories
as he should discover, and the title was to pass on his death
to his heirs. As admiral he was given the right to be sole
judge of all cases arising in connection with the trade and

---

[1] Vignaud, ii, pp. 47–70.

[2] At least so say Vignaud, ii, p. 75,
note, and Harrisse, *Christophe Colomb*, i,
p. 389; without any further references
for the statement. Strictly speaking,
'Royal Council' or 'Consejo Real'
means the 'Council of Castile' in this
period, and it seems doubtful whether
Santangel belonged to that body : more

probably he was a member of one of the
other councils, very likely of the Council
of Aragon. He was also treasurer of
the Hermandad, and Chancellor and
contador mayor of Aragon.

[3] *Ante*, p. 176, and Vignaud, ii, pp.
71–88.

[4] Vignaud, ii, pp. 90–93.

commerce of the territories in question. He was to be viceroy and governor general in the lands he expected to find, and was to have the right of presenting three candidates for any post of profit and emolument under him, from whom their Majesties should select one. He was to have one tenth of all the products drawn from the said lands, and the right, if he contributed one eighth to the cost of the expedition, to receive one eighth of the profits resulting from it.[1] It used to be the fashion to represent Ferdinand as indifferent, or even positively hostile, to the whole enterprise, and to give all the credit of the affair to Isabella; but more recently strong reasons have been advanced for thinking that the king of Aragon bore an important part in the whole negotiation.[2] That his signature is affixed to all the documents and capitulations relative to the expedition may not count for much, and the story that he employed the first gold brought to Spain from the Indies to gild his royal palace at Saragossa is not particularly significant; but the fact that his own officials found most of the necessary money for the voyage is an evidence of interest too substantial to controvert.[3] The whole matter is of great importance as leading up to the question of how far the realms of the Crown of Aragon were subsequently permitted to take part in the conquest and colonization of the New World — a problem which goes down to the very foundation of the Spanish Empire. We shall return to this matter in another place. For the present we need only observe that though the privilege of emigration and

---

[1] Vignaud, ii, pp. 97–101.
[2] Vignaud, ii, pp. 128–134.
[3] V. Balaguer, *Castilla y Aragón en el Descubrimiento de América*; Mir, *Influencia de los Aragoneses en el Descubrimiento de América*; Ibarra y Rodríguez, *D. Fernando el Católico y el Descubri-miento de América*. There seems little, if any, foundation for the tale that Isabella pawned her jewels to pay for the enterprise. Vignaud, ii, pp. 114–116; C. Fernández Duro, *Las joyas de Isabel la Católica* (Madrid, 1882).

settlement was with rare exceptions restricted to the inhabitants of the western kingdom from the time of the announcement of the discovery to the death of Queen Isabella in 1504, it was gradually thrown open to the inhabitants of the other Spanish kingdoms in the succeeding years, until, by the end of the sixteenth century, they enjoyed absolute equality in this respect.[1]

The story of the preparations for the voyage and the equipment of the three caravels [2] has been often told. So great was the prevalent distrust of the issue of the expedition, that it is more than doubtful whether, even with the backing of the crown, Columbus could have successfully organized it, without the precious aid of the pilot Martin Pinzon.[3] The Catholic Kings were scrupulously careful not to permit the explorer to trespass on the Portuguese territories in Africa; he was specifically forbidden to go to the Guinea coast.[4] The contemporary accounts vary widely as to the number of persons who went with him. Probably the total was rather less than more than one hundred and twenty, of whom ninety were sailors of one sort or another. The majority came from the towns of southwestern Andalusia, but there were apparently a Genoese and a Portuguese among their number, and possibly an Englishman and an Irishman. Strangely enough, no priest accompanied the expedition.[5] The little fleet sailed at dawn on August 3, 1492, from Palos, put in six days later at the Canaries for repairs, and finally departed thence on September 6 for the unknown seas. Doubts, discouragements, and proposals to turn back, grumblings

[1] Cf. infra, p. 221.
[2] The Santa Maria was much the largest of the three and the only one that was decked. She may perhaps be more accurately described as a car-rack than as a caravel. Cf. Channing, History of the United States, i, p. 20.
[3] Vignaud, ii, pp. 135–171.
[4] Vignaud, ii, p. 136.
[5] Vignaud, ii, pp. 163–167, 526–532.

and mutinous threats from the crews were the daily accompaniments of the next five weeks, but the sublime faith of the Admiral triumphed, and at last, on the evening of October 11, a flickering light was perceived in the darkness ahead. The following morning revealed the low-lying shores of one of the Bahamas, which the majority of modern scholars have agreed in identifying as Watling's Island, and which Columbus significantly named San Salvador. Whether we accept the older notion that the object of the Admiral's expedition was to reach the east by way of the west, or follow M. Vignaud's more recent argument that he had started out with the idea of finding new lands which he had reason to believe existed some seven hundred and fifty leagues west of the Canaries, it seems clear that Columbus, having already progressed some two hundred leagues farther than he had ever expected to go, was persuaded that he had reached the confines of the eastern world.[1] At any rate he dubbed the natives he encountered 'Indians,' a name which had hitherto had an exclusively Oriental connotation, though Ferdinand Columbus tells us that his father adopted it because it was suggestive of great riches; and as 'Indians' the aboriginal inhabitants of the Western Hemisphere have continued to be known until this day.[2]

Of course the adventurers soon discovered that the land they had found was merely an outlying islet. They therefore continued their voyage westward to look for the larger territories which lay beyond. On October 28 they struck the northern shore of Cuba and explored it; and

---

[1] Vignaud, ii, pp. 170–210; cf. also E. G. Bourne and E. L. Stevenson in *American Historical Review*, viii, pp. 341–346; xvii, pp. 610–613. M. Vignaud's theories are hard to refute, but he fails to account for the fact that Columbus received from Ferdinand and Isabella a gracious letter to be presented to the Great Khan. Is it not probable that the explorer had *both* ends in view?

[2] Channing, i, p. 24.

so sure was Columbus that he had reached the mainland, and that the realms of the Great Khan could not be far away, that he sent off two of his followers to seek for the court of that potentate and carry him the compliments of the sovereigns of Spain.[1] From Cuba he sailed southeast to Haiti, in which he fancied he recognized both the island which he had expected to discover and the Cipango which Martin Pinzon believed had been reached; on account of its similarity, at first appearance, to Spain, he named it Española.[2] Off the coast of this island his largest ship, the *Santa Maria*, ran aground on Christmas Day and was wrecked. Ready aid from the friendly Indians, however, made possible the saving of the cargo and provisions, and the Admiral finally became convinced "that God had permitted the disaster in order that the place might be chosen for a settlement."[3] Some forty of his followers agreed to remain and await his return; the construction of a stronghold to give them shelter was begun; every effort was made to urge upon them the importance of preserving the friendliest possible relations with the natives; finally, on January 4, 1493, after duly impressing the cacique with a sense of his power by a salvo from his cannon, Columbus set sail for home. He took with him specimens of gold which his followers had collected, and also a few Indians; the number of these was increased during the first week of the homeward voyage when he touched at several other points on the northern shore of Española, and came for the first time into hostile collision with the natives.[4] The return voyage was beset by gales. Columbus was obliged to stop at the Azores on the way, where the Portuguese governor apparently had some thought of apprehending

[1] Gaffarel, *Histoire de la découverte de l'Amérique*, ii, pp. 110 f.
[2] Vignaud, ii, pp. 191–194, 208.
[3] Gaffarel, ii, pp. 120 f.; Winsor, *Christopher Columbus*, p. 233.
[4] Winsor, *op. cit.*, pp. 235 f.

him; moreover, when he finally landed at Lisbon and told his story to the Portuguese sovereign, there was talk of King John's laying claim to the lands he had discovered, and even of provoking the explorer into a quarrel and compassing his death. Clearly the Portuguese were jealous of Columbus's good fortune, and of the fact that Spaniards rather than themselves were to profit by it; and the remembrance that the explorer had originally applied to them for aid in his great enterprise, long before he had visited the Castilian court, must have added to the bitterness of their reflections. But Ferdinand and Isabella were now far stronger than they had been during the War of Succession. King John could not afford to quarrel with them, and he knew it; he therefore wisely determined to bide his time, and leave the substantiation of any claims he might have to a more favorable opportunity in the future. Columbus was accordingly permitted to depart with a splendid escort of knights; two days later he again embarked, and finally, on March 15, 1493, dropped anchor in the harbor of Palos, whence he had set sail over seven months before. The people received him with enthusiasm and thanksgivings, and he was speedily summoned to report to their Catholic Majesties at Barcelona.[1]

Before pursuing further the fortunes of the explorer, we must examine the measures taken by the Catholic Kings to guarantee their possession of the lands he had discovered; for they did not wait to see Columbus before applying for papal confirmation of their right to the new territories. Dread of Portuguese competition was, of course, the explanation of their haste. The news of the Admiral's adventures at Lisbon on his homeward voyage had brought the dangers of it forcibly to their minds, and there were

[1] Gaffarel, ii, pp. 121-127; Winsor, pp. 238-242.

also other memories of earlier days which strengthened their determination to guard themselves against it. Bulls of Martin V, Eugenius IV, Nicholas V, and Calixtus III had granted the Portuguese such lands as they might discover from Capes Nun and Bojador southward towards Guinea and beyond, and there was a general impression that their claims under these bulls extended as far as the Indies.[1] In 1479–80 the Catholic Kings had specifically recognized by treaty the exclusive rights of Portugal to all lands she should discover in Guinea and off the coast of it, except the Canaries;[2] and on June 21, 1481, Pope Sixtus IV had confirmed this treaty, and also the grants under his predecessors' bulls.[3] Since that time the Portuguese had rounded the Cape of Good Hope and followed up the east coast of Africa to a point beyond Algoa Bay; clearly, in view of the prevailing ignorance of geography and the doubts as to the exact location of the lands Columbus had found, it was essential that Rome be immediately notified of the Spanish pretensions. Ferdinand and Isabella had every reason to believe that their claims would not fare ill at the hands of the recently elected pontiff, Alexander VI, who, in addition to being of Valencian birth, was beholden to them in a variety of different ways. Their foresight was justified by

---

[1] The bulls *Romanus pontifex* (put forth by Nicholas V on January 8, 1455) and *Inter caetera* (promulgated by Calixtus III, on March 13, 1456) are printed with full notes and English translations in Miss F. G. Davenport's recent volume of *European Treaties bearing on the History of the United States and its Dependencies*; cf. also J. Ramos-Coelho, *Alguns Documentos*, pp. 14–22. The statements in these bulls in regard to the Indies are exceedingly vague — the most definite being that which vests "ecclesiastical and all ordinary jurisdiction, lordship, and power, in ecclesiastical affairs only" in the lands "to be acquired from capes Bojador and Nam as far as through all Guinea, and past that southern shore all the way to the Indians" in the Military Order of Christ. Yet the fact that Ferdinand and Isabella, in their letter to Alexander VI, referred to Columbus's voyage as only "versus Indos," looks as if they feared that if they definitely stated that he had actually reached them, they would be adjudged to have trespassed on Portuguese territory.

[2] Cf. *ante*, p. 173.

[3] J. Ramos-Coelho, *Alguns Documentos*, pp. 47–55; Davenport, *op. cit.*, pp. 49–55.

the event; in all the ensuing negotiations the pontiff was less an arbiter, than an instrument in the hands of the Catholic Kings.[1] In April, 1493, he put forth the first of the two famous bulls *Inter caetera*, granting to the Spanish sovereigns exclusive right and possession in all the lands and islands discovered in the West, towards the Indies, in the Ocean Sea, as well as in all others yet to be discovered in that region. On May 17 the bull was dispatched to the papal nuncio in Spain.[2] It was doubtless Alexander's hope that the very vague phraseology which had been employed would safeguard the rights already granted by his predecessors to Portugal "from Cape Bojador towards Guinea and beyond," and at the same time satisfy the demands of Ferdinand and Isabella; but he was destined to be disappointed. By the time that the bull arrived in Spain, the sovereigns had had time to discuss the whole affair with Columbus, and to learn the full extent of his achievements and of his hopes. They had also opened negotiations with John II of Portugal, and had been informed of the counter-claims which that monarch had to urge. The wording of the first bull was clearly inadequate: it did not settle the question of the dominion of the Atlantic, particularly to the southward, which Spain was most desirous to secure. Columbus urged the advisability of a demarcation line; and the sovereigns, acting on his suggestion, again applied to Rome for an amplification and extension of the rights already conferred upon them.[3] The

[1] H. vander Linden, "Alexander VI and the Demarcation of the Maritime and Colonial Domains of Spain and Portugal," in *American Historical Review*, xxii, pp. 13 f. (October, 1916). It is also worth noting, in this connection, that all the papal bulls on this question are directed solely to Ferdinand and Isabella.

[2] This bull was formally dated May 3, and is commonly referred to as of that day. Vander Linden, *op. cit.*, p. 6, has clearly proved, however, that it was expedited in April, and finally sent off on May 17. For its text, and that of its successors of May 4 and September 26, see Navarrete, *Viajes*, ii, pp. 23–35; Davenport, *op. cit.*, pp. 56–83.

[3] Vander Linden, *op. cit.*, pp. 16 f.

result was the second bull *Inter caetera,* which was issued in June and reached Spain in the middle of July.[1] It granted to their Catholic Majesties all lands found or to be found both to the west and to the south towards India and all other regions, provided they had not been occupied by any other Christian prince previously to Christmas, 1492; and it established a line to be drawn, north and south, a hundred leagues to the westward of the Azores and Cape Verde Islands,[2] beyond which no foreigner was to venture without a license from the Spanish sovereign. Furthermore, a supplementary bull *Eximiae,* issued in July,[3] reiterated and emphasized the rights and privileges to be enjoyed by Ferdinand and Isabella in the territories in question; while a final one, dated September 26, provided — in flat contradiction to the earlier instrument — that previous occupation by other Christian potentates should not constitute a title, and annulled all grants "to kings, princes, infantes, or religious or military orders" in the regions assigned to the king and queen of Spain.[4]

Clearly all these stipulations were aimed directly at the Portuguese; Alexander, who, on account of the political situation in Italy, was like wax in the hands of Ferdinand and Isabella, was being steadily led on to more and more open infringement of the rights of their rival. Naturally, under the circumstances, King John regarded the course of the negotiations between Spain and the Vatican with steadily increasing dissatisfaction. In addition to all their

[1] Vander Linden, *op. cit.,* pp. 6, 18. This bull is usually referred to as of May 4, its formal date.

[2] As there is a difference in longitude of at least eight degrees between the westernmost of the Azores and the easternmost of the Cape Verde Islands, it is futile to attempt definitely to locate this line. If one measures a hundred leagues west of St. Antonio, the westernmost and largest of the Cape Verde group (which is perhaps a fair average), the line would fall well to the east of the eastern point of Brazil.

[3] Vander Linden, *op. cit.,* pp. 6, 10. It was formally dated May 3.

[4] Vander Linden, *op. cit.,* p. 10.

other advantages, the fact that the Catholic Kings were holding their court at Barcelona, whence they could reach Rome twice as quickly as could the Portuguese monarch, doubtless convinced the latter that little was to be gained by an attempt to outbid them there; his best hope was to deal directly with Ferdinand and Isabella themselves. He therefore instructed Ruy de Sande, his representative at the Spanish court, to lay his case before them; moreover he assembled a powerful fleet, probably with the idea of threatening a descent on Columbus's discoveries if his protests should not be heard.[1] The negotiations dragged slowly along far beyond the date of Columbus's departure on his second voyage,[2] but both parties were desirous to avoid a quarrel, and Ferdinand and Isabella saw no harm in yielding to the argument of King John that the original line — one hundred leagues west of the Azores and Cape Verde Islands — limited too closely Portugal's opportunities for expansion in the Atlantic.[3] On June 7, 1494, a treaty between the monarchs was accordingly signed at Tordesillas, by which the line of demarcation of their respective claims was drawn north and south at a point three hundred and seventy leagues west of the Cape Verde Islands — that is, about half way between them and the islands that Columbus had discovered; everything beyond that line was to fall to the Catholic Kings, everything to the east of it was to belong to the Portuguese.[4] The line hits the north coast of South America just east of the mouth of the Amazon, and of course ultimately served to secure the Portuguese title to Brazil. On the other side of the globe it passes just west of New Guinea, but it was a long time before the facts were accurately determined, and in the meantime

[1] Gaffarel, ii, p. 136.
[2] Winsor, pp. 254 f., 305, 310.
[3] Lannoy and vander Linden, *Expan-* *sion coloniale de l'Espagne et du Portu-gal*, p. 54.
[4] Davenport, *op. cit.*, pp. 84–100.

Spain made good her hold on the Philippines, which lie on the Portuguese side of it.[1]

We now return to the career of Columbus, who was most graciously received by their Catholic Majesties at Barcelona; indeed, the months immediately succeeding his triumphal return from his first voyage were unquestionably the happiest in his life. But the sovereigns were even more concerned with the vigorous prosecution of the advantages already won than with rewarding the Admiral for his energy and faithfulness. On May 23, 1493, it was announced that a new and much larger expedition to the Indies would be sent out, and no less than sixteen royal orders were issued on that same day in regard to the preparations for it.[2] Other *cartas* and *cedulas* on the same subject followed in large numbers during the next three months, and bear witness to the immense enthusiasm which the whole affair had roused. The principal object of them all seems to have been to secure over every phase of the enterprise the largest possible measure of royal control and supervision compatible with the privileges granted to Columbus in 1492. The name of Juan Rodríguez de Fonseca, archdeacon of Seville, appears in the majority of these documents as a sort of superintendent of Indian affairs resident in Spain, and links this earliest period of discovery with the beginnings of the regular political and commercial organization of Spanish America in the next century. From

[1] In view of the difficulty of ascertaining exact positions in the Pacific, the sovereigns of Spain and of Portugal made a treaty in 1529, by which a line was drawn from north to south 297 leagues east of the Moluccas, to serve as a boundary between the areas claimed by the two realms pending a scientific and accurate determination of their respective rights. This arrangement put the Philippines in Portuguese territory even more conclusively than the Tordesillas line would have done; but the Spanish monarchs chose to ignore the facts, and tacitly assumed the right to conquer them. Cf. Blair and Robertson, *The Philippine Islands*, i, pp. 29 f., 222–239; also frontispiece to H. Harrisse, *The Diplomatic History of America: its first chapter*, London, 1897.

[2] Navarrete, ii, pp. 37–54.

1493 until after the death of Ferdinand the Catholic, Fonseca was, in fact, the crown's chief minister for colonial affairs. The duty of converting the Indians to Christianity was emphasized again and again, and a Catalan monk of the Benedictine order, named Boyl, was especially intrusted with it. The expedition numbered seventeen ships and some fifteen hundred men, among them soldiers, artisans, and laborers, and it carried all sorts of building and agricultural implements, seeds, and livestock. Clearly it was intended that a permanent colony should be founded. On the other hand the enterprise was regarded as so hazardous that it was deemed unwise that any women should accompany it; the lack of them goes far to account for the miserable broils of the colonists with the natives in the succeeding years.[1]

The adventurers set sail from Cadiz on September 25, 1493. On November 3 they sighted one of the Lesser Antilles, which, as it was on a Sunday, they named Dominica; the inhabitants, however, were so hostile that they did not remain there long, but passed over in the latter part of the month to Española, where Columbus had left a portion of his company on his previous expedition. Much to his horror, not a trace of them was to be found. Throwing off all discipline after his departure, they had assaulted and maltreated the natives; a few of them had been massacred in return, and the rest had been driven off and perished in the wilderness.[2] It was both an earnest of far worse difficulties of the same sort that were to come in the near future, and the beginning of immediate troubles for Columbus, which were to make his second expedition a very different affair from the first. In December the Spaniards

---

[1] Navarrete, ii, pp. 54–110, *passim*, especially pp. 66–72.
[2] Gaffarel, pp. 145–151.

passed along the north coast of Española to a more favorable site, and set about the construction of a permanent town, which they named Isabella. But the heavy labor in the strange climate played havoc with their health. Columbus himself was prostrated for prolonged periods. Discipline broke down, and the punishments the Admiral inflicted kindled the resentment of his followers. Explorations into the interior brought back encouraging reports of gold, but not enough specimens to satisfy the sceptics. Worst of all were the relations of the Spaniards with the Indians. The disappearance of the first colony had raised dark suspicions and deep resentment in the hearts of the newcomers: even Fray Boyl had counselled measures of vengeance and terrorization. A few of the natives, who were believed to be cannibals, were taken prisoners and sent back to Spain in January, 1494, with a recommendation from the Admiral that they be Christianized and taught Spanish, in order to make them available as interpreters; and Columbus further advised that more of them be captured and sold as slaves to pay for the supplies of various kinds that the colonists so sorely needed. All this was glozed over by much discussion of the spiritual welfare of the Indians, but it marked a wide departure from the line of policy advocated by the sovereigns less than six months before, and the clash of conflicting views on this most difficult subject was to constitute one of the hardest problems of Spanish colonial administration.[1] During the summer of 1494 the Admiral made a voyage of discovery to Jamaica and along the Cuban coast. After his return he was once more overtaken by a long and painful illness; and before his recovery was complete some of his followers, among them Fray Boyl, deserted and went back to Spain, where they

[1] Bourne, pp. 36–39; MacNutt, *Las Casas*, 23 ff.

roundly declared that the Indies were not worth retaining. The remaining colonists were in a sorry plight. Provisions ran short. Relations with the natives went steadily from bad to worse. It became necessary to raid the interior, and to terrorize the Indians into submission by the exaction of heavy tributes. In the spring of 1496 things were in such evil case that Columbus determined that he must go back to Spain to seek help and advice. Leaving his brother Bartholomew, who had come out in 1494, in command at Isabella in his absence, he set sail with two caravels, bearing about thirty Indians and upwards of two hundred homesick and discontented colonists, and reached Cadiz on June 11.[1]

His detractors had not been idle in his absence. Instead of the triumphant welcome accorded him in 1493, he now had hard work to regain the badly shaken confidence of the Catholic Kings, and to secure the maintenance of his original rights and privileges. More serious still, the fascination of the Indies for the mass of the Spaniards seemed temporarily dead; the Admiral was reduced to the most desperate extremities to find colonists to accompany him on a third voyage; most of those who finally went were paid by the crown, and the rest were criminals and jailbirds, who were sentenced to transportation in lieu of prison or execution. An advance guard of two ships was despatched in January, 1498, Columbus himself following with six more in May; but half of these were sent straight to Española from the Canaries, while the Admiral with the rest took a more southerly course across the Atlantic.[2] The first land he sighted was the island of Trinidad (July 31), and a little later he descried the continent of

[1] Bourne, pp. 39–44; Gaffarel, ii, pp. 154–162.

[2] Bourne, pp. 45 f., and references there.

South America beyond it. At first he took it for another
island, and named it Isla Santa, but a little later the enormous volume of fresh water pouring out of the mouths of
the Orinoco convinced him that he had reached the mainland.[1] Passing on up the coast to the northward and westward, he discovered the islands of Tobago, Granada, Mar-
garita, and Cubagua, and finally arrived at the newly founded
town of Santo Domingo on the southern shore of Española
in the end of August, after an absence of nearly two years
and a half, to find conditions even worse than he had feared.
Difficulties with the natives were more threatening than
ever : and far graver still, dissension and insubordination
had broken out among the Spaniards themselves ; some
ninety of their number, led by a certain Francisco Roldan,
had become so enraged at the strict discipline of Bartholomew Columbus that they had gone off into the interior
of the country and abandoned themselves to a life of violence and debauchery. After long negotiations, the Admiral determined that it would be expedient to pardon these
rebels and restore them to favor, and he finally did so ; but
long before this had occurred, he realized his powerlessness
to set affairs permanently to rights in the colony without
aid from home, and consequently sent back to Spain in the
autumn of 1498 a full account of the insurrection, with
vigorous demands for reënforcements, and for a *letrado*
of experience, who should be capable of fulfilling the duties
of a judge.[2] But Columbus had enemies as well as friends
on the returning ships, and also at court, who made the most
of his absence to traduce him. He had also sent back a large

---

[1] Gaffarel, ii, pp. 195 f. It does not
seem possible to determine whether
Columbus himself actually set foot on
the shore. The probabilities are that
he did not.

[2] Las Casas, *Historia de las Indias*
(edition of 1875), ii, p. 370, "un letrado,
persona experimentada para ejercer el
oficio de la justicia."

cargo of Indians, with an assurance that the continuance of the practice of enslaving them was the best possible means to preserve the existence of the colony; and these arrived, most unfortunately for him, at a juncture when the proverbially sensitive conscience of the queen had been vigorously aroused on the ethical questions involved.[1] The net result of this welter of conflicting circumstances, reports, and arguments was that the sovereigns in May, 1499, intrusted the government of the Indies to Francisco de Bobadilla, a knight of Calatrava and ancient servant of the crown, and sent him out there in January, 1500, armed with several alternative commissions, to be used according to his discretion.[2] This was a gross infringement of Columbus's rights and monopolies in the Indies, as defined in the grant of 1492, and can scarcely be justified on the ground of the request in his letter to the sovereigns for a *letrado*; but the Catholic Kings had already made up their minds that, whatever his services to them as an explorer, the Admiral had no talent for ruling men. The appointment of Bobadilla marks, indeed, the beginning of the taking over of the administration of the Indies by the crown. It seems clear that the new governor was prejudiced against Columbus before he started, and his impressions were strengthened by what he found on his arrival. The Admiral was speedily clapped in irons and sent back to Spain; and though liberated and granted an interview by the sovereigns soon after he landed, he never regained anything approaching the position he had previously held. No more political authority of any kind was ever vouchsafed to him. His original rights and privileges were more and more shamefully invaded. From henceforth he was merely one (and

[1] Bourne, pp. 49–51; Gaffarel, ii, pp. 200–205.
[2] Navarrete, *Viajes*, ii, pp. 235 ff.

by no means the most conspicuous) of a number of explorers of the Western Hemisphere. He made one last voyage to the Indies in 1502, on which, after being refused permission to land at Española, he followed down the east coast of Central America from Honduras to Panama; but so many others had reached other portions of the mainland before him that this final venture attracted but little attention. The very month of his return (November, 1504) saw the death of his best friend and patron Isabella; Ferdinand for the moment was far too much absorbed in his efforts to retain possession of the Castilian throne to pay any attention to him; and on Ascension Day, 1506, the great discoverer passed away at Valladolid, in an obscurity which, under all the circumstances, may well have been more grateful than the reverse.[1]

We must now briefly run through the achievements of the other explorers in the New World down to the death of King Ferdinand in 1516. The first of these was a certain Alonso de Ojeda, who had distinguished himself by his bravery and resourcefulness on Columbus's second voyage. He was in Spain at the time that the report arrived of the Admiral's discovery of the mainland of South America in 1498, and being himself a favorite of Fonseca, boldly asked leave, in defiance of the exclusive rights of Columbus, to undertake a voyage into the west for his own profit and advantage.[2] With an injunction to avoid all Portuguese possessions, and any lands discovered by Columbus previous to 1495, the desired permission was accorded him, and on May 20, 1499, Ojeda set sail.[3] He struck the north shore

[1] Bourne, pp. 52 f., 77–81; Winsor, pp. 390–490, *passim*.
[2] Navarrete, iii, pp. 538 ff.; Herrera, dec. i, lib. iv, cap. i.
[3] He was accompanied on this voyage by the famous mapmaker Juan de La Cosa, and by the Florentine Amerigo Vespucci, whose name was finally attached to the Western Hemisphere. We need not enter into the prolonged

of South America well to the east of the point reached by Columbus in the previous year — probably somewhere in the Guianas — and coasted along to the northward and westward as far as Cap de la Vela[1] — thus covering wide strips on both sides of the coast previously traversed by the Admiral. In the Gulf of Maracaibo he found a native village built on piles, which so reminded him of Venice that he bestowed upon the region the name Venezuela, which it bears today. A visit to Española not unnaturally involved him in a vigorous dispute with Columbus, after which he returned to Spain, where he was warmly received and granted new privileges of exploration and conquest.[2] But long before Ojeda could profit by this fresh patent, other explorers were in the field. Indeed, it seems probable that he was actually anticipated on the Venezuelan pearl coast by the pilot Alonso Niño, who left Cadiz with a single caravel in the early summer of 1499; though unimportant from the point of view of exploration, the expedition apparently brought back much treasure, and thus raised the badly shaken prestige of the Indies in Spain.[3] In the late autumn of 1499 Vicente Yañez Pinzon, a brother of Columbus's associate Martin, and, like him, a companion on his first voyage, sailed in a more southerly direction than any of his predecessors, struck the coast of Brazil, probably near its easternmost point, and followed the coast some two thousand miles north and west, discovering the Amazon (which he took to be the Ganges) by the way, and returning via Española to Spain. He was followed a few weeks later by a certain Diego de Lepe, who made the Brazilian shores

and acrimonious controversies which have centred around the latter's career and claims, but there seems no reason to place any credence in his alleged voyage of 1497. Cf. Bourne, chapter vii, and Channing, i, pp. 42–47, 55–57.

[1] Near Punta Gallinas, in Colombia, the northernmost point in South America.
[2] Gaffarel, ii, pp. 213–224.
[3] Bourne, p. 69.

still farther to the south, and got back to report before
Pinzon. Finally, a Sevillan notary, by name Rodrigo
Bastidas, sailed in October, 1500, explored the coast from
Cap de la Vela to the Isthmus of Panama, and returned
to Spain in 1502. The last voyage of Christopher Columbus
along the Central American shore fell in the same year,
so that the entire coast of the Western Hemisphere, from
Honduras to beyond the eastern point of Brazil, had now
been visited by the Spaniards.[1]

Meantime, while all these Castilian adventurers had been
flocking to the New World, the Portuguese, who had relapsed into temporary inactivity during the ten years
following Bartholomew Diaz's famous expedition of 1486,
gave signs of reawakening interest in the acquisition of new
and unknown lands. In 1495 King John had died, and was
succeeded by his energetic and enthusiastic cousin Emmanuel the Fortunate; in 1497 Vasco da Gama was despatched on the memorable voyage which carried him to
the Malabar coast of India. In 1500 another expedition
was sent out by the king of Portugal under Pedro Alvares
Cabral to follow up the advantage that da Gama had
already gained. Probably on the advice of his predecessor,
Cabral steered well out westward into the Atlantic after
leaving the Cape Verde Islands, in order to avoid the calms
of the Gulf of Guinea, and on April 21 sighted the east
coast of Brazil, near Porto Seguro, some five hundred miles
the south of the point reached by Diego de Lepe a few
weeks before.[2] Of course no one knew at that time that
the line of demarcation established by the treaty of Torde-

---

[1] Gaffarel, ii, pp. 225–231; Bourne,
pp. 69–71.

[2] Bourne, p. 74; Gaffarel, ii, pp.
258–266. When we remember that a
line dropped due south from New York
falls for the most part *west* of the continent of South America, we shall realize
how narrow the Atlantic is in the lati-
tude of Brazil, and understand how
Cabral's accidental discovery of it was
possible.

sillas fell far to the west of the landings of Lepe and Pinzon, but it was probably altogether fortunate for the later substantiation of the Portuguese rights to Brazil that Cabral chanced thus accidentally to light on its coast as early as 1500. Had the Portuguese claims under the treaty of Tordesillas not been backed up by actual discovery at this critical moment, they might well have been subsequently forgotten.[1]

For six years after Columbus's departure on his last voyage in 1502 there is a curious lull in Spain's exploring activities. Only one or two scattering expeditions were undertaken, and with practically no results. Ferdinand's preoccupation with domestic troubles and European politics was doubtless the chief explanation, and the Archduke Philip died before he could carry out any of his American projects. In 1508, however, the work of discovery was actively taken up again, a large portion of the voyages for the next decade and more being directed toward the finding of a passage through the continent which would give the Spaniards access to still richer lands beyond. Cuba was circumnavigated in 1508 by Sebastian de Ocampo, and conquered and settled in the succeeding years by Diego Velasquez, Pánfilo de Narvaez, and others.[2] In 1508–09 Vicente Yañez Pinzon and Juan Diaz de Solis followed the American coast from Honduras down probably somewhat beyond the extreme eastern point of Brazil: those who maintain that they attained the fortieth parallel are confronted with the difficult problem of showing why they failed to discover the Rio de la Plata.[3] In 1509 comes the first permanent effort of the Spaniards to settle on

[1] Cf. Bourne, p. 31. Discovery was of course essential in order to give final and unquestioned title.

[2] Bourne, pp. 104 f., 149 f.

[3] As, for example, Bourne, p. 105. The best account is that in J. T. Medina's *Diaz de Solis*, especially p. clxx, where he says that the explorers did

the mainland. The energetic and popular Ojeda, who seemed to bear a charmed life, and had never once been wounded in his many encounters with the Indians, was granted a strip of the coast line from Cap de la Vela to the Gulf of Darien, with the name of New Andalusia, while a rich planter of Española, called Diego de Nicuesa, received the stretch northward from the Isthmus to the eastern point of Honduras, with the title of Castilla del Oro. An attempt of Ojeda to make a settlement near the modern town of Cartagena was frustrated by the hostility of the Indians, who with their poisoned arrows slew some seventy of his followers; he therefore moved west to the extreme limit of the territory assigned to him and built there a fort, which he called San Sebastian, on the eastern side of the Gulf of Urabá.[1] But the marvellous good luck which had hitherto accompanied him seemed to have turned at last. The Indian attacks continued, and Ojeda himself was struck by an arrow; only by cauterizing the wound with plates of white hot iron was he able to preserve his life. He had lost most of his followers, and the survivors had become restless and discouraged. Finally he determined to leave the settlement in charge of his friend and supporter, an attorney named Enciso, and himself to repair to Española for aid; but he failed to obtain the help he sought, and died some years later in poverty and wretchedness. Nicuesa had meantime striven valiantly to develop his section to the northward, and founded the town of Nombre de Dios just east of the present city of Colón; moreover he subsequently attempted to extend his authority over the remnant of Ojeda's colony, which had by this time moved from San Sebastian across the Gulf of Darien into territory

not get farther south than the seventh parallel (near the modern town of Parahyba).

[1] Herrera, dec. i, lib. vii, caps. vii, xvi; Helps, *Spanish Conquest in America*, i. p. 214.

which fell within Nicuesa's jurisdiction. But Ojeda's
men would have nothing to do with him; his own followers
were decimated by disease; and finally the unhappy ad-
venturer was forced to sail for Spain in an unseaworthy
ship, and was never heard of again.[1]

The dominant personality in the remnant of Ojeda's
little colony at Darien was a certain Vasco Nuñez de Balboa,
who had escaped from his creditors in Española to the
mainland, concealed in a cask, on a ship that bore Ojeda's
lawyer lieutenant Enciso to his destination. It was at his
suggestion that the settlement had been removed from San
Sebastian to Darien; having earned the gratitude of the
company by proposing this wise change of abode, he refused
obedience to Enciso, and finally shipped him off to Spain,
with a letter to Ferdinand ringing with the scorn of the man
of action for the legist 'who tries to do everything from his
bed.' [2] With the reins of authority securely in his own
hands, Balboa made a vigorous attempt to secure provisions.
This naturally brought him into conflict with some of the
Indians, but he strengthened himself for any struggle that
might ensue by a close alliance with one of the native chieftains, who even went so far as to give him his daughter.[3]
The intimate knowledge of the aborigines which resulted
from these events brought to the Spaniards constant rumors
of 'regions flowing with gold,' and another great sea to the
westward; and on September 1, 1513, Balboa, with a picked
company of one hundred and ninety of his followers and a
number of Indian servants, started off through the tropical
forests to substantiate them. So dense was the undergrowth
that the explorers made on the average less than two miles a

[1] Herrera, dec. i, lib. viii, caps. iii,
iv; Helps, i, pp. 214–235.
[2] Navarrete, *Viajes*, iii, pp. 375–386.
[3] Doubtless as his mistress, though
the Indian chieftain believed that he
had taken her as his wife. Herrera, dec.
i, lib. ix, cap. i.

day; but on September 25 they were rewarded by coming
out on a summit whence they could gaze upon "the other sea
so long looked for and never seen before of any man coming
out of our world." Four days later Balboa waded into
the waters of the Mar del Sur, or Southern Ocean, as he had
already named it, holding aloft a banner and a sword, and
solemnly took possession of the portentous Pacific and the
adjacent lands in the name of his royal master, the king of
Spain.[1]

But it seemed to be for the most distinguished of the
Spanish explorers that the cruellest of fates were reserved.
Columbus had been cheated out of his rights and suffered
to die in oblivion; Balboa, who next to the Admiral had
perhaps rendered the most notable service, was to be rewarded for his achievements with death. In April, 1515,
before the news of the discovery of the Pacific had been
reported in Spain, King Ferdinand, whose most recent
information concerning the state of affairs at the Isthmus
had been received through the report of the rancorous
lawyer Enciso, sent out a stern and truculent official, Pedrarias Davila, as governor of the colony with full powers
and a large military force, and special instructions to take
the residencia of Balboa.[2]   On his arrival a trial was instituted, but the prestige which Balboa had won by his discoveries and his obvious popularity with his followers
discouraged Pedrarias from pushing it to its conclusion;
and his perplexities were increased in 1515 when news came
from Spain that Ferdinand had at last received word of
Balboa's achievement, and had rewarded him with the title
of *adelantado de la Mar del Sur*.[3] But Pedrarias was profoundly jealous of the man he had been sent out to supplant,

[1] Bourne pp. 110 f. and references
there.

[2] Herrera, dec. i, lib. x, caps. vi, vii, xi.
[3] Herrera, dec. ii, lib. i, caps. i, iii.

and vowed his ruin. There was indeed an official reconciliation between them, and Balboa was sent off on a fresh
exploring expedition; but a report from a treacherous subordinate that he entertained plans of regaining independent
authority for himself gave his enemy an excuse for arresting him again. After a humiliating trial, he was beheaded,
with four of his companions, sometime in the year 1519.
Had his discovery of the Pacific been reported a little earlier
in Spain, Pedrarias would in all probability never have
been sent out, and Balboa might well have anticipated the
work of Pizarro. It was a sad earnest of the tragic results
which were bound to ensue from the extreme slowness
and difficulty of communication between the now widely
scattered portions of the Spanish Empire.[1]

Two more expeditions, one to the north and one to the
south, complete the tale of the exploring activities of Spain
in the New World during the period at present under review.
Rumors of an island called Bimini to the north of Española,
which contained a spring or fount of eternal youth, so
fascinated a certain Juan Ponce de Leon, who had come out
in 1493 and since risen by his own energy and valor to the
headship of the island of Porto Rico, that he applied for a
patent to discover and colonize it; and this was granted
him by the king at Burgos on February 23, 1512.[2] The
voyage he undertook in pursuance of this license brought
him in April of the following year to the northern part of
the eastern [3] shore of the present state of Florida. He took
the land he had found to be an island, and christened it
with the name it bears today, probably because he had

---

[1] Herrera, dec. ii, lib. ii, caps. xi, xiii,
xxi, xxii; Helps, i, pp. 292–303.
[2] Bourne, pp. 133 ff.; Woodbury
Lowery, *Spanish Settlements*, pp. 135,
437 ff.
[3] W. Lowery, p. 138, says in "lati-
tude 38° 8'," but surely this is a mis-
take for "30° 8'": cf. Herrera, dec. i,
lib. ix, caps. x, xi. Herrera wrongly
puts the expedition in 1512: it should,
of course, be 1513.

discovered it on Easter Sunday — the Spanish Pascua de Flores — or possibly on account of the luxuriance of its vegetation. During the next two and one-half months he coasted down along the eastern shore, rounded the point, and followed the western side up possibly as far as Appalachee Bay. Thence he returned, still obsessed with the idea of discovering Bimini, for further exploration among the Bahamas, and finally got back to Porto Rico in September. He still cherished the delusion that Florida was an island, as is proved by the terms of the patent for its settlement which he secured in Spain in the following year (1514)[1]; but as he did not actually return thither until 1521, the remainder of his career must be reserved for another volume.

Meantime to the southward the news of Balboa's discovery of the Pacific gave fresh impetus to the old quest for a strait; and on November 12, 1514, King Ferdinand commissioned Juan Diaz de Solis, the companion of Vicente Yañez Pinzon's famous voyage of 1508, and now chief pilot of Spain, to explore the coasts of South America, to a distance of seventeen hundred leagues or more beyond the Isthmus of Panama, if possible, taking great care not to trespass on the territories of the king of Portugal.[2] With three small ships and seventy followers, Solis left San Lucar on October 8, 1515,[3] struck the Brazilian coast just north of Rio de Janeiro — well to the south, indeed, of the point reached by Cabral fifteen years before, but still east of the line of demarcation — and coasted along until in February, 1516, he reached the estuary of the Rio de la Plata.[4] Sur-

[1] Herrera, dec. i, lib. x, cap. xvi; W. Lowery, p. 146.

[2] Navarrete, iii, pp. 134 ff.; Herrera, dec. ii, lib. i, cap. vii; Medina, Solís, caps. vi, vii, viii. There had been a project, shortly before, of sending Solis west to discover the actual location of the Tordesillas line, but it was never carried out.

[3] Medina, p. ccxlix.

[4] Medina, p. cclxxx.

prised at the great volume of fresh water, but not sus-
pecting at first that it could be the mouth of a river, he
called it the Mar Dulce. On landing, the adventurers were
suddenly assaulted by a great host of cannibal Indians, and
Solis and some of his men were slain; the rest of the company, fearful that a similar fate would overtake them if
they attempted to avenge the death of their comrades,
sorrowfully departed, and after loading their vessels with
Brazil wood, made the best of their way back to Spain.[1]

Thus far did the exploration and settlement of the New
World progress under the Catholic Kings; the first years
of their imperial successor were to witness fresh strides
in advance. To complete the picture of Spanish America
at the death of King Ferdinand, we must now briefly
sketch the growth of a system of administration of the new
territories after the abolition of the monopolistic privileges
of Columbus.

It is scarcely possible to overemphasize the obvious truth
that the Spanish colonial system was an exceedingly gradual
development. No one could have had any notion at the
time of Ferdinand and Isabella of the immense importance
of the place the Indies were ultimately destined to occupy
in the Spanish Empire. The policies and institutions under
which they were administered grew up little by little, *pari
passu* with the extension of the domains of the Crown of
Castile in the Western Hemisphere. The methods adopted
by Ferdinand and Isabella were no more than the earliest
beginnings. They bear little resemblance to the full-fledged
colonial system as it appears in the end of the sixteenth
century.

Yet, on the other hand, there were certain dominant

[1] Medina, pp. cclxxx–ccxcv.

principles of colonial policy initiated by the Catholic Kings which lasted right down to the days of the Bourbons, though the methods of applying them changed greatly as the years went by. Some of them, indeed, go back to the heyday of the fortunes of Columbus. The motto subsequently added to the coat of arms granted to the Admiral in 1493 hints at one of the most essential of them:

> Á Castilla y á León
> Nuevo mundo dió Colón; [1]

and the same idea appears again and again in the Laws of the Indies and in the writings of contemporary historians and legists. The American possessions were not, strictly speaking, Spanish; in a sense they were Castilian, though even that statement can only be accepted with reservations; but with the realms of the Crown of Aragon they had nothing whatever to do. Down to the death of Queen Isabella, indeed, even the privilege of emigration was not granted to the inhabitants of the eastern kingdoms. There may be some ambiguity in the phraseology of the famous ordinance granting to 'cualesquier personas' liberty to go and settle in the Indies and to 'cualesquier personas nuestros subditos e naturales' the right to go and make discoveries there; [2] but Herrera and Oviedo are perfectly definite in their statements that only Castilians were permitted to pass over to the Indies in these early years.[3] After 1504, when Ferdinand obtained control of the western kingdom, it seems clear that the restrictions were considerably re-

---

[1] On this cf. Helps, i, p. 90, note.

[2] Navarrete, *Viajes*, ii, p. 166.

[3] Herrera, dec. i, lib. iii, cap. ii; Oviedo, lib. iii, cap. vii. These assertions are further confirmed by a passage in Isabella's will (Dormer, *Discursos Varios*, p. 344), and by certain petitions from the colonists that their trade be thrown open to all Spaniards (C. H.

Haring, *Trade and Navigation between Spain and the Indies*, pp. 8 f.). It is true that Veitia Linaje (*Norte de la Contratacion*, lib. i, cap. xxxi) says that from the beginning the Aragonese had equal rights with the Castilians in the Indies, but his testimony is not of much value for this early period.

laxed, at least in practice, by frequent utilization, for the benefit of the inhabitants of the realms of the Crown of Aragon, of the royal right to grant special exemptions from the operation of existing laws;[1] but it was not till the year 1596 that all the inhabitants of Spain were legally given the same privileges of emigration to the New World.[2] And in matters of government and administration the realms of the Crown of Aragon were much more completely and permanently shut off from participation in American affairs; the laws and institutions of the Indies continued throughout to be modelled on those of Castile. It is not difficult to see the reason. Geographical considerations doubtless counted for something; but a far more fundamental explanation of the unwillingness of the sovereigns to permit any of the political methods of the eastern kingdoms to percolate to the Indies was their dread lest the new territories should be contaminated by coming in contact with the 'Aragonese liberties' which they had not been able wholly to subvert. It was their ultimate object to maintain absolute control of their American possessions for themselves: therefore the government of those possessions was to be modelled on that of Castile, which had been reduced to a satisfactory condition. The system which these statements imply was not fully set up until Hapsburg days; but the idea of keeping the administration of the realms of the Crown of Aragon and their dependencies in Italy and the Mediterranean rigidly apart from that of the territories that had been acquired in the New World goes back to the reign of the Catholic Kings. Spanish separatism had in

[1] Gómara, *Historia General de las Indias*, cap. xvii; also Herrera, dec. iii, lib. x, cap. xi.
[2] *Recopilación de Leyes de las Indias*, lib. ix, tit. xxvii, ley 28. This law forbids all except natives of Castile, Leon, Aragon, Valencia, Catalonia, Navarre, and the Balearics to go to or settle in the Indies; and a clause was added to it in 1614 specifically excluding the Portuguese.

fact begun to make itself felt in the initial stages of the development of the Indies : the new empire that was opening up to the westward was not to be permitted to learn anything from that portion of Spain which had hitherto enjoyed by far the largest measure of imperial experience.

It must not, however, be inferred from the foregoing that the Indies in any sense belonged to Castile as a whole, or that any Castilian institution except the crown had the smallest vestige of authority there. Spanish colonial laws and institutions were to be brought into the closest alignment with those of Castile, in sharp contrast to their many divergences from those of Aragon, but save for the sovereign at the head of them all, they did not possess a single authority in common. The Castilian Cortes, councils, and audiencias were not to have an atom of power in America (save, possibly, in the very early days through an occasional appeal from the Casa de Contratación to the royal justices in Seville) :[1] the crown proposed to maintain exclusive control of the new possessions — to manage them as another hereditary domain, through a totally new set of institutions, without doubt closely similar to, and in fact modelled on, those of Castile, but entirely separate from them.[2]

This determination of the crown to supervise every phase of the development of the American possessions manifests itself first of all in economic affairs, a fact which has been adduced by some authors to prove that the primary object of the sovereigns in the new territories was to derive revenue from them. The political authority conferred on the Admiral in the capitulations of 1492 was quite

[1] Haring, *op. cit.*, pp. 41 f. I can find no case of an appeal from the Council of the Indies to the Council of Castile. The former, like the latter, was a 'Real y Supremo Consejo,' and exercised a coördinate, not a subordinate jurisdiction.

[2] Bourne, p. 221.

adequate to the needs of the first settlement in Española, and he had not yet demonstrated his failings as a ruler of men; but the monarchs were much concerned that the revenues of the little colony should be developed to the full, and that only the right sort of men for that purpose should be permitted to emigrate. They therefore appointed Juan Rodríguez de Fonseca in 1493 to supervise the preparations for Columbus's second voyage, as we have already seen, and to issue licenses to those who were to accompany him; furthermore, acting on a suggestion from the Admiral, they gave orders that all ships returning from the Indies should enter and unload at Cadiz alone.[1] From the very beginning the entire trade of Spanish America was concentrated at a single port — for when Cadiz was abandoned in 1503, its place was immediately taken by Seville — in order to facilitate the rigid supervision which the crown was resolved to maintain. This system was, of course, most detrimental in its economic effects, both on the mother country and on the colonies — the more so because of the immense difficulties of communication in separatistic Spain — and there were petitions that other seaports might be permitted to share in the American trade.[2] No attention, however, was paid to these requests. The government was definitely launched on its policy of strict supervision and monopolistic control, and all other considerations were to be sacrificed to the maintenance of it.

All this, however, was the merest preliminary. The early years of the sixteenth century were to witness a much further development of the machinery of royal control of American affairs. In the first place, Columbus's rights and privileges had by this time been entirely abrogated, so that the crown had matters completely in its own hands. In the second,

<hr />

[1] Thacher, *Columbus*, iii, p. 112.   [2] Bourne, p. 282, and references there.

other explorers had been sent out, and new lands had been discovered, so that Fonseca, energetic man-of-all-work though he was, had become absolutely overwhelmed with the multifarious tasks that were imposed upon him.[1] In 1503, accordingly, it was determined to relieve him of a large share of his economic responsibilities by the erection of a *Casa de Contratación,* or Board of Trade. This body, which was at first composed of a treasurer, a comptroller (*contador*), and a business manager (*factor*), was established in June, 1503, in the Alcazar Real at Seville, where it remained until the days of the Bourbons.[2] Besides the three officials above named, a chief pilot made his appearance in 1508 (the office was first bestowed on Amerigo Vespucci),[3] and the beginnings of a sort of a school of navigation took shape before the close of the reign ;[4] a postmaster-general (*correo mayor*) was also appointed in May, 1514 ;[5] and as the business of the Casa increased, a number of secretaries and legal counsellors naturally had to be added. But the original division of the functions of the Casa into three main parts remained virtually undisturbed for over a hundred years. The *tesorero, contador,* and *factor* became each the head of a department in which subordinate officials found their places.

From the composition of the Casa de Contratación we pass to the more difficult and important subject of its functions. Our chief source of information concerning these is the ordinances of January 20, 1503, and of June 15, 1510,[6] which have been preserved to us in full ; and also that of 1504, of which we have an abridgment.[7] At the outset the

[1] Bourne, pp. 221 f., and references there.

[2] Veitia Linaje, lib. i, cap. i, par. 2 ; see also the original ordinance creating it, dated January 20, 1503, and printed in Navarrete, ii, pp. 285–292.

[3] Navarrete, iii, pp. 297 f.

[4] Puente y Olea, *Trabajos geográ-*ficos, pp. 60–63.

[5] Solórzano, *Política Indiana,* lib. ii, cap. xiv ; Veitia Linaje, lib. i, cap. xxxii ; Moses, *Spanish Dependencies,* i, pp. 388–391.

[6] Navarrete, ii, pp. 285–292, 337–344, 345–349.

[7] *D. I. I.,* 2d ser., v, pp. 94–97.

crown probably had some idea of retaining the American trade entirely within its own hands. Experience, however, soon proved that this was impracticable, so that the Casa fell heir to the exceedingly onerous task of supervising all the ships and merchants that carried goods and passengers to and from the Indies, and seeing to it that all the laws and ordinances relative to navigation, emigration, and commerce with the new territories were fully and exactly carried out. It has been well described as "at once a Board of Trade, a commercial court, and a clearing house for the American traffic." [1] The chief duty of the treasurer was to receive and care for all the gold, silver, and precious stones which were due to the royal treasury from the American mines.[2] These were regarded, in this period, as belonging to the crown, though the latter rarely exploited them on its own resources. The regular practice was to turn them over to private persons to operate, but to demand that a large share of the product (two thirds at first, though the proportion was gradually reduced until, in 1504, it reached one fifth) be paid over to the Hacienda Real for the privilege.[3] To the *factor* fell the function of outfitting and provisioning ships, of purchasing supplies and armament of all kinds, and the care of all merchandise, except gold, silver, and precious stones, that was remitted from the Indies to the Crown.[4] The *contador*, meantime, discharged the very difficult duty of registering all persons and commodities carried by outgoing or incoming ships. Every person wishing to emigrate

[1] Armstrong, *The Emperor Charles V*, ii, p. 47. The Casa also had charge of the trade with the Canaries and with the adjacent African coast, though this amounted to less than 2% of its entire duties: it even collected the tax due on the tuna fisheries of Andalusia, and, after its discovery in 1555, on the famous mine of Guadalcanal in the Sierra Morena. Cf. Haring, *op. cit.*, pp. 25, 47.
[2] Veitia Linaje, lib. i, cap. xi.
[3] *Recopilación de leyes de las Indias*, lib. iv, tit. xix, *passim*; Haring, *op. cit.*, pp. 155 ff.; Gallardo Fernández, *Rentas Reales*, vi, pp. 1–19.
[4] Veitia Linaje, lib. i, caps. xxii–xxiii.

was obliged to obtain a license from the crown, which had to be duly authenticated. No infidels or heretics, or their descendants down to the fourth generation, were permitted to go, and it was the *contador's* business to see that they were kept out.[1] The meticulous paternalism which characterized every phase of the Indian administration of the late sixteenth and seventeenth centuries was indeed not fully developed in the period of the Catholic Kings; but an excellent foundation for it had unquestionably been already laid. The precision and detail with which it was expected that the different officials of the Casa should discharge the functions assigned to them can be best appreciated by careful perusal of the ordinance of 1510; that their task was no sinecure may be judged from the fact that they were expected to come together for consultation and joint action twice a day, morning and afternoon, every day in the year except holidays.[2] In this connection it may also be observed that the Casa as a body attempted from the very beginning to exercise some measure of judicial authority over Indian affairs, and as a result soon found itself involved in quarrels with the municipal authorities of Seville. In September, 1511, a royal proclamation attempted to define the Casa's jurisdiction as a court of law, and the nature of the cases that should come before it; but interference by the local judiciary continued until the Casa's powers were amplified and the Council of the Indies was definitely established in the reign of the Emperor Charles V.[3] The collection of the *averia*, or toll for the convoy of the fleets, and of the *almojarifazgo*, or duty on commodities imported from the Indies, was also to form an important branch of the

[1] Navarrete, ii, pp. 257–259; Veitia Linaje, lib. ii, caps. xvii (especially paragraphs 14–16) and xxvii (especially paragraph 16).

[2] Navarrete, ii, pp. 337 ff.
[3] D. I. I., 1st ser., xxxi, pp. 242 ff., 248 ff.; 2d ser., v, pp. 146 ff., 247, 299–303.

Casa's activities; but as these imposts were not established till the succeeding reign, we do not need to consider them here.[1]

From matters economic we pass to the political administration of the Indies. The original concessions to Columbus in 1492 gave him supreme authority over such territories as he should discover; then on his return in the following year Fonseca was appointed, as we have already seen, as the royal representative in Indian affairs resident in Spain; and the terms of the various commissions issued to him show that he was clothed with wide powers of government as well as of economic supervision. The gradual withdrawal of the privileges of the Admiral in the succeeding years, as well as the rapid progress of American exploration, naturally increased the burden of Fonseca's responsibilities, and a number of subordinate persons were associated with him; a certain Gaspard de Gricio appears in 1501 as secretary for the affairs of the Indies, and was succeeded, on his death in 1507, by the Comendador Lope de Conchillos.[2] At the same time the officials of the Casa de Contratación, which had been formally established four years before, were ordered to keep close in touch with these men, as was also Governor Ovando in Española; and in 1514 we learn that in affairs of great importance Doctors Zapata and Palacios Rubios, and the Licenciados Santiago and Sosa, all of them members of the Council of Castile, were called in by Fonseca and the secretary to give their advice.[3] This group of men formed the germ of the future Council of the Indies, or supreme authority in the management of the Spanish possessions in the

---

[1] *Avería* began in 1521; *almojarifazgo* in 1543. The latter, however, was collected in the American ports during the reign of Ferdinand and Isabella, at the rate of 7½%. Cf. Scelle, *Traite négrière*, i, p. 70; Haring, *op. cit.*, pp. 59–95, *passim*.

[2] Navarrete, ii, p. 411; Herrera, dec. i, lib. vii, cap. i.

[3] Herrera, dec. i, lib. x, cap. vi.

New World down to the end of the old régime; but since that body was not permanently organized until 1524, we may postpone further consideration of it until the succeeding reign.[1] A number of orders and injunctions from Ferdinand relative to the Indies, some of them of an extremely minute and detailed character, plainly show that the king kept close watch over the administration of the American possessions; certainly this first amorphous committee on the Indies, from which the full-fledged Consejo de Indias was subsequently evolved, enjoyed little independent authority apart from the crown. The king's concession in 1507 of coats of arms to fourteen different 'cities' of Española is an interesting indication of the way in which the Spaniard carried his ancient love of emblems and dignities with him across the sea.[2]

So much for the organs of Spanish American government which remained resident in Spain. We now turn to the representatives of the crown in the Indies themselves. In later days, after the Spanish American administration had got into full working order, these consisted of viceroys, captains-general, audiencias, and their subordinates, but this was not until the time of Charles V and Philip II; for the present we are concerned merely with the methods in vogue during the period intermediate between the withdrawal of the privileges of Columbus and the end of the reign of Ferdinand and Isabella. Our chief source of information concerning these is the instructions issued to Francisco de Bobadilla, who was sent out to supersede Columbus in 1500, and subsequently to Nicolas de Ovando and Diego Columbus, who followed him in turn in 1501 and in 1509; the orders borne by Pedrarias Davila in 1514 to the

[1] It was proleptically, though inaccurately, referred to as the Consejo de Indias as early as 1509: cf. Bourne, p. 224; Lannoy and vander Linden, p. 340.

[2] Herrera, dec. i, lib. viii, caps. i, ii.

colony at Darien also contain items of interest.[1] Aside from their precepts for the treatment of the Indians, which is a matter of such importance as to demand separate consideration, the following features of these instructions are particularly worthy of attention. In the first place, the powers granted to the new governor in each case were practically all-inclusive: all subordinate officials were to take their orders from him, but he was beholden to no one, and was not compelled to take any one's advice. A plan of controlling Pedrarias at Darien by forbidding him to act without the consent of certain important lay and ecclesiastical officials who were sent out with him was tried, indeed, but was soon abandoned as useless;[2] and for a long time afterwards the governor was left to manage affairs alone. Only in the nascent municipal constitutions did any vestige of ancient Castilian democracy or self-government permanently survive;[3] it is interesting to observe that the inhabitants of the settlement at Darien elected Balboa as their alcalde in 1510, and that we hear of procuradores chosen to inform the crown of the desires of the inhabitants of the cities of Española as early as 1508.[4] All the royal orders laid great stress on the necessity of strict and impartial administration of justice; and the practice of taking the residencia of outgoing officials became firmly planted in the Indies from the very beginning, with all its attendant benefits and disadvantages. It must be confessed, however, that the latter were considerably greater than the former under the system as it operated in the American territories; for so great was the dread in those

[1] Cf. Navarrete, ii, pp. 235 ff., 255 ff., 322 ff., 327 ff.; iii, pp. 344 ff.; Herrera, dec. i, lib. iv, caps. vii, viii, xii, xiii; lib. vii, cap. viii; Helps, i, pp. 126 ff., 167 ff., 263 ff.

[2] Herrera, dec. i, lib. x, cap. vii.
[3] Bourne, p. 235, and references there.
[4] D. I. I., 2d ser., v, p. 125.

distant regions of complaint by some malicious foe that
the majority of the magistrates feared to deviate in the
slightest degree from instructions composed, often quite
ignorantly, in Spain; with the result that healthy initiative
was checked, evils of which the home government knew
little or nothing were perpetuated, and a sort of creeping
paralysis ultimately came to pervade the entire structure
of the Spanish Empire in the New World. Finally, the
instructions to the successive governors reveal plain traces
of the crown's burning desire to extract revenue from the
American lands at any and every possible opportunity. In
1501, Ovando was ordered to try to levy a *servicio volun-
tario* on the inhabitants of Española to defray the expenses
of the 'wars against the Turks'; in 1509, we hear of the same
thing again under the name of an *empréstito*, or loan.[1] On
the other hand, it is fair to say that one of the commonest
privileges offered to induce men to go and settle in the New
World was exemption for a more or less prolonged period
from the *alcabala*.[2]

Lastly we come to the difficult question of the treatment
of the Indians and the various attempts to reconcile the
sovereigns' firm determination to deal kindly with them,
and ultimately to convert them to Christianity, with their
desire to see the colonies self-supporting and, if possible, a
source of profit. No one who has read the documents can
doubt the sincerity of the good intentions of the Catholic
Kings in their policy toward the natives, who were regarded
from the outset as subjects of the crown of Castile, and not,
as by the English colonists farther north, as independent
tribes, hostile or friendly as the case might be. The major
part of the instructions to practically every explorer and

[1] Herrera, dec. i, lib. iv, cap. xii;   1508–09; cf. Herrera, dec. i, lib. vii,
dec. i, lib. vii, cap. viii.   cap. vii.
[2] As, e.g., to Ojeda and Nicuesa in

governor sent out from Spain under Ferdinand and Isabella is occupied with exhortations and commands to be kind and just to the Indians, and to bring them as soon as possible to the Christian faith. But the church itself was the means on which the sovereigns chiefly relied to accomplish their purposes in this respect. Their control over the ecclesiastical revenues and appointments in the Indies was even more complete, as we have already seen, than that which they exercised in Spain, and they utilized it with an eye to the welfare of the natives, as well as to that of the emigrant Spaniards. At least two bishoprics were set up in the islands in the course of the years 1512–13,[1] and their occupants were chiefly concerned with the superintendence of the work of conversion; but an earlier and more active agency in this, and also in the protection of the Indians from maltreatment by the newcomers, was the contingent of monks which came out with almost every fresh party of settlers. Some of these, indeed, like the Benedictine Fray Boyl who accompanied Columbus's second expedition, were quite unworthy of the high task that had been laid upon them; but the majority were of better stuff, and certainly meant to do their duty, though their achievements did not always correspond to their intentions. The foremost champions of the rights, and also of the conversion of the Indians, were the Dominicans, whose zeal for the welfare of the natives ultimately obtained "such root in that brotherhood as almost to become one of the tenets of their faith"; [2] unfortunately, however, the jealousies of the other orders, particularly of the Franciscans, were so aroused by their activities in this direction that the cause for which they labored not seldom

---

[1] Santo Domingo and San Juan de Puerto Rico. Lannoy and vander Linden, p. 408, give a third, that of Concepción de la Vega in Española, but I can find no mention of it in Gams, *Series Episcoporum*.

[2] Helps, i, p. 174.

suffered from having been permitted to become the subject of bitter monkish quarrels.[1]

Nevertheless the actual facts of existence in the Indies were strangely at variance with the indubitably benevolent intentions of the home government. Columbus himself, who in 1492 was apparently imbued with the sovereigns' humanitarian views, had become as early as 1494 at least temporarily a convert, as we have already seen, to the necessity of enslaving the Indians. The perilous condition and scanty resources of the colony at Española were of course the cause of the change. Gold had not been found in any· thing like the quantities that had been expected. If the settlement was to be maintained at all, means must speedily be devised to make life there profitable and attractive, and the method finally adopted was to parcel out the land and the enforced labor of the Indians resident upon it in so-called *encomiendas*, or *repartimientos*, among the Spaniards who went out to the New World. This system, which did not reach its full development until the time of Ovando, is said to have been suggested by a tribute which had been imposed on certain Indians in 1495 as penalty for a revolt, and which had been rendered by them in the form of manual labor;[2] but certainly the idea of dividing up conquered territory into *repartimientos* between those who had won it goes back to a much earlier period of Spanish history, and was employed by James the Conqueror when he captured the Balearics and Valencia.[3] Obviously the character of

[1] MacNutt, *Bartholomew de las Casas*, p. 80; H. C. Lea, "The Indian Policy of Spain," in *Yale Review*, viii (1899), pp. 129 f.
[2] Bourne, pp. 206, 210, and references there; Helps, i, pp. 138 ff., 263, note; Lannoy and vander Linden, pp. 370 ff.
[3] Cf. Vol. I, p. 315. I can find no specific statement in the *Liber Parti-* *tionis Regni Maiorice* (*D. I. A.*, xi, pp. 7 ff.) or in the *Regestrum Donationum Regni Valentie* (*ibid.*, pp. 151–656) as to whether or not the services of any captured and enslaved Moors ever went with the different parcels of land into which the conquered territories were divided; but it seems inherently probable that they did. Swift, *James the First of Aragon*, p. 54.

this practice as ultimately developed in the Indies would depend primarily on whether the emphasis was laid on the allotment of the land, or on that of the compulsory services that went with it; and as time went on it was the latter that became the increasingly predominant factor. It is true that Ferdinand and Isabella strove to make the *encomienda* system actively promote their plans for the conversion of the natives to Christianity, for in all the patents the grant of their services was made conditional on the grantees' teaching them "the matters of our holy Catholic Faith."[1] Indeed, one of the reasons for the establishment of the *encomiendas* was that the Indians had withdrawn into the interior to avoid all contact with the Spaniards, and consequently were inaccessible to missionaries. The sovereigns were also careful to insist that the Indians on the *encomiendas* should be paid for their work at a reasonable rate, for in addition to their desire to Christianize them the monarchs were determined that the natives should not be enslaved.[2] In 1501 they had even gone so far as to authorize the importation of negro slaves into the New World in order to spare the Indians, and though the license was temporarily revoked in the last years of the life of the queen, it was renewed in 1505, and the practice it sanctioned gradually established itself in the succeeding years.[3] Yet despite all these precautions to safeguard the welfare of the natives, the tendency of the settlers to exploit them for their own advantage, to the prejudice of their health and their instruction, proved too strong to be effectively resisted. The royal arm could not reach across the sea and bring the offenders quickly to justice. The period of labor in the fields, and still worse in the remote mines in the interior, was gradually

[1] Bourne, p. 270, and references there.

[2] Herrera, dec. i, lib. v, cap. xi.

[3] Scelle, *Traite négrière*, i, pp. 122 ff.

lengthened; wages were not regularly paid; and the precepts of kind treatment and instruction were neglected. So cruelly were they abused, in fact, that the Indian inhabitants of the islands began to dwindle away; according to an admittedly partisan witness the existence of similar conditions throughout the world would soon cause the human race to die out.[1]

A violent sermon delivered by the Dominican monk Fray Antonio de Montesinos to the inhabitants of Santo Domingo on the fourth Sunday of Advent, 1511, served to bring clearly into relief this wide discrepancy between the home government's programme for the Indians and the facts as they actually were. The preacher fiercely rebuked his auditors for their oppression and neglect of the natives, and when the colonists demanded that he retract what he had said, he repeated his discourse on the succeeding Sunday with redoubled emphasis, and ended by announcing that the sacraments of the church would thenceforth be refused to those who did not amend their ways.[2] The colonists replied by sending a Franciscan monk to Spain to complain of the Dominicans; and the latter naturally retorted by despatching Montesinos to defend them. The Franciscan had every advantage over his adversary at the court, but the vivid horror of Montesinos's recital led Ferdinand to appoint a commission of inquiry, whose labors finally resulted in the publication, on December 27, 1512, of a brief code — generally known as the Laws of Burgos, from the place in which it was put forth — which has justly been described as "the first public recognition of the rights of the Indians, and an attempt at least to amend their wrongs."[3] Limita-

---

[1] Bourne, pp. 210 f. and references there; Lannoy and vander Linden, p. 372.

[2] Herrera, dec. i, lib. viii, cap. xi; Las Casas, *Historia*, lib. iii, caps. iii-

v (vol. iii, pp. 361–375, in the five-volume edition of 1875–76).

[3] MacNutt, *Las Casas*, p. 58; H. C. Lea, "The Indian Policy of Spain", in

tion of the periods of the labor of the natives, regulations concerning their food and shelter, and a provision for the nomination of inspectors to see that the orders of the crown were actually carried out, are the principal feature of this theoretically admirable ordinance;[1] but as the inspectors were themselves *encomenderos*, they had every inducement to neglect the discharge of their functions. We have here again, in fact, the selfsame difficulty which crops up in every phase of the Spanish administration of the New World to the very end. The regulations made by the home government were usually excellent, but distance and defective means of communication rendered it wellnigh impossible to carry them out.[2] The best evidence of the nonobservance of the Laws of Burgos is the fact that less than three years after their passage a certain settler of Cuba, by name Bartholomew de las Casas, whose conscience had been aroused by the exhortations of the Dominicans, surrendered his *encomienda* and made his way back to Spain to plead for the Indians before the king. Powerful interests in the Casa were opposed to him, and Ferdinand died before this future apostle of the Indians could be fully heard, but the work which he had so nobly begun was to be carried much further in the succeeding reign.[3] — All the fundamental difficulties of the Indian question had, in fact, been clearly recognized under the Catholic Kings, but practically no progress whatsoever had been made towards its solution. The circumstances of the reign of the Emperor Charles V were destined greatly to increase the complexity of the issues involved in the problem which his grandparents had bequeathed to him.

Yale Review, viii, pp. 129 ff., and references there.

[1] Las Casas, *op. cit.*, lib. iii, caps. xiii, xv, xvi (vol. ii, pp. 417-438); Moses,

Spanish Dependencies, i, pp. 206-208.

[2] Lea, in *Yale Review*, viii, p. 155.

[3] Lea, in *Yale Review*, viii, p. 132; MacNutt, *op. cit.*, pp. 59-75.

This is not the place to attempt any extended estimate of the position and significance of the Indies in the fabric of the Spanish Empire. Only the surface had as yet been scratched. The real wealth and extent of the new possessions remained hid for many years to come, and the system under which they were to be administered was still in its infancy. Yet one brief comment may be added here, if only to emphasize the tremendous importance of the achievement of Christopher Columbus. More than sixty years ago a shrewd and observant writer advanced the theory that the possession of the Indies was the determining cause of the ruin of Spain in the succeeding centuries, that it diverted her from her normal and traditional lines of development, caused her to neglect excellent chances nearer home, and forced her to bleed herself white in the effort to maintain her remote acquisitions in the New World.[1] There is much to be said for this argument. The number, variety, and coincidence of Spain's opportunities, as we have often remarked, was one of the most potent causes of her decline, and it was the American possessions which caused her to deviate the furthest from the paths she had trodden before. Had she kept out of the New World she would doubtless have led a more comfortable existence in the Old. She would not have been so easily induced to attempt impossible tasks. She would not have drawn down on herself the jealousy and hatred of neighboring states. She would probably have avoided the fatal trial of strength with England. She might well have been more powerful today. Yet when all is said and done, it was the Indies that account for her greatness during the brief period that it lasted. If they were a principal cause of her subsequent decay, they were also

[1] J. Arias y Miranda, *Examen Crítico Histórico del influjo que tuvo en el Comer-* *cio Industria y Poblacion de España su Dominacion en América.*

the primary source of her temporary preëminence. Without them she would never have been able to retain the hegemony of Europe so long as she did; without them the Spanish Empire would scarcely have been worthy of the name. What seemed to contemporaries but a fortunate incident was really the great turning point in the reign of Ferdinand and Isabella. The day that Christopher Columbus set sail from Palos was the most fateful in the history of United Spain.

BIBLIOGRAPHICAL NOTE

In view of the fact that the matters dealt with in the foregoing chapter are so much more familiar to the general reader than the other parts of this book, I have felt that it was needless to enumerate in this note the standard collections and authorities such as the *Documentos Inéditos* . . . *de Indias*, the *Recopilación de Leyes de las Indias*, Herrera, Oviedo, Las Casas, Solórzano, Veitia Linaje, Navarrete, Helps, Winsor, Gaffarel, and the rest. Those who desire further information on this topic will find it in the late Professor E. G. Bourne's admirable " Critical Essay on the Authorities," on pages 320 to 337 of his *Spain in America* (New York and London, 1904). All that I have attempted to do here is to name a few books and articles which deal with subjects outside the field covered by Professor Bourne, and consequently were not mentioned by him, and also those which have appeared since the publication of his book.

The most important collection of sources on the early history of America which has been compiled since Bourne wrote is Miss F. G. Davenport's recent volume of *European Treaties bearing on the History of the United States and its Dependencies to 1648*. It has just been published by the Carnegie Institution of Washington, and I am greatly indebted to Professor J. F. Jameson for permitting me to see it in page proof. It contains the text and English translation of 40 important documents — bulls, treaties, etc. — beginning with the bull *Romanus pontifex* of January 8, 1455; and its value is greatly enhanced by numerous explanatory notes and bibliographical references.

Among general works that have been put forth during the last fourteen years may be mentioned Edward Channing, *A History of the United States*, vol. i (New York, 1905), which presents, in condensed but attractive form, the results of many years of study and research; Charles de Lannoy and Herman vander Linden, *Histoire de l'expansion coloniale des peuples européens : Portugal et Espagne* (Paris and Brussels, 1907), which gives a good account of the Spanish colonial system; and Bernard Moses. *The Spanish Dependencies in South America* (New York, 1914, 2 vols.), which deals chiefly with the later period, but contains much that is valuable on the age of discovery and conquest.

Of the more special works, Henry Vignaud's *Histoire critique de la grande entreprise de Christophe Colomb* (Paris, 1911, 2 vols.) is probably the most important; it marks an epoch in the study of the career of the discoverer (cf. *American Historical Review*, viii, pp. 341–346; xvii, pp. 610–613). Much new light has been thrown on the difficult subject of the Demarcation Line by an article of Herman vander Linden on

"Alexander VI and the Demarcation of the Maritime and Colonial Domains of Spain and Portugal, 1493-1494," in the *American Historical Review*, xxii, pp. 1-20. J. T. Medina's *Juan Diaz de Solís* (Santiago de Chile, 1897) and F. A. MacNutt's *Bartholomew de las Casas* (New York, 1909) are useful biographies. Two notable contributions to the history of the economic policy of Spain in the new world are Georges Scelle's *La traite négrière aux Indes de Castille* (Paris, 1906, 2 vols.) and C. H. Haring's *Trade and Navigation between Spain and the Indies in the Time of the Hapsburgs* (Cambridge, Mass., 1918). The former contains one of the best short accounts of the policy and government of Spain in the New World, and the latter sheds a flood of new light on a hitherto neglected topic of fundamental importance. I am much more deeply indebted to it than I have been able to indicate in the footnotes. Víctor Balaguer, *Castilla y Aragón en el Descubrimiento de América* (Madrid, 1892); Miguel Mir, *Influencia de los Aragoneses en el Descubrimiento de América* (Palma de Mallorca, 1892); Eduardo Ibarra y Rodríguez, D. *Fernando el Católico y el Descubrimiento de América* (Madrid, 1892); and Manuel de la Puente y Olea, *Los Trabajos Geográficos de la Casa de Contratación* (Seville, 1900), are useful monographs on more special topics. José Arias y Miranda, *Examen Crítico Histórico del influjo que tuvo en el Comercio Industria y Poblacion de España su Dominacion en América* (Madrid, 1854), presents a number of interesting arguments from a rather novel standpoint.

CHAPTER XVIII

NORTH AFRICA

THE Spanish possessions in the New World did not so monopolize the attention of Ferdinand and Isabella as to prevent them from laying plans for the conquest of another region, whose destinies, from time immemorial, had been intimately connected with those of the Iberian Peninsula. The task of carrying the Christian arms across the Mediterranean into North Africa was the obvious and logical sequel to the capture of Granada; it was dictated by every consideration of sentiment and of expediency; in 1493, as we have already seen, the Catholic Kings had sent out a trusty official, Lorenzo de Padilla, in disguise to reconnoitre.[1] The kingdom of Fez, directly across the Strait, was closed to him by virtue of the provision in the treaty of 1479 which had assigned it to Portugal.[2] He therefore set his course farther eastward and finally penetrated to Tlemcen, whence he returned with much useful information. In the following year (1494), the Spanish ambassador at Rome reminded the Pope of the many historical ties that united Spain to Mauretania, and demanded that his Holiness should concede to their Catholic Majesties the exclusive right of conquest of the North African coast. Portuguese representatives were, of course, on hand to insist on the priority of their rights in the western part of the territory in question, and on the Atlantic seaboard; they were finally brought to agree, however, that

---

[1] *Ante*, p. 74.   [2] *Ante*, pp. 172 f.

everything east of and including the town of Melilla should be assigned to Spain, though they took a mild revenge by challenging the Spanish claims to the possession of lands on the west coast opposite the Cañaries.[1] The Pope also handed over to the Spanish sovereigns and their heirs the *tercias* of Castile, Leon, and Granada *in perpetuo*, to aid them in the prosecution of the Holy War, and in 1496–97 the town of Melilla was seized by a representative of the Duke of Medina Sidonia, who subsequently turned it over to the Catholic Kings.[2] Yet despite all these early activities, it was almost ten years later before the Spanish conquest of North Africa can be said to have really begun. The chief cause of the delay was unquestionably the Italian wars, which absorbed all the available resources of the Catholic Kings during the decade following the memorable raid of Charles VIII on Naples. Not until the year after the final conquest of that kingdom by the troops of Gonsalvo de Cordova was it possible to launch the first regular expedition against the Barbary coast.

The real hero of the story of Spanish expansion in North Africa during the first ten years of the sixteenth century is neither King Ferdinand nor Queen Isabella, but Cardinal Francisco Ximenes de Cisneros. His fame as a churchman and as regent of Castile during the twenty months that elapsed between the death of Ferdinand and the arrival of his grandson Charles from the Netherlands will doubtless long outlive his reputation as a builder of the Spanish Empire; but it is in the latter capacity that we have to consider him here, and it is no reason to depreciate its significance that the cardinal accomplished still greater things in other directions. A well established tradition, accepted by a contemporary biographer, pictures him on

[1] Zurita, v, ff. 48 f.   [2] Mercier, ii, p. 417.

the southern slope of the Sierra Vermeja, in the year of the conquest of Granada, pointing out to an attendant monk the distant promontories of the opposite shore beyond the blue waves of the Mediterranean, and solemnly urging upon him the glorious duty of carrying the Christian faith into the country of its infidel foes.[1] It was doubtless his enthusiasm that inspired the monarchs to take the first steps towards the realization of this project in the years that followed the conquest of Granada; and more important still, it was his insistence that prevented the whole matter from being quite forgotten in the whirl of European diplomacy which occupied the next decade. Isabella was certainly a far more ardent supporter of the cardinal's plans than was her husband. Her attention was not centred, as was his, on the prosecution of the Italian campaigns; and it is one of the ironies of history that she died before the first expedition against Mers-el-Kebir was actually sent forth. "I beg my daughter and her husband," so runs a memorable passage in her will, 'that they will devote themselves unremittingly to the conquest of Africa and to the war for the faith against the Moors";[2] and her words may well have been an inspiration to Ximenes in the hard struggle to enlist the sympathies of the cautious Ferdinand in his crusading schemes, which he was henceforth left to carry on alone. It is perfectly clear that the North African enterprise did not commend itself to the king of Aragon on religious grounds alone, and also that he failed at first to perceive its political and economic advantages. The cardinal won his consent to it at last by pointing out that an attack on the Barbary coast was the best means of defending the Spanish ports from the ravages of Moorish

---

[1] A. Gomecius, *De Rebus gestis a Francisco Ximenio*, f. 7; N. Blum, *Croisade de Ximénès en Afrique*, pp. i f.

[2] Isabella's will in Dormer, *Discursos varios*, pp. 348 f.

pirates, which had increased in frequency since the fall of
Granada; and still more by promising to advance to the
royal treasury the sums necessary to pay for the requisite
number of troops during the first two months.[1] But
though Ximenes was quite capable of utilizing political
and financial arguments in order to secure the consent
of his sovereign, his own enthusiasm for the North African
campaign was primarily of a religious character. It was
as a crusade, and as a final and glorious consummation of
the great work of the Reconquest, that he regarded it, and
he succeeded in imbuing the soldiers who were collected
for the purpose with the feeling that they were sent forth
to fight for a sacred cause. There can be no question that
the militant religious fervor which inspired these last crusades of the West went far deeper than that of the period
of the Reconquest as a whole, and the influence of Cardinal
Ximenes was one of the principal causes of the change.

On the advice of a Venetian merchant named Geronimo
Vianelli, who had traded all along the North African coast,
and also served under Gonsalvo de Cordova in the Italian
wars, the cardinal selected the fort of Mers-el-Kebir as the
point that it would be most profitable to attack.[2] It lay
just west of the far more important town of Oran, which
was the key to all the country round about, and which was
so strongly fortified that a direct assault from the sea was
foredoomed to failure. Only by land could Oran be attacked
with any reasonable prospect of success, and a land attack
necessitated a base at Mers-el-Kebir. Some 10,000 troops
were accordingly collected at Malaga in August, 1505,[3]

---

[1] Blum, pp. 11 f.

[2] Mercier, ii, p. 420.

[3] A letter from the sovereigns to
Gonsalvo de Cordova, dated April 30,
1504, ordering him to send home 2000
soldiers for the African war, shows that
Ferdinand and Isabella had determined
to wage it a year and a half before the
expedition against Mers-el-Kebir was
actually sent out. Cf. R. A., 3d ser.,
xxv, pp. 426–427; xxvi, p. 309.

under the lead of Diego Fernández de Cordova, a distant
kinsman of the Great Captain, and embarked on a fleet of
140 ships commanded by Ramón de Cardona.[1] Passing
up the coast to Cartagena to take on their pilots, they
finally set sail on September 3, and after being driven about
in the Mediterranean by bad weather, arrived eight days
later off Cape Falcone, at the entrance to the Bay of Mers-
el-Kebir. The disembarkation was effected through the
heroism of 180 Spaniards, who made their way to shore in
small boats and by swimming, and fell upon a vastly superior body of Moors with such fury that they soon cleared
a space for others to follow them. The next step was the
occupation and fortification of a hill dominating the city,
and the repulse of a violent counter-attack. A vigorous
bombardment of the fortress itself was soon after begun,
and preparations to storm it hurried forward. But a
Moorish soldier who had fallen (perhaps not unintentionally)
from the battlements of Mers-el-Kebir into the sea and
swum out to the Spanish fleet, brought news of the wretched
state of the garrison. They had been overwhelmed and
discouraged by the suddenness of the Spanish assault;
they were divided among themselves; their leaders had
been killed; and they were ready to treat. Desirous to
avoid unnecessary slaughter, and fearing the arrival of
Moorish reënforcements from the interior if he delayed too
long, the Spanish general sent his informant back to the
fortress to offer the defenders generous conditions in return for immediate surrender. The details were soon arranged. The Moors were accorded free leave to evacuate
the place with their wives and children, and all the belong-
ings that they could carry away with them. They gave
up the keys of Mers-el-Kebir to their conquerors, and

[1] Blum, pp. 14, 17.

liberated thirty-five Christian captives who had been taken from the Portuguese on the occasion of an unsuccessful attack by them in 1501. A solemn entry of the triumphant troops followed, and was accompanied by a great profusion of religious ceremonies and thanksgivings. The news of the victory, when reported in Spain, evoked fervent rejoicing. Even the unemotional Ferdinand yielded temporarily to the popular enthusiasm.[1]

Mers-el-Kebir was not, however, an end in itself. For Ximenes and his most ardent supporters it was merely a stepping stone, as we have already seen, to the capture of Oran. Indeed, there is strong reason to believe that the plans of the cardinal had already begun to go much further than the mere control of the coast.   " Africa, Africa for the king of Spain, our sovereign lord ! " [2] echoed the shouts of his troops as they entered the conquered fortress ; and there are plenty of other indications in the contemporary historians that Ximenes was already contemplating the foundation of a Hispano-Mauretanian empire stretching southward to the confines of the Sahara.[3]   Moreover, it soon became evident that Mers-el-Kebir itself could not long be retained, unless the Christian territories round about it were enlarged. The Moors of Oran were constantly on the watch to cut off any foraging expeditions into the interior ; and more important still, the king of Tlemcen, whose access to the coast was menaced by the hold the Christians had already won, was moving heaven and earth to expel them.[4] Most serious of all was the question of supplies. Cooped up in Mers-el-Kebir, it was impossible for the

[1] Blum, pp. 15–34. The standard contemporary account of the expedition is the letter of Gonzalo de Ayora to Ferdinand, dated September 15, 1505, printed in *D. I. E.*, xlvii, pp. 536–555 ; cf. E. Cat, *Essai sur Gonzalo de Ayora* (Paris, 1890), p. 12.
[2] Blum, p. 32.
[3] Blum, p. 70.
[4] Blum, pp. 42 f., 47, 63.

Spaniards to maintain themselves on what they had already won; before June, 1506, it had been found necessary to send over to them no less than 12,000 bushels of grain from Barcelona.[1] If the captured *presidio* was to be made self-supporting, as it was clearly desirable that it should be, further conquests were indispensable; advance was essential as the sole way to prevent retreat. For a long time, however, it was impossible to bring King Ferdinand to see this. He was glad that Mers-el-Kebir had been taken, for its capture had cost him practically nothing; but the North African enterprise had never fired his imagination as it had the cardinal's, and in the months that followed its initial success he was deeply absorbed in his quarrels with his son-in-law, Philip, over the Castilian regency, and afterwards with his journey to Naples. Even Ximenes himself was obliged to neglect the Barbary conquests in this period, owing to the multitude of problems that claimed his attention in Spain.[2] Throughout the year 1506 and the early part of 1507 the garrison of Mers-el-Kebir was shamefully neglected, despite urgent messages despatched by the gallant Diego Fernández de Cordova to beg for reënforcements. Finally, the news of a Moorish victory over a Christian detachment which had been sent out to seize provisions, coupled with a personal visit of the Spanish general to the Castilian court during the absence of Ferdinand in Italy, elicited from the cardinal a substantial body of troops; but the *razzia* in which they were utilized soon after their arrival resulted in a terrible disaster. The Moors let them plunder at will, and then, as they were retiring to their base, led them into an ambush in the ravine of Fistel, where they slew or captured nearly all of them; Diego Fernández de Cordova managed almost alone to escape

[1] Blum, p. 37.   [2] Blum, p. 40.

by night to Mers-el-Kebir. Encouraged by this success, the Moors of Oran attacked the Spaniards in the fortress itself; though they were repulsed, the episode served to clinch the argument of the Spanish leader that unless more troops and munitions were speedily sent out from home, the loss of all that had been already gained was inevitable. Ferdinand had by this time returned from Italy. The European situation was temporarily quiet, and he was free to devote more of his attention to North African affairs. The last months of the year 1507 saw vigorous preparations for a renewal of the Barbary campaign on a much larger scale.[1]

But when it came to settling the details of the arrangements for the new attack, all the old difficulties and divisions broke forth afresh. First, there was the inevitable question of funds. The royal treasury had been emptied by the Italian campaigns; and Ximenes, as previously, had to come forward with an independent offer. After long negotiations, it was finally agreed that he should pay the entire cost out of the revenues of his archiepiscopal see, and should receive in return supreme command, under the crown, of the forthcoming expedition, together with the royal promise that all conquests made should specially appertain to the diocese of Toledo.[2] Then came the problem of finding a competent military leader. Diego Fernández de Cordova would have been the best possible choice on account of his previous experience, but the failure of his last raid had discredited him, and both king and cardinal were resolved to make a change. Ximenes wanted the Great Captain, but Ferdinand, suspicious of the latter's schemes for personal aggrandizement, would have nothing to do with him, and insisted instead on nominating Pedro

[1] Blum, pp. 49–68.   [2] Blum, pp. 72, 88 f.

Navarro, renowned indeed as a soldier and engineer in the Italian wars, but altogether too untrustworthy and rapacious for leadership in an enterprise like this.[1] Nay more, Navarro, from the moment of his appointment, lent himself obediently to the private schemes of Ferdinand, who, though ostensibly an enthusiastic convert to the plans of the cardinal, was still much of the time secretly working against him.[2] Ximenes had powerful enemies about the Castilian court; and the king, who lived in perpetual terror of having his authority overshadowed by that of some subordinate, was easily led to believe that Ximenes was aiming at the conquest of an independent empire. Indeed, it is not impossible that it was chiefly with the idea of putting a spoke in the cardinal's wheel, and of delaying the departure of the main enterprise against Oran, that Ferdinand sent off Navarro, in July, 1508, on the pretext of a punitive raid against the Moorish pirates, to attack the island and town of Velez de la Gomera, far to the westward, in the regions which had been assigned to the Portuguese. The expedition was brilliantly successful.[3] The island was captured, and the town on the opposite shore bombarded and destroyed. But the Portuguese at once complained of this invasion of their sphere of influence, as they had done in 1494 when the Spaniards laid claim to Melilla; and they were apparently further irritated, rather than grateful, when Navarro relieved the Portuguese garrison of the fortress of Arzila on the Atlantic coast, which was being besieged by the Emir of Fez.[4] Long negotiations naturally

---

[1] M. de los Heros, *Historia del Conde Pedro Navarro*, in *D. I. E.*, xxv, *passim*; Blum, pp. 74 f.; L. de Torre, "Pedro Navarro," in *R. A.*, 3d ser., xxii, pp. 198–214.

[2] Blum, pp. 75–79; *Cartas del Cardenal Jimenez*, edd. P. Gayangos and

V. de la Fuente (Madrid, 1867), pp. 1–20.

[3] Zurita, vi, ff. 168–169; Blum, pp. 77 f. ; M. de los Heros in *D. I. E.*, xxv, pp. 106 ff., 420 ff.

[4] Zurita, vi, ff. 169–170; Bernáldez, cap. ccxvii; Mercier, ii, pp. 406, 417.

ensued before the two nations could come to an agreement; and, as before, the Portuguese attempted to bring the Spanish rights on the mainland opposite the Canaries into the discussion, in the hope that if they lost at one point they would gain at another. Eventually they were defeated at both ; for the boundary between the territories claimed by the two states in the Mediterranean was ultimately moved west to Velez, which remained in Spanish hands till recaptured by the Moors in 1522, while the Spanish possession of the Atlantic coast opposite the Canaries was confirmed, as we have already seen, in 1509.[1] The chief immediate result of the whole episode, however, was a long postponement of the main enterprise against Oran. It was a striking instance of the way in which the whole North African policy of Spain in this and in the succeeding reigns was made to suffer as a result of jealousies and divided councils at home; certainly nothing short of the heroic determination of Ximenes could have set the expedition in motion at all. Not until May 16, 1509, were the last pretexts and excuses of his enemies exhausted, so that the great army, 14,000 to 20,000 strong, was enabled to embark for the Barbary coast, in a huge fleet of ninety great ships and several hundred transports.[2]

The crossing this time was so speedily accomplished as to leave the Moors but little time for preparation. On the second night after its departure from Spain, the bulk of the army was landed on the shores of Mers-el-Kebir. The activities of certain Christian captives within the walls of Oran had apparently won over some of the Moors inside the fortress from their allegiance, so that the Spaniards were

---

[1] Mercier, ii, p. 425 ; R. Donoso-Cortés, *Zonas Españolas de Marruecos*, p. 75 ; *ante*, p. 189.
[2] The authorities differ as to the numbers. See Prescott, iii, p. 284, and references there ; Blum, pp. 95 f., 101 ; E. Froelicher, *Domination espagnole en Algérie et au Maroc*, p. 14.

measurably aided in their enterprise by treachery in the ranks of their foes; [1] but all accounts agree that the really crucial factor in the conflict was the enthusiasm evoked by the dauntless bearing of Cardinal Ximenes. Despite his seventy-three years, his bodily infirmities, and the dubious loyalty of some of his subordinates, the cardinal insisted in sharing all the hardships of the expedition. Mounted on a mule, and preceded by the great silver cross of Toledo, he rode along the ranks exhorting the soldiers to do or die for the faith. Only the assurance that solicitude for his personal safety would divert his followers' attention from the battle could dissuade him from taking active part in the attack, and it was his urgency that saved the less zealous Navarro from the fatal error of postponing it. [2] The plan of the operation comprised two distinct parts. The first and most important was the assault and capture of the high ridge that separates Mers-el-Kebir from Oran and completely dominates the latter; the second was a bombardment of Oran itself from the ships in the bay, to be followed, if successful, by a landing of troops and a storming of the walls. The attack on the ridge, delivered late in the afternoon and with great desperation, finally attained its objective, owing largely to the cover which a thick mist afforded to the advancing troops, and to a battery of heavy guns which Navarro turned loose at a critical moment on the Moorish flank. The Spaniards reached the summit in time to gaze down upon the minarets of Oran flashing in the level rays of the dying sun. But in order to make the most of the advantage already gained it was essential to press on, and capture the town before its defenders could recover from their surprise. The fleet had meantime done

[1] Blum, p. 107.
[2] Prescott, iii, pp. 286 f., and references there; Blum, pp. 110–112.

its part, by drawing the fire of the cannon on the walls, and landing a large detachment on the shore at the foot of the ridge; it was by joining with this force in a sudden desperate attack that the troops on the summit could best hope to carry the city then and there. Down the eastern slopes, therefore, they rushed, and, uniting with the detachment at the base, went forward against the fortifications of Oran. The lack of storming ladders did not stop them. Thrusting their long pikes into the crevices of the rocks, they surged over the walls with an impetuosity that nothing could resist, and, led by the captain of the cardinal's bodyguard, planted the cross and the arms of the primate on the ramparts. Leaping down on the inside, the soldiers soon overwhelmed the Moors at the gates, and a few moments later the entire Christian army poured through into the streets. The massacre and pillage which ensued form one of the darkest blots on the Spanish arms in the reign of Ferdinand and Isabella. Neither age nor sex exempted any one from the outrages of the brutal soldiery; the streets were filled with corpses, and thousands of Moors were captured to be sold as slaves; Navarro was totally unable to maintain discipline. A pleasanter feature of the conquest was the liberation of the three hundred Christian prisoners confined in the Casbah, or citadel of the town; for Ximenes, who made a solemn entry into Oran two days after its capture, this ceremony was the culmination of the whole expedition. The booty taken was considerable. A large portion of it was devoted by the cardinal to the maintenance of his army, and the rest he turned over to the royal treasury. An army sent by the king of Tlemcen for the relief of Oran retreated in hot haste when it learned that the town had already been taken; the episode furnished the best possible vindication of the wisdom of Ximenes's refusal to permit Navarro to postpone the attack.[1]

The completion of the conquest of Oran brought once more to the fore all the old differences between the two leaders. In the eyes of the cardinal it was merely an entering wedge, like Mers-el-Kebir, for the foundation of a Spanish empire in North Africa. He wished to import colonists to settle it as a permanent Spanish outpost; and he desired to penetrate at once to Tlemcen.[2] But Navarro, like Ferdinand, was very sceptical about the possibilities of a North African empire. Like most professional soldiers of his day, his immediate interest in the campaign he had undertaken was the prospect it offered of booty and reward. Having captured Oran, he wanted to move on and attack and plunder other rich ports to the eastward; and he showed no enthusiasm for the more difficult and permanent projects which fascinated Ximenes. These antagonisms came to a head in a violent scene between the two leaders, a day or two after the capture of Oran, over the limits of their respective jurisdictions. A proclamation of Navarro, in defiance of the conventions signed by Ximenes and Ferdinand, that the conquered city belonged to the crown, and was in no wise attached to the see of Toledo, carried the quarrel somewhat further, and the climax was reached when one of Ximenes's servants laid before him an intercepted letter from the king to Navarro, in which the latter was urged to amuse the cardinal with various projects and detain him as long as possible in Africa, thus preventing his return to Spain, where his presence was not desired. Naturally the suspicions of Ximenes were at once aroused. He had always been rather the counsellor of

[1] Prescott, iii, pp. 286–291; Hefele, *Cardinal Ximenes*, pp. 376–387; Blum, pp. 112–127, and references there.

[2] Blum, pp. 129 f.; *Cartas de Jimenez*, p. 47.

Isabella than of her husband: what black treachery was Ferdinand meditating against him now? The only way to meet such treatment was to return at once and ascertain the facts, and this with characteristic promptitude the cardinal resolved to do. At a council of the officers he designated Navarro as commander-in-chief, and urged him, with all the eloquence he could command, to continue the campaign; then, with many promises to watch over and provide for the needs of the expedition at home, he set sail on Wednesday, May 23, after a sojourn in North Africa of less than one week. Disdaining an invitation to visit the king, he despatched one of his subordinates to Ferdinand to report; and then, after occupying himself for a couple of weeks with the collection of supplies and equipment for the army that he had left behind, he retired on June 12 to his beloved university at Alcalá.[1] A bitter quarrel, arising out of an odious attempt to deprive him of the rights over Oran which had been guaranteed to the see of Toledo in the original convention with Ferdinand, pursued him to his quiet retreat. The king made no pretence of keeping either to the letter or the spirit of his agreement in the matter; and the feud lasted without definite settlement beyond the limits of the cardinal's life.[2] It was another example, perhaps even more striking than those contemporaneously afforded in the Indies and in Italy, of the suspicion and distrust with which Ferdinand in his later years regarded any evidence of independence or initiative in the representatives of his authority in distant lands. Unfortunately these traits were inherited and magnified by his successors until they became a distinctive

---

[1] Prescott, iii, pp. 292 ff.; Hefele, pp. 389 ff.; Blum, pp. 131–137, and references there. Also *Cartas de Jimenez*, pp. 50–58; M. de les Heros, in

D. I. E., xxv, pp. 124–128.
[2] Blum, pp. 140–142, and references there.

and ultimately ruinous feature of Spanish colonial and imperial policy.

After the withdrawal of Ximenes the whole aspect of the North African campaign changed. No one else had taken the possibilities of a Spanish empire in North Africa as seriously as he. Few but himself had cherished any thought of penetrating inland. Had he remained in command, an expedition against Tlemcen would almost infallibly have followed the capture of Oran, and there is every reason to think that it would have been successful, so thoroughly were the Moors demoralized by the losses they had already sustained. But with the cardinal in retirement the opposition had its innings. Ferdinand, and under him Navarro, were now the guiding minds. With the king the principal motive of the North African campaign had doubtless been the suppression of piracy; [1] for Navarro, as we have already seen, the capture of booty was the main consideration; and both these ends could be far better attained by attacking other seaports than by advancing inland. In the autumn of 1509, therefore, it was decided that Navarro should attempt the capture of Bugia, just east of Algiers, leaving Oran in charge of Diego Fernández de Cordova, who was recommended for the purpose by the cardinal before his retirement, and invested with the imposing title of 'Captain General of the town of Oran, the fortress of Mers-el-Kebir, and the kingdom of Tlemcen.' In 1510 the ruler of the latter place recognized the sovereignty of Spain, and gave a solemn

[1] Even in this matter of checking piracy the cardinal had far more extensive plans than his sovereign. From 1509 till the day of his death he kept urging the crown to establish at Oran a branch of the Military Order of Santiago, to serve, like Rhodes under the Knights of St. John of Jerusalem, as a military outpost in infidel territory, with the special duty of putting an end to the ravages of the Barbary corsairs. The consent of Ferdinand was apparently secured, but he died before the project could be realized and Ximenes never had a chance to broach it to Charles V. Froelicher, *Domination espagnole*, pp. 24 f.

promise, which he shortly afterwards broke, to furnish aid to the Christians against their foes. Some of the neighboring tribes also made political and commercial treaties with the invaders in the succeeding years, but this and the emigration to Oran of six hundred Spanish families were all that the cardinal was able to accomplish towards the permanent foundation of the empire of which he had dreamed. For all practical purposes the control had passed into the hands of men who had much less ambitious ends in view.[1]

The rest of the story of Spanish expansion in North Africa during the reign of Ferdinand and Isabella may be briefly told. On January 1, 1510, Navarro set sail for Bugia with a large force, and a few days later dropped anchor in the bay before it. There is much discrepancy among the different accounts of the capture of the place. According to some authors the entire population fled at the sight of the Spanish fleet, and Navarro was able to take possession without striking a blow; it seems more probable, however, that the fugitives were merely the women and children, for there is good evidence that a vigorous resistance was made, under the lead of a Hafside prince named Abd-el-Aziz, before the invaders finally entered the place.[2] Curiously enough, it was soon after, and as a direct result of their capture of Bugia, that the Spaniards first came in contact with the power which was ultimately to be their most effective foe in North Africa — the famous Barbarossa brothers. These two, whose names were Arudj and Khaireddin, were sons of a potter of the island of Mitylene, and after a stormy career as pirates in the Levant had transferred the scene of their operations to the western Mediterranean. It was soon after their arrival off the North African coast that the

[1] Zurita, vi, f. 225; Mercier, ii, p. 423, and references there; Froelicher, pp. 26 f.

[2] Mercier, ii, pp. 423 f.; Froelicher, pp. 17 f.

dispossessed ruler of Bugia applied for their aid in the recovery of his dominions. The elder lost no time in seizing
the opportunity that chance had thrown in his way. With
a thousand Turks he joined forces with Abd-el-Aziz, and,
probably in 1512 — the date is somewhat uncertain — assaulted the Spaniards in Bugia. The assailants were repulsed with great slaughter; Arudj had his arm shattered
by an arquebus shot, and his younger brother had to remove him to Tunis to recuperate.[1] But he was anxious to
repeat the experiment, and in the following year (1513)
was again in the field. This time he resolved to proceed
more methodically. He began by establishing himself
on the island of Gerba, where the Moors had remained in
unchallenged possession since the expedition of Alfonso the
Magnanimous in 1432,[2] and where Barbarossa could effectively organize an expedition at his leisure. Next he
assaulted and captured Jijeli, just east of Bugia, from the
Genoese (1514), who in a fit of jealousy at the recent Spanish
conquests on the Barbary coast had possessed themselves
of it the year before. Having obtained this solid base on
the mainland, he returned in 1515 to the attack of Bugia,
with the aid of a host of plundering Berbers who rallied to
his standard. The town was heroically defended by a
small garrison under Don Ramón Carroz for three months,
at the expiration of which time Christian reënforcements
arrived in such numbers that Barbarossa deemed it prudent
to retire; but the Spaniards had by no means seen the last
of him, as they were to learn to their cost in the succeeding
reign.[3]

Meantime the great majority of the adjacent Berber

---

[1] Mercier, ii, pp. 426 ff.; Froelicher,
p. 18. I have been unable to see M.
Féraud's *Histoire de Bougie*; on it cf. de
Grammont, *Histoire d'Alger*, p. 14, note.

[2] Cf. Vol. I, p. 418.
[3] Mercier, ii, pp. 425–428, and references there.

tribes were far too much terrified by Navarro's victories to contemplate further resistance. They deemed it more prudent to acknowledge Spanish overlordship, at least for the present, than to fight for their independence under the aegis of a Turkish corsair. Algiers was convinced that submission was the sole way to avoid the fate of Bugia. On January 31, 1510, a capitulation was signed by envoys whom the town had dispatched to Navarro to sue for peace, promising the recognition of the sovereignty of Spain, friendship with her friends, enmity to her foes, payment of tribute, and liberation of all Christian captives. Furthermore, the Algerians made haste to confirm their surrender to Navarro by despatching an embassy to Ferdinand in Spain to ratify what they had done, and to offer costly presents to their new master.[1] But Navarro believed in making assurance doubly sure. He realized that as the submission of Algiers had been rather compulsory than voluntary it was more likely to be temporary than permanent; he therefore took measures which he hoped would serve to hold his new vassals permanently to their allegiance. He seized and fortified an islet — the famous Peñon d'Algel — in the harbor directly opposite the town, and left a strong garrison there, in the belief that it would keep the inhabitants in perpetual terror of the Spanish arms; but it was only six years afterwards that Arudj Barbarossa entered Algiers in the face of the Spanish guns, while in 1529 his brother captured the Peñon itself, and built the mole which connects it with the mainland today.[2] Certainly the Barbary coast was not to be permanently held by any such devices as these. Systematic conquest and colonization of the interior were the only way; but the sole advocate of

[1] Mercier, ii, p. 426.
[2] A. Berbrugger, Le Pégnon d'Alger (Algiers, 1860), p. 94; Élie de la Primaudaie, Histoire de l'occupation espagnole en Afrique (Algiers, 1875), pp. 32 f.

such a policy as this was now in retirement at Alcalá, and for the time being Navarro's methods seemed amply sufficient. Tenes and Dellys made haste to follow the example of Algiers and send in their submission; and before the year 1510 was over Navarro was able to follow the injunctions of Ferdinand, and, discreetly avoiding the powerful fortifications of Tunis, to pass on to the conquest of Tripoli farther east. After a desperate resistance the town was captured. In deference to traditions inherited from Norman days, it was placed in the succeeding year under the jurisdiction of the viceroy of Sicily, and accounted thenceforth an integral part of that kingdom until its cession to the Knights of St. John of Jerusalem in 1528.[1] It was the last conquest of the reign on the Barbary coast; moreover it was almost immediately followed by a very serious reverse. Together with García de Toledo, the father of the famous Duke of Alva, who had been sent over from Spain with seven thousand men for the purpose, Navarro attempted to capture the island of Gerba; but the expedition was most rashly launched, without adequate preparations or knowledge of the country, and was finally beaten off by inferior forces with a loss of several thousand men. The disaster was not retrieved in Ferdinand's day. Navarro was called off to Italy by the war of the Holy League in the following year, and North African affairs were neglected during the rest of the reign.[2]

The verdict which the student of history will pass on the whole North African enterprise under the Catholic Kings will depend primarily on the standpoint from which he regards it.[3] Looked at as an isolated affair, or even as a phase

[1] Zurita, vi, ff. 225–227; M. de los Heros, in D. I. E., xxv, pp. 143–147; G. Longo, La Sicilia e Tripoli, pp. 22 ff.
[2] Zurita, vi, ff. 230–232: M. de los Heros, in D. I. E., xxv, pp. 149–163; L. de Torre, in R. A., 3d ser., xxii, p. 210.
[3] Cf. C. Rosell, Discurso de Recepcion, R. A. H., 31 May, 1857.

of the development of the regions in question, it seems certain that the Spaniards would have done better to have followed the more ambitious programme of Cardinal Ximenes and striven to establish a real Mauretanian Empire. The enterprise was hallowed by the most ancient of the national traditions: if the thing were worth doing at all, it certainly seems, when regarded as a separate problem, as if it would have been worth doing far better. But when we come to fit these North African campaigns into their proper setting in the general development of the Spanish Empire, we shall not be at a loss to find plenty of reasons, if not ample justification, for the somewhat halting method in which they were conducted. They formed, after all, only one, and perhaps on the whole the least important, of a vast number of problems that simultaneouly claimed the attention of the Catholic Kings. Without even going into the question of internal affairs, it was inevitable that the responsibilities of maintaining and strengthening their political, territorial, and dynastic position in Europe, as well as the development of their newly discovered domains in the Western Hemisphere, should occupy a far larger share of the attention of the Spanish monarchs than the possibilities of further expansion on the Barbary coast. Had Oran or Mers-el-Kebir been captured before Columbus reached the Indies, or even before the beginning of the Italian wars, they might possibly have taken precedence; but as it was, these North African campaigns were started last of the long list of memorable enterprises which distinguish the reign of the Catholic Kings: under all the circumstances they were bound to be subordinated to the others. Indeed, the mere effort of retaining the few strongholds which had been won diverted energy and resources which were badly needed elsewhere. Superadded to the multitude of other cares and responsibilities which had so recently and so suddenly been saddled upon Spain, they constituted a burden which was ultimately to prove too heavy for her to bear. It was really a case of the last pound that breaks the camel's back.

BIBLIOGRAPHICAL NOTE

Sources and Contemporary Authorities. — *Cartas del Cardenal Francisco Jimenez de Cisneros á Diego Lopez de Ayala* (edd. Pascual Gayangos and Vicente de la Fuente, Madrid, 1867) contains letters from the cardinal about the expedition against Oran. A " Carta de Gonzalo de Ayora a Rey Fernando sobre la toma de Mazalquivir," in *D. I. E.*, vol. xlvii, pp. 536–555; and the documents accompanying the *Historia del Conde Pedro Navarro* by Martin de los Heros, in *D. I. E.*, vol. xxv, pp. 405–582, are also valuable. Alvarus Gomecius (Alvaro Gomez de Castro), *De Rebus gestis a Francisco Ximenio Cisnerio libri octo* (Alcalá de Henares, 1569; also printed in Schott, vol. i, pp. 929–1156), is the standard contemporary life of the cardinal, and the basis for most of the subsequent biographies of him. Cf. Prescott, ii, p. 368. Zurita is also indispensable on the North African campaigns.

Later Works. — The lives of Ximenes by Pedro de Quintanilla y Mendoza, Esprit Fléchier, and Jacques Marsollier (cf. Prescott, ii, p. 369) have been superseded by C. J. von Hefele's *Der Cardinal Ximenes* (2d edition, Tübingen, 1851; French translation, Paris, 1856; English translation, London, 1860), which, however, leaves much to be desired. In addition to the above-mentioned life of Navarro by Martin de los Heros, a recent article on him by Lucas de Torre in the *R. A.*, 3d series, xxii, pp. 198–214, should be consulted. Nelly Blum, *La croisade de Ximénès en Afrique* (Oran, 1898), is the standard authority on the subject, and contains a useful bibliography, marred by numerous misprints. Émile Froelicher's *La domination espagnole en Algérie et au Maroc* (Paris, n. d.); Giovanni Longo's *La Sicilia e Tripoli* (Catania, 1912); L. Charles Féraud's *Histoire de Bougie* (in vol. xiii of *Recueil de la Société Archéologique de Constantine*, 1869); H. D. de Grammont's *Histoire d'Alger sous la domination turque* (Paris, 1887), and his translation of Fray Diego de Haedo's *Epitome de los Reyes de Argel*, entitled *Histoire des rois d'Alger* (Algiers, 1881); and numerous articles in the *Revue Africaine*, of which the most important are indicated in the bibliography at the end of Blum's book, and in the footnotes to Mercier, are all useful. Of the general works Prescott and Mercier are the most valuable.

NAPLES AND SICILY

IN 1504

SCALE OF MILES

0 10 20   40   60   80   100

14°   16°

42°

42°

40°

38°

38°

Umbria
Assisi
Foligno Camerino
Spoleto Ascoli
Terni
Ndrni Aquila
L. di Tagliacozzo Sulmona
Bracciano
ROME
Anagni
Velletri Sora
Roccasecca
Pontecorvo
Fondi Terra
Terracina Trajetto
Gaeta Sessa
R. Garigliano Capua
I. Ponza R. Volturno Caserta
Aversa Nola
Naples
I. Procida Nocera
I. Ischia Sorrento
I. Capri Amalfi Salerno
R. Sele

Abruzzi
Chieti
R. Sangro
Molise
Termoli
S. Severo R. Candela
Campobasso
Foggia Manfredonia
Capitanata Barletta
Benevento Cerignola Bisceglie
Giovinazzo
Trani Bari
Bitonto Mola
Avellino Atella Monopoli
Venosa Altamura
Castellaneta Brindisi
Potenza Oria
Taranto Lecce
Basilicata R. Bradano Ofranto
Agri R. Gallipoli
Policastro
Lauria
Castrovillari R. Crati
Cosenza Cotrone
Calabria Catanzaro
Aeolian Is. Tropea Squillace
Maida
Terranova
Seminara Gerace
Scylla Reggio
Messina

R. Pescara
Atri
R. Pescara
Fermo
The Marches
Teramo
APENNINES

Neapolitan Apennines

Campania

Aspromonte Mts.

Palermo Cefalù
Trapani Termini Taormina
Mazara SICILY
Caltanissetta Catania
R. Giarretta
R. Platani Girgenti
Terranova Syracuse
R. Salso Ragusa
Avola

Longitude 14° East   from   16° Greenwich SUFFOLK, BOSTON

CHAPTER XIX

MARRIAGE ALLIANCES AND THE CONQUEST OF NAPLES

No plainer evidence of the rapid rise of Spain's power and prestige in the reign of Ferdinand and Isabella could be desired than the immense increase in the activity of her foreign policy. It has, perhaps, been the fashion somewhat to exaggerate the measure of the isolation of the mediaeval Spanish realms — to forget the conquests of Aragon in the Mediterranean and in Italy and to remember only the Moorish wars and the domestic troubles of Castile; but it is undeniable that the part played by the Iberian kingdoms in the general history of Europe down to the end of the fifteenth century was insignificant in comparison to that of England, France, or the Empire. Before the death of Ferdinand the Catholic, however, all this was radically changed. From comparative obscurity Spain leaped forward to a position of acknowledged prominence in the family of European states, and in the succeeding reigns she was, for a brief space, to attain primacy. On her relations with her neighbors the whole course of European history in the sixteenth century turned, and it was in the effort to prevent her from becoming omnipotent that the principle of the balance of power was gradually evolved. Her chief rival for the hegemony of Europe was France. England, at first her friend and ally, gradually became her foe, and finally dealt her the stroke which rendered ultimately inevitable the ruin of her dominion overseas. With the

Empire she was accidentally brought into intimate dynastic relations which proved disastrous to both. Italy was the principal theatre of her continental wars. With Portugal, the most obvious menace to the even tenor of her imperial way, she consistently pursued a policy of friendship, and later of annexation by marriage, which was finally rewarded by temporary success in 1580–81. Against the Turk, after considerable hesitation, she declared the Holy War and announced herself the champion of Christendom. All, or nearly all, the issues involved in these momentous developments had proclaimed themselves before the end of the reign of the Catholic Kings; in fact most of the chief international problems of modern times were stated in the course of the first two decades of the sixteenth century, though the solution of them was reserved for later generations. And the man who set the stage for the great drama that was to unfold itself in Europe in the period when his country reached the highest pinnacle of her glory was King Ferdinand the Catholic. By him Spain was dragged forth from obscurity, and irrevocably committed to that immensely active foreign policy, which, under less sympathetic and skilful guidance, she followed unfalteringly for the next one hundred years. He took the lead in external affairs even more markedly than Isabella had done in domestic ones. The fortunes of the nation abroad could not, in the nature of things, be vigorously pressed until the great internal problems of the time had been solved. Then, when these necessary preliminaries had been cleared away, the queen became so absorbed in the affairs of the Indies and of North Africa that she left her husband a free hand to deal with his fellow potentates of Europe according to his own desires. Finally, after her death in 1504, that is, during the twelve last and most difficult years of the reign, Ferdinand had exclusive control of every phase of the policy of his native land. Thus the story which forms the subject of this and of the succeeding chapter begins inconspicuously, and for a long time is overshadowed by that of Spain's activities at home and in the Western Hemisphere; but it gradually emerges from obscurity into prominence, until at the end it takes precedence of everything else; and it is dominated throughout by the figure of the Catholic King.[1]

It will be convenient to clear away the account of Spain's relations with Portugal at the outset; for these constitute an episode by themselves, apart from the general current of European affairs, and almost unaffected by the history of Spain's dealings with the larger states. Since Portugal had declared her independence in the twelfth century, Castile had often longed to win her back, and had several times taken steps, both peaceful and warlike, to attain that end. Castile's weakness and ill fortune, however, had invariably caused these efforts to fail, and when, in the latter part of the fifteenth century, she suddenly turned her face to the eastward and united her destinies to those of Aragon, the opposition of Portugal had nearly succeeded in subverting the thrones of Ferdinand and Isabella. But after the final defeat of the projects of Affonso the African, it was natural that the more ancient traditions of intimate alliance, if not of unity, should be revived. The expansion of Portugal down the West African coast made her friendship more desirable than ever for Castile, while the triumphant union of the Spanish kingdoms rendered it hopeless for Portugal to oppose them in war. It may indeed seem strange that Ferdinand and Isabella did not anticipate by a century

[1] On this paragraph cf. G. Sela y Sela, *Política internacional de los Reyes Católicos* (Madrid, 1905), *passim.*

the work of their great-grandson, Philip II, and deliberately invade and overwhelm their western neighbor by irresistible military force; and their failure to do so is the more difficult to explain when we remember the rapidity with which the value of the reward increased before their eyes, through the immense expansion of the Portuguese empire overseas. Excess of responsibilities and opportunities in other directions, rather than any hesitancy on grounds of international morality, was doubtless the principal cause; but one cannot help wondering whether it would not have been sounder policy for Spain to have sacrificed the Italian programme of the latter part of the reign to a more vigorous prosecution of her ends in Portugal; and whether indeed she would not have done so, had King Ferdinand happened to be a Castilian. Be that as it may, the sovereigns were certainly too busy at home, at the time of the repulse of Affonso the African's last raid into Castile in 1479, to think of retaliating by a counter-invasion of Portugal. An honorable and secure peace was, for the time being, all that they cared to demand; and this, as we have already seen, they shortly afterwards obtained. At the same time it was arranged that their eldest child, Isabella, born October 1, 1470, should be married, when she had reached a suitable age, to Affonso, the grandson of Affonso the African, and the son of the future King John the Perfect.[1] An intimate dynastic alliance, such as had frequently been made in early days, once more united the two realms; but whereas hitherto it had usually been the Castilian Infante who had wedded the Portuguese princess, now, for the first time since the middle of the fourteenth century, a Portuguese Infante had found a wife in Castile. The primary cause of the change was unquestionably the fact that there was not at that time

[1] Cf. *ante*, p. 54, and Prescott, i, p. 208 n.

available any Portuguese princess of a suitable age for Ferdinand and Isabella's only son John, who was born June 30, 1478; had a favorable opportunity offered they would doubtless have been glad to continue the policy of their predecessors. Yet in their readiness to marry Isabella to the Portuguese Infante, as well as in the fact that they subsequently arranged for their son John an alliance in a very different quarter of Europe, we have evidence that their chief object for the moment was rather to conciliate Portugal, and to win her friendship, than to prepare the way for reannexing her. It is also clear that in view of the great increase of strength which had resulted from the union of Aragon and Castile, they felt that they could face with equanimity the very slight risk that their daughter's marriage might some day threaten the independence of Spain by giving her a Portuguese sovereign.

The wedding of Isabella and Affonso was finally celebrated in the autumn of 1490; but the bridegroom died a few months afterwards, and the Infanta returned to her native land, to forget her grief in works of charity and devotion.[1] Her father-in-law, King John the Perfect, continued to reign in Portugal until his death on October 25, 1495, when he was succeeded by his cousin, Emmanuel the Fortunate, hitherto Duke of Bejar, and at that time twenty-six years of age. Emmanuel, it would appear, had become enamored of Isabella during her previous residence in Lisbon. Immediately after his accession he sent an embassy to the Castilian Court to ask for her hand and to offer a renewal of the ancient alliance. His overtures were finally rewarded by success, but not until the autumn of 1497; and the contemporary chroniclers assure us that the cause of the long delay was the reluctance of the Infanta

[1] Bernáldez, cap. xcv; Prescott, ii, p. 320.

to marry again, which was only overcome at the last by the earnest entreaties of her parents.[1] It seems highly probable, however, that political considerations had much to do with the whole affair. The Portugal of 1495 was far stronger than that of 1479. In 1484 Diogo Cam had discovered the Congo ; in 1486 Bartholomew Diaz had doubled the Cape of Good Hope. The new king was known to cherish most ambitious projects, and to be haunted by the idea that he might some day unite all the Iberian realms under his own sceptre.[2] In Spain, on the other hand, the dynastic situation was critical in the extreme. No other sons, except John, had been born to the royal pair, and as their youngest daughter, Catharine of Aragon, was by this time ten years old, they had little hope of further issue. If by any chance John should die childless, such offspring as Isabella might have by Emmanuel would inherit the Spanish thrones, and Portugal would become, theoretically at least, the head of a united Iberia. Such a prospect would of course be most unwelcome to the Catholic Kings, and it seems probable that they deliberately postponed the union of Isabella and Emmanuel until they should be sure of the marriage of John with Margaret, the daughter of the Hapsburg Emperor, Maximilian. This match, as we shall subsequently see, had been under consideration for several years past. It had been practically settled in the early part of 1495, but the vacillations of the Emperor had postponed the final ratification until the fifth of the following November ;[3] and the anxieties of the Catholic Kings concerning it were not absolutely set at rest until the actual celebration of the marriage on April 3, 1497. Margaret's pregnancy was an-

[1] Zurita, v, f. 128; Peter Martyr, *Opus Epistolarum*, ep. 146.
[2] It was probably for this reason that he drew near to France in 1496; cf.

Zurita, v, f. 88.
[3] H. Ulmann, *Kaiser Maximilian*, i, pp. 241 ff.

nounced in the course of the summer, so that Ferdinand and Isabella felt reasonably safe in going ahead with the Portuguese match; in September Isabella was finally wedded to Emmanuel at Val de Alcántara near the frontier. But the sovereigns were keenly alive to the possible dangers inherent in the alliance to which they had consented, and were resolved to extort an important concession in return. Apparently on the plea that the marriage of Emmanuel and Isabella might some day result in the union of all the Iberian realms under a single sceptre, and that conformity of action in racial and religious matters was therefore imperative, they demanded, and Emmanuel agreed, that all the Jews in Portugal should promptly be expelled, as they had already been, five years before, from Aragon and Castile.[1]

Then, like a bolt from the blue, came that truly terrible series of deaths which ruined all the carefully laid plans of Ferdinand and Isabella, and ultimately brought to pass a catastrophe far more serious than that which they had feared. The wedding ceremonies of Emmanuel and Isabella were clouded by the news of the dangerous illness of the Infante John: on October 4, 1497, he died.[2] Shortly afterwards his widow, Margaret, was delivered of a stillborn child; and all the direct descendants of the Catholic Kings in the male line were thus wiped out.[3] Isabella, the wife of Emmanuel, now became the legal heiress of her parents, and she and her husband were promptly summoned over from Portugal and solemnly recognized as the lawful successors to the Castilian throne by the Cortes, assembled at Toledo. An attempt to extort a similar acknowledgment from the more obstinate representatives of Aragon

[1] Zurita, v, f. 124.
[2] Zurita, v, ff. 127–128.

[3] Zurita, v, f. 137; E. E. Tremayne, *Margaret of Austria*, pp. 27 ff.

elicited vigorous opposition, owing to the doubts cast
upon female rights of inheritance; but the discussion was
closed in tragic fashion on August 23, 1498, by the death
of Isabella in childbirth.[1]   Her baby, a boy, who was named
Miguel, received the recognition that was denied to his
mother, so that the crowns of Aragon, Castile, and Portugal were now, as Prescott says, "suspended over one head";
but the situation was not destined to endure, for on July
20, 1500, before he had completed his second year, the
Infante followed his mother to the grave.[2]   This event
terminated, of course, all danger of a Portuguese monarch's
falling heir to the Spanish throne, but it also, unfortunately,
confronted the nation with a far more grievous peril — the
succession of the foreign Hapsburg offspring of the marriage
of the sovereign's third, and oldest remaining child, Joanna,
to the Archduke Philip the Handsome.[3]   In view, therefore,
of the distressing prospect that the sovereignty of Spain
might one day be carried across the Pyrenees, there was
every reason why Ferdinand and Isabella should wish to
draw near to Portugal, in order to make a united stand for
the cause of Iberian freedom from the matrimonial entangle-
ments of the house of Hapsburg.   The fresh strides of
Portugal's territorial advance in distant lands since the
marriage of Emmanuel to Isabella were an added argument
for the renewal of the ancient bonds.   Vasco da Gama had
reached India in 1497; Pedro Alvares Cabral discovered
Brazil, and Gaspar Cortereal, Labrador, in the spring and
summer of 1500; for one brief moment it almost seemed as
if the imperial prospects of the little western kingdom were
destined to eclipse those of Spain itself.   Consequently,
when Emmanuel, still fascinated with the dream of possibly

[1] Zurita, v, ff. 152–156.   p. 339.
[2] Bernáldez, cap. cliv; Prescott, ii,   [3] Gómara, *Annals*, p. 48.

placing his descendants on the thrones of Castile and Aragon, approached their Catholic Majesties with a proposal to marry their fourth child, Maria, they did not hesitate to accept; and the wedding was celebrated in October, 1500.

From that time onward, until the end of the reign, the relations of Spain and Portugal call for no special remark. It was to the interest of both states to keep on the friendliest possible terms with one another. Both were exceedingly busy in extending their possessions in distant lands; neither had any time to spare for bickerings with its next-door neighbor. Even in their new dominions overseas they scrupulously avoided collisions in this period. There was a notable cessation of Portuguese raids on the Canaries, and the boundary between the Portuguese and Spanish spheres of influence in North Africa was amicably settled, as we have already seen, in 1509. Emmanuel continued to the last to cherish the hope of ultimately winning the Spanish thrones for his descendants, and when his second wife, Maria, died in 1517, he immediately took steps to renew the tie that had been broken by marrying for the third time into the royal family of Spain.[1] The bride that was selected for him on this last occasion was Eleanor, the niece of his first two wives, and elder sister of the Emperor Charles V, who was struggling for recognition as king by the Cortes of the different Spanish realms at the time that the marriage took place; but Emmanuel died in 1521,[2] and was succeeded by John III, the offspring of his union with Maria. In the following reigns, as we shall later see, the policy of intermarriage between the two royal families was carried further still — so far indeed as ultimately to transgress the laws of nature; moreover, in the next generation the Spanish monarchs turned the tables on Emmanuel, and themselves

[1] Gómara, pp. 48, 56.   [2] Gómara, p. 65.

reverted to the ideas of reannexation by dynastic unions that had animated the mediaeval Castilian kings. Charles V married the sister of John III; the first wife of his son Philip II was the Empress's niece and the Portuguese king's daughter; finally, when the 'curse of the Jews'[1] had carried off all the other direct descendants of Emmanuel the Fortunate, the Spanish sovereign was able to realize the hopes and ambitions of a multitude of his predecessors, and seat himself at last upon the Portuguese throne.

When we contrast the Portuguese policy of the Catholic kings with that of their predecessors and successors, we note, in the first place, that they were obliged to abandon their aims of annexation by marriage for lack of opportunities to carry them out; but that on the other hand they saw that it was essential to terminate the ancient quarrels that had divided the two states in previous generations and to cultivate friendly relations.[2] To attain this end they even risked the danger of Spain's being united to Portugal, but they accomplished their object, and broke, for the time being, the miserable tradition of hostility that stretched back for so many years. When we recall the fact that the crucial lap in the race for imperial domain was being run by the two nations at the very moment that this happy change was being effected in their relations at home, we shall appreciate more fully the wisdom and importance of the policy of Ferdinand and Isabella in this regard. The treaty of Tordesillas would, in all probability, have been a scrap of paper before the reign was finished, if it had not been strengthened and supported by the consistent maintenance

[1] Supposed to have fallen on the Portuguese royal house because of the expulsion which accompanied the marriage of Emmanuel and Isabella.

[2] "The Portuguese are not naturally friendly to the Castilian nation," as Zurita (v, f. 88) remarks; it needed strong efforts to reverse the ancient traditions.

of cordial friendship between the high contracting parties in the Iberian Peninsula. That peace with Portugal was also absolutely essential to the effective handling of Spain's different problems in other parts of Europe is too obvious to need further emphasis here.

The dealings of Spain with the various non-Iberian nations are so closely interrelated that it is useless to attempt to follow the course of the Catholic Kings' policy toward any one state without keeping in touch with their contemporary dealings with all the rest. From first to last, however, the story revolves around their rivalry with France. There lay the gist of the whole matter, and Spain's attitude towards the other countries was primarily governed by it.

We have already seen that Castile, the larger and dominant portion of Spain, had enjoyed an unusually long and uninterrupted tradition of amity with France during the later Middle Ages, but that in the third quarter of the fifteenth century the friendship between the two countries had been severely strained.[1] The immediate reason for this was the various efforts of Louis XI, already described, directly or indirectly to prevent the marriage of Ferdinand and Isabella, and to frustrate the ends for which it stood. Another cause of a more general nature, yet certain to be exceedingly effective in the long run, was the fact that with the close of the Hundred Years' War and the expulsion of the English from Gascony the two kingdoms became for the first time contiguous to one another at the western end of the Pyrenees.[2] By the realms of the Crown of Aragon, on the other hand, France had been regarded for more than two centuries past almost in the light of an hereditary foe.

[1] Cf. ante, Vol. I, pp. 132–139.
[2] H. Lemonnier in Lavisse, Histoire de France, v, 1, p. 21.

The princes of the house of Anjou had been the chief rivals of Aragon in Italy, and there was an even more ancient tradition of hostility with the French crown over the lands north of the Pyrenees which had been claimed at one time or another by the Aragonese kings. Furthermore, these enmities had all been accentuated and brought to a head by events of the latter part of the reign of John II and of the early years of that of Ferdinand. There was, in the first place, the bitter memory of the way in which Louis XI had tried to make capital for himself out of the Catalonian revolt in the reign of John Il. Despite all the latter's energy and skill, he had been obliged to endure the humiliation of leaving Cerdagne and Roussillon in French hands at the time of his death, and to hand on the task of reconquering them to his son; certainly the French king's coöperation in John's Navarrese policy had not been hearty enough to efface the remembrance of his treachery farther eastward. Then, in 1480–81, with the deaths of old King René and of his nephew Charles, the ancient line of the counts of Anjou had become extinct, and Louis XI fell heir to the Angevin lands in Provence and also to the Angevin pretensions to Naples. The Neapolitan question did not directly influence the course of Franco-Spanish relations for many years to come, but the effect of the acquisition of Provence was felt at once. It gave the French monarchs a long and valuable stretch of seacoast on the western basin of the Mediterranean — a coign of vantage from which they could deal deadly blows to the progress of the Aragonese Empire. Never before, in fact, had there been anywhere nearly so many opportunities for dissension between France and Spain as at the accession of the Catholic Kings; never had the interests of the two nations threatened to conflict at so many different points. It is true that the large majority of these causes of quarrel pertained only to the realms of the Crown of Aragon; but with Ferdinand in control of the foreign policy of united Spain it was inevitable that they should become the dominating factors in the situation. Under the circumstances, the ancient traditions of Franco-Castilian friendship and alliance were bound to be forgotten, and France and Spain to engage in a desperate struggle for supremacy.

It was a long time, however, before that struggle declared itself in open war. From 1480 to 1495 it was essentially a battle of secret diplomacy and intrigue, such as was dear to the heart of the crafty king of Aragon. On the Spanish side the cause of the long delay in appealing to arms is obvious at a glance — the imperative need of restoring order and strong government at home, and of expelling the Moors from Granada, before launching the united kingdoms on the perils of a foreign war. In France, also, the desire to attain internal unity accounted for much. The last three years of the life of Louis XI were chiefly occupied in reaping the rewards of his earlier efforts to ruin his feudal vassals; and his son Charles VIII, who succeeded him in August, 1483, devoted the first part of his reign to the termination of the independent existence of the duchy of Brittany. Indeed, the struggle over Brittany (1485–91) became for a time the storm centre of European politics during the period immediately previous to the opening of the Italian wars. Spain, England, and the Hapsburgs were all intimately concerned in it, each striving to utilize the embarrassments of the king of France in such a way as to extort concessions valuable to themselves. It thus forms an admirable starting point for our examination of the foreign policy of Ferdinand and Isabella, and a glance at it will enable us to get a clear idea of the aims and relative positions of the differ-

ent European powers on the eve of the famous raid of
Charles VIII on Naples.

The first object of the Catholic Kings was to get back
Cerdagne and Roussillon, whose recovery was regarded by
Spain as almost equally important with the conquest of
Granada. There had apparently been some talk of
Charles VIII's voluntarily restoring them at the beginning
of the reign;[1] but as nothing ever came of it, the episode
merely had the effect of whetting the appetites of Ferdinand
and Isabella. Then arose the struggle in Brittany, which
offered the sovereigns a splendid opportunity to fish in
troubled waters, to increase the difficulties of their rival the
young king of France, and perhaps indirectly to accomplish
the end which was nearest their hearts. They themselves
were far too busy actively to interfere in such a remote
region; but there were two other powers already involved
in the contest, either one of which might conceivably be
induced by a suitable reward to do for the Catholic Kings
the work which they were at present unable to perform.
The first of these two powers was Maximilian, the Hapsburg
King of the Romans, the son of the Emperor Frederick III,
and, through his marriage in 1477 with Mary the daughter
of Charles the Bold, the heir to all the ancient Burgundian
quarrels with the crown of France. His wife had died in
1482, leaving him as regent in the Netherlands for their
son Philip; moreover he had been in close relations with
the duke of Brittany since 1486, and had even gone so far
as to promise to marry the latter's daughter Anne in order
to cement their alliance against their common enemy
Charles VIII.[2] The other was Henry Tudor, king of England since 1485, who, though he was greatly indebted to
the French monarch for timely aid in his final and suc-

[1] Zurita, iv, ff. 327-328.   [2] H. Ulmann, *Kaiser Maximilian*, i, pp. 1-14.

cessful attempt to win the English throne, had also spent no less than twelve of the earlier years of his exile in Brittany, where he had been most hospitably treated by the duke.[1] Of the two sovereigns, Maximilian seemed at first to have more causes of quarrel with the French king than did Henry VII, and, consequently, to promise better for the purposes of Ferdinand and Isabella. In the spring of 1488, however, an unexpected event occurred which determined them to try to make use of the king of England instead.

This event was the arrival of proposals from the English court for a close political and commercial alliance between the two kingdoms and the marriage of Arthur, the eldest son of the English monarch, to Catharine, the youngest daughter of the Catholic Kings.[2] No one realized more thoroughly than Ferdinand and Isabella that Henry came to them with these friendly overtures as a suppliant. The new Tudor dynasty was not yet firmly seated on the English throne. It was threatened by pretenders, and by the hostility of neighboring states. Moreover the realm had fallen so low during the anarchy of the Wars of the Roses that it had forfeited the respect of continental Europe, and desperate efforts were necessary to enable it to regain its badly shaken prestige. In an intimate alliance with the Spanish sovereigns, whose fame had already begun to spread beyond the boundaries of their realm, the English king saw the chance for which he had been waiting; in no other way could he so significantly assert his right to be treated as an equal by the other monarchs of the time. But upstarts have to pay heavily for recognition, and Ferdinand and Isabella did not propose to permit the case of Henry Tudor to prove an exception to the rule. They determined, as the

---

[1] W. Busch, *England under the Tudors*, tr. Todd, i, pp. 12–20.
[2] Busch, *op. cit.*, pp. 50. 329 f.

price of the union for which the English king was so desirous, to demand that he break with Charles VIII, by whose help he had won his throne, enter the Breton war against him in alliance with the King of the Romans, against whom he bore a grudge — in fact that he so embarrass the king of France in the northwest of his dominions, that Ferdinand and Isabella should be able to gain with a minimum of effort the southern counties on which their hearts were set. Henry VII, in other words, was to win Cerdagne and Roussillon, for Spain, from France, in Brittany. Such was the real significance of the famous treaty signed at Medina del Campo, March 27, 1489, between the Catholic Kings and the English ambassadors, in which the latter finally agreed to the conditions imposed by the former in return for their alliance and the hand of their daughter.[1]

The war in Brittany which ensued on the conclusion of this treaty was slackly conducted by all the participants, save possibly the king of France. Maximilian, blow hot, blow cold, at one moment deserted the allies, and at the next returned to the attack, thus convincing every one with whom he dealt of his absolute untrustworthiness. The Spaniards sent a bare thousand men into the duchy to besiege Redon, and also to keep watch on the conduct of their English allies, whom they expected to do most of the work. But Henry Tudor was no novice at the game of diplomacy. He was exceedingly loath to break with Charles VIII at all, and made the most of every opportunity to delay the opening of the war which he had bound himself to wage. Not until 1492 did he seriously take the field. The fate of Brittany had already been decided by that time. On December 6, 1491, the Duchess Anne had been married to Charles VIII,

[1] Busch, pp. 53 f., 330, and references there.

and the way had thus been paved for the union of the province to the domain of the Crown of France. But the international issues which had become involved in the struggle still remained unsettled, and there is no knowing when the solution would have been reached had not the young French king, in defiance of sound precedent and the advice of his wisest counsellors, abandoned the work of internal consolidation, which had been bequeathed to him by his father, and begun to prepare for his memorable raid on Naples. Peace with his neighbors was of course the obvious prerequisite to an expedition into distant lands, and as Charles was all on fire to depart, he naturally paid the price demanded by those with whom he dealt.[1] To Henry of England, by the peace of Étaples (November 3, 1492), he promised 745,000 crowns of gold as reimbursement for the expenses of his campaign. To Ferdinand and Isabella, by the treaty of Barcelona (January 19, 1493), he restored Cerdagne and Roussillon without even demanding payment of the 300,000 crowns for which John of Aragon had pawned them to Louis XI.[2] The sole compensation which Charles received for his surrender of the counties was a promise, soon to be broken, that the Catholic Kings would make no marriage alliances with the King of the Romans without his consent, and would consider themselves the enemies of all those, save the Pope, who should be at war with France.[3] The definitive handing over to the Catholic Kings of the lands for which the Tudor sovereign, in order to get his marriage treaty, had entered the war, was thus postponed until two and a half months after the English monarch had

---

[1] Zurita, v, ff. 1–10, *passim*; Busch, *op. cit.*, p. 333, and references there.

[2] H. Lemonnier in Lavisse, *op. cit.*, v, 1, pp. 22 f. The original debt of 200,000 crowns to the king of France had been augmented to 300,000; cf. J. Calmette, *Louis XI, Jean II, et la révolution catalane*, pp. 84–92, 373 f.

[3] H. F. Delaborde, *L'expédition de Charles VIII*, p. 256.

withdrawn from it; but as the cession had been discussed between the representatives of France and Spain since the year 1491,[1] Henry VII must have known, when he signed the treaty of Étaples, that with Charles's attention riveted on Naples, the Catholic Kings would obtain what they desired. The result of the Italian projects of the young king of France was really a windfall for the sovereigns of both England and Spain. The latter got back the lands on which they had set their hearts far more easily and swiftly than they had any right to expect; the former obtained his marriage treaty without the serious military effort which, at one time, had seemed inevitable — indeed, without permanently imperilling his friendly relations with France. Finally, the treaty of Senlis (May 23, 1493), by which Charles VIII purchased peace with Maximilian before his departure for Italy, had an important bearing on the subsequent fortunes of Spain. By it Margaret, the daughter of Maximilian, who had been destined for Charles VIII, and had resided in Paris since 1483, was handed back to her father; and with her went the lands which were to have constituted her dowry.[2] The way was thus opened for her subsequent marriage to the Infante John in 1497, and the continuation of the territorial jealousies of France and the Hapsburgs was insured for the future.

The Breton war had served in fact to place the pieces for the great game of international politics which was to be played during the critical period of the Italian wars. It gave renewed proof of the irreconcilability of the ambitions of Spain and France. The treaties with which it ended had no element of permanence. It had merely served to reveal to Ferdinand and Isabella the gross incompetence of the French king, and was the prelude to a fresh outburst of

[1] Zurita, v, ff. 5, 9.   [2] H. Lemonnier, in Lavisse, v, 1, p. 23.

hostilities in another place. Moreover the course of the struggle in Brittany had also shown the Catholic Kings where to look for allies in their forthcoming duel with the kings of France. They had been able to bring the English monarch into the war on their side and hoped to do so again. This hope was not invariably realized in the succeeding years; in fact, some of the most serious mistakes of Spanish diplomacy in the sixteenth century arose from deficient comprehension of the fact that the Tudors, save for a few temporary aberrations, had thrown over the mediaeval English tradition of enmity to France. Still, for the time being, it is no wonder that Spain thought she could gain many advantages by keeping the ancient animosities alive. From Maximilian also something might reasonably be expected. There was no question of his hostility to France ; the danger was lest his versatility and ubiquitousness might destroy the value of his alliance for Spain. In any case, the plan of a marriage between the Archduke Philip, son and heir of the King of the Romans, and one of the daughters of Ferdinand and Isabella was under discussion at least as early as the autumn of 1491, and even spoken of as a settled matter in the following February.[1] The origins of the most fateful dynastic union of the sixteenth century are thus to be traced back to the period of this Breton war. Finally, the years of this singular conflict saw Ferdinand and Isabella reach a satisfactory solution of their internal problems, and consequently set them free to devote a far larger share of their energies to foreign affairs. Hitherto they had been obliged to do most of their work through others. Henceforth they were able to enter the lists themselves, with all the power and prestige which their domestic triumphs had insured them. The preliminary period was in fact over,

[1] A. Rodríguez Villa, *Juana la Loca*, p. 11; Ulmann, *op. cit.*, i, pp. 241 f.

the main events were about to begin, and with the change the scene of interest shifts from northwestern France to southern Italy.

We left Italian affairs in 1458, at the death of Alfonso the Magnanimous, who had bequeathed Naples to his illegitimate son, Ferrante, while the rest of his domains were inherited by his brother John. For the next thirty years the two Aragonese courts in Spain and in Naples were united in most intimate friendship and alliance; they maintained a regular family compact. John was too busy at home to interfere actively with Italy, though he had numerous interests there; it was consequently essential for him to keep on the best of terms with his nephew, who could represent him on the spot. Ferrante needed the aid of his uncle against hostile Angevins and Turkish corsairs, and welcomed his advances. In all the 'leagues for the preservation of Italian peace' which succeeded one another in such bewildering confusion at this time, the name of John of Aragon is invariably found together with that of his nephew. In 1476 Ferrante married, as his second wife, Joanna, the daughter of his uncle, and a sister of Ferdinand the Catholic.[1] The objects of this intimate alliance were defensive rather than offensive. Maintenance of the status quo was at that period all that either partner could reasonably expect. The alliance was founded, moreover, essentially on practical considerations, rather than on any real affection. John doubtless coveted Naples for himself, and would have been only too glad to expel Ferrante if he could. Ferrante, on his part, bore no love to his uncle and would willingly have thrown him over had he dared. But as a matter of fact neither sovereign was strong enough to do without the other; and

---

[1] *Nouvelle Biographie Générale*, xvii, col. 401.

on John's death, in 1479, his son inherited the Neapolitan alliance.[1]

Though Ferdinand the Catholic was no less busy in Spain during the early part of his reign than his father had been before him, he was obliged from the very beginning to take a somewhat more active part in Italian affairs. Every time he interfered there, however, in this first period, he did so on behalf of his Neapolitan kinsman; in fact the sole object of his Italian policy seemed to be to defend Ferrante against his various foes. When the Turks took Otranto in 1480, Ferdinand was the chief agent in forming the league of princes that expelled them in the following year; moreover he dispatched no fewer than seventy ships from Castile to aid the Christian forces.[2] Still more significant was the action of the Spanish monarch in a small conflict of the characteristic Italian sort which broke out in the northern part of the peninsula in 1482. On May 2 of that year, Venice, land-hungry and insolent, and supported by Pope Sixtus IV, declared war on Ercole d'Este, duke of Ferrara; the Pope moreover solicited the aid of Louis XI, offering in return to help him to assert the French claims in Naples against the house of Aragon.[3] Wide ramifications of the impending struggle were obviously possible; and Ferrante of Naples, who, besides being threatened in his own domains, was father-in-law to the duke of Ferrara, applied for the support of the Catholic Kings. The latter, totally unprepared at that juncture for any considerable military effort

[1] For many of the conclusions reached in this and in the following paragraphs, I am indebted to an article by M. Joseph Calmette in the *Revue des Pyrénées* for 1904, entitled "La France et l'Espagne à la fin du quinzième siècle." The elaborate volume which he has been preparing in support of the views there advanced has not yet been published, but no one who is familiar with his work can doubt that he will make out his case.

[2] Zurita, iv, ff. 308, 311; Pulgar, *Crónica*, pt. ii, cap. xcix (*B. A. E.*, lxx, pp. 358 f.).

[3] J. Calmette, "La politique espagnole dans la guerre de Ferrare," in *Revue Historique*, xcii, p. 227.

beyond the boundaries of their realm, were yet most un-willing to see their Neapolitan kinsman deprived of his dominions.   Accordingly they strove at first to prevent the conflict by conciliatory means, and by reminding the Pope of his duty to maintain peace among Christian princes. Meantime they became convinced that Louis XI was so old and feeble that there was no danger of the French inter-ference which they dreaded most of all.   Consequently when the Venetians, scorning arbitration, invaded Ferrara in the course of the summer, the Spanish sovereigns adopted a more vigorous attitude, threatened commercial war with the republic, and spoke of armed intervention to the Pope. The latter was so impressed by these menaces that he promptly ratted to the side of Naples and Ferrara.   By the end of the year 1482, Venice had not a single ally left among the Italian states, save Genoa ; but she was still too proud to lay down her arms, and attempted to strengthen herself by begging for the intervention of France.   The war, then, was by no means over, though the ultimate issue could not long remain in doubt.   During the whole of the year 1483, the sovereigns, busy with the Granadan campaign, strove their hardest to put on others the work of bringing the republic to its senses.   They even advised Ferrante of Naples to consider a league with the Turk against Venice, and gave him full power, in case it should be con-cluded, to enroll the realms of the Crown of Aragon among its members.[1]   But more vigorous measures than these were necessary on the part of the Spanish monarchs to bring the Ferrara war to a close.   Early in 1484 they fulfilled their

[1] The proposed alliance was never actually made, but the fact that Fer-dinand formally approved of it shows that Francis I was not the earliest Chris-tian monarch to consider a treaty with the infidel as a means of solving his difficulties in Western Europe.   It also indicates that the Catholic King was far less squeamish about the orthodoxy of his foreign relations than were Charles V and Philip II.

threat of a commercial campaign against the republic, and expelled all Venetians from their territories. In the following June they sent a fleet into Italian waters to cooperate with that of Naples. Finally, on August 7, they had the extreme satisfaction of compelling Venice to sign a treaty which granted all their demands and reëstablished the status quo. The whole episode had demonstrated the vigor of the Spanish-Neapolitan alliance and greatly enhanced the prestige of Ferdinand and Isabella. They had asserted in dramatic fashion their right to be consulted in future settlements of Italian affairs.[1]

Just ten years later the two ends of Spain's foreign policy were most unexpectedly drawn together by the French king's crossing the Alps at the head of a large army, intent on possessing himself of Naples as heir of the house of Anjou : fascinated, as Comines says, "with the smoke and glories of Italy." [2] The strength of the Spanish-Neapolitan alliance was now to be tested again. To all the old causes of Franco-Spanish hostility which had come to the surface in the struggle for the throne of Castile and in the Breton war, another was now to be added — and in view of the memories it awakened, it was perhaps the most potent of them all. And now for the first time the Catholic Kings were able to give their chief attention to the direction of foreign affairs. The Granadan war was over. Their thrones were secure. Neither the Indies nor North Africa had yet begun to occupy a large share of their attention. They had a well trained and efficient army and could back up their

---

[1] Calmette in *Revue Historique*, xcii, pp. 227-253. Cf. also "La politique espagnole dans l'affaire des barons napolitains," by the same author, in the *Revue Historique*, cx, pp. 225-246, for another case of effective diplomatic intervention of the Catholic Kings in Italy, this time to protect their kinsmen against a revolt which was supported by the Pope and threatened to have the backing of France.

[2] On the origin and validity of this claim, cf. H. Lemonnier in Lavisse, *op. cit.*, v, i, pp. 13-16, and references there given.

diplomacy by military force. Opportunity came in a way that no one could have anticipated, simultaneously with the ability to utilize it. The intensity of the struggle with France increased with the enlargement of its scope.

But though Spain was now far stronger than ever before, and though Ferdinand fully realized the rashness and incompetence of Charles VIII, his conduct at this crisis was marked with even more than his usual caution. He was the last man in the world to play carelessly when the game was in his own hands; and besides, might there not be a double stake to be won from the French king's descent into Italy? Hitherto, as we have seen, the Neapolitan alliance had been almost a necessity for Spain; but now, with her internal problems solved, it might safely be thrown over — the more so, since the able though vicious Ferrante had been succeeded, in January, 1494, by his much less valorous son Alfonso. Neither Ferdinand nor his father before him had given up hope of ultimately reuniting Naples to their own dominions; at the bottom of their hearts they had always regarded the illegitimate Neapolitan dynasty as usurpers;[1] but they had both realized that to quarrel with it before they had set their own house in order would be madness. Now at last the chance had come. Coincident with the termination of the domestic difficulties of the Catholic Kings, their arch enemy, the king of France, was voluntarily setting out on an expedition directed against their ally of the past, whom they now were quite ready to cast aside. On the face of it, the situation gave the Spanish sovereigns every pretext for declaring war on Charles VIII, whom it was essential sooner or later to expel from Italy; but on the other hand, there was obviously much to be gained by delaying the opening of hostilities until the Valois

---

[1] Cf. here Zurita, v, ff. 23–25.

monarch should have attacked and weakened for them the
Neapolitan dynasty which they were now most desirous to
displace. And the supreme cleverness of the Italian diplomacy of Ferdinand the Catholic during the next ten years
consists in the fact that he timed the ebbs and flows of his
policy in just such a way as most effectively to compass
both these ends.[1]

At first the Catholic Kings seemed anxious above all
things to prevent the French king's expedition. In the
winter of 1493–94 they despatched their ambassador Diego
López de Haro to the Vatican to counterwork the envoys
of Charles VIII, and to keep the new Pope, Alexander VI,
on the side of the Neapolitan king.[2] Six months later they
sent a special envoy, Alfonso de Silva, to the French monarch at Vienne, to warn him to desist from his enterprise
and to recommend that he devote all his forces to a war
against the Turk. When Charles replied that by the peace
of Barcelona Ferdinand had bound himself to treat the
enemies of France as his own, Silva reminded him that
since Naples was a fief of the Holy See, it was not affected
by the provisions of that instrument.[3] Yet, on the other
hand, the Spanish sovereigns carefully avoided giving effect
to their threat for many months to come. They had formally taken their stand against the French invasion; but
they suffered Charles to cross the Alps unopposed in August,
1494, and to proceed as far as Rome before he heard from
them again. Then at last, in January–February, 1495,
just as the young monarch was about to enter the kingdom of Naples, the ultimatum came. Ferdinand's envoys,
Juan Albion and Antonio de Fonseca, gained access to the
French king, roundly accused him of insulting their master

---

[1] Calmette, "La France et l'Espagne," in *Revue des Pyrénées* for 1904.

[2] Zurita, v, ff. 26–27, 34–35.
[3] Zurita, v, ff. 37–39.

and maltreating the Pope, warned him again to abandon the Neapolitan enterprise, and finally threatened, in case he persisted with it, to throw over the treaty of Barcelona: the older historians tell us that on receiving an angry reply from Charles, the ambassadors dramatically produced the original copy of that agreement and tore it in pieces before his eyes.[1] Whatever the precise manner in which the interview ended, its purport could not possibly be misunderstood; it was nothing more nor less than a frank declaration of war. Yet it is important to notice that the climax had been postponed until the other aim of the Spanish monarch's Italian policy had been at least partially accomplished. On January 23, while Charles was still at Rome, Alfonso of Naples had voluntarily abdicated the throne of that kingdom in favor of his son, Ferrante II, and retired to Sicily.[2] Not until the Neapolitan dynasty had begun to totter was the challenge of Spain hurled at the king of France. Of course the extreme slowness of communication between Spain and Italy renders it impossible that Ferdinand should have planned the timing of the ultimate defiance of Charles to accord so exactly with his own desires. It was owing to good luck, rather than to foresight, that it occurred precisely when it did. Nevertheless, the fact that he had delayed it so long may reasonably be taken to indicate that he was not unwilling to see Charles temporarily attain the goal of his ambition. The ulterior objects of Ferdinand the Catholic in Naples, quite as much as the difficulties and delays of military preparation, were unquestionably

---

[1] *Crónicas del Gran Capitán* in *N. B. A. E.*, x, p. 19 f., 276; Zurita, v, ff. 54–55; Prescott, ii, pp. 263 f., and references there; Delaborde, *L'expédition de Charles VIII en Italie*, pp. 542–545. Of course this tearing up of the treaty of Barcelona put the whole question of Cerdagne and Roussillon, theoretically at least, again in doubt; though practically the chances of France's recovering them were almost nil. Cf. L. G. Pélissier, *Louis XII et Ludovic Sforza*, i, p. 107.

[2] Zurita, v, f. 56.

responsible for the fact that the king of France had been allowed to get so far.[1]

Ferdinand of Aragon was not the man to issue a challenge without being ready to fight. As in the Breton war, however, he determined, as far as possible, to put the work on others. Since the autumn of 1494 he had been planning the formation of a league against Charles VIII, in order to make sure of victory when the time for action should come. The question was where to look for allies; and among the Italian states he quickly decided that Venice, his enemy in the Ferrara war, was the most suitable for his purpose. The republic was probably the most powerful of all the states in the peninsula at the time, and political combinations shifted far too rapidly in the Italy of those days for her to cherish any lasting resentment against Spain for the quarrel of ten years before. She was out of the line of march of the French king, and consequently could make her preparations undisturbed. She was also, for the moment, on excellent terms with Lodovico il Moro, duke of Milan, whose sister, Hippolita, had married Alfonso of Naples.[2] In the autumn of 1494, accordingly, Ferdinand despatched an ambassador, Lorenzo Suarez de Figueroa, to Venice to propose to that power a league with the Pope against Charles VIII, and to promise the coöperation of a Spanish fleet and troops under Gonsalvo de Cordova. On January 5,[3] 1495, Figueroa reached his destination and immediately set to work. In order fairly to estimate the situation with which he was confronted, we must leave him for a moment at Venice, and examine the ramifications of the policy of his wily master in other parts of Europe.

---

[1] Calmette, op. cit., in Revue des Pyrénées for 1904.
[2] Delaborde, op. cit., pp. 530–533.
[3] Zurita, v, ff. 47, 59–60; M. Sanuto, La Spedizione di Carlo VIII in Italia, p. 178. Delaborde, p. 538, has mistranslated the date "5 Zener," in Sanuto, and made it "5 juin."

In the Breton war, it will be remembered, Ferdinand had
been greatly aided in his efforts to embarrass the French
monarch by Henry VII of England, and also by Maximilian, King of the Romans, who now, since the death of
his father on August 19, 1493, was Holy Roman Emperor
in all but name.   It was therefore natural that in the present
crisis he should turn to them again.   From the former he
was able to gain nothing of substantial value.   The Tudor
king was by this time far too firmly set upon his throne to
be induced, as before, to break with France.   He did, indeed,
finally adhere to the league against Charles VIII which
Ferdinand was striving to create, but not until September,
1496, long after it had accomplished its purpose.[1]   With
the versatile Maximilian, Ferdinand was much more successful.   Even before Charles VIII had begun to think of his
descent on Naples, there had been talk of a marriage between
Maximilian's son, the Archduke Philip, and one of the
daughters of the Catholic Kings; and in 1492 embassies
had been exchanged between the two powers for the purpose
of settling the terms.[2]   No very rapid progress was made
in these early stages, chiefly for the reason that Charles
VIII had refused to give up Cerdagne and Roussillon
until assured that Ferdinand would make no marriage
alliances with the Hapsburgs without his consent: such,
it will be remembered, was the stipulation in the treaty
of Barcelona of January 19, 1493.   But now, with the
coveted territory safe within their grasp, the Spanish sovereigns were perfectly ready, in case any advantage could
be gained by so doing, to tear up the agreement they
had made.   They consequently despatched another envoy, Francisco de Rojas, to the court of Maximilian in

[1] Busch, *op. cit.*, p. 128.
[2] Cf. *ante*, p. 279, and A. Rodríguez Villa, *Juana la Loca*, p. 11.

November, 1493, to bring the matrimonial negotiations to a conclusion.[1]

The task was not an easy one. The plan of marrying the Infante John to the Archduchess Margaret had by this time taken shape and had to be considered in conjunction with that of the union of Joanna and Philip. Maximilian, as usual, changed his mind almost every day. Philip's Francophile leanings made matters doubly complicated and led to constant bickerings with his father. Furthermore, Rojas was greatly embarrassed by the fact that down to the final denunciation of the treaty of Barcelona, in February, 1495, the Catholic Kings insisted on continuing the pretence of demanding the consent of Charles VIII.[2] By the spring of 1494, however, the Spanish ambassador had successfully concluded his business, at least with the Hapsburgs. A letter of the Catholic Kings to their envoy, dated July 1, from Arevalo, indicates that the only thing lacking was the approbation of the king of France.[3] Failure to obtain this was doubtless responsible for the postponement of the final ratifications until the time that Ferdinand was ready openly to break with Charles VIII; and the exciting events that followed further delayed matters until November 5, 1495, when the treaties were finally confirmed at Malines.[4] But though the last formalities were not complete until after the French king had been driven out of Italy, the alliances were practically certain before he entered it, so that King Ferdinand had every reason to hope for the active support of Maximilian in his Italian schemes. Furthermore his new intimacy with the Emperor had a most important effect on his negotiations with Venice. We have already

---

[1] A. Rodríguez Villa, "Don Francisco de Rojas," in *Boletín de la R. A. H.*, xxviii, p. 183.
[2] Rodríguez Villa in *Boletín de la* *R. A. H.*, xxviii, pp. 183 f.
[3] *Ibid.*, pp. 297 f.
[4] A. Rodríguez Villa, *Juana la Loca*, p. 13.

seen that the republic was in many respects admirably
fitted to be the instrument of Ferdinand's plans for opposing
Charles VIII; but there had been one serious difficulty
in the way. For years Venice had lived in terror of invasion
by Maximilian, who had repeatedly announced his intention of conquering her; not until she was relieved of that
menace could the republic devote her energies to making
war on the king of France. Now, in November, 1494, she
was most agreeably surprised to receive friendly overtures
from the Emperor, which were gladly accepted by the Doge,
and ripened in the following January into proposals for a
regular alliance.[1] Though we have no document to prove
it, there seems every reason to believe that this change
in the attitude of Maximilian, so convenient for the realization of Ferdinand's Italian aims, was effected through
the skilful ambassador of the Catholic Kings in the Netherlands.

It was almost three months later, however, before the
confederates could be brought together in a formal treaty
to attain their ends. Suarez de Figueroa labored for it
with might and main, but there were still many difficulties
to be overcome. Philippe de Comines had been posted
in Venice by the king of France to watch developments
and report, and it was by no means easy to hoodwink him
into believing that all was well.[2] Moreover both the Venetians and the duke of Milan, though they had been brought
to good terms with Maximilian, showed a decided repug-
nance to having the armies of the Emperor cross the Alps.
"If the Germans descend upon Italy," said Lodovico il
Moro, "they will be in no wise preferable to the French;
instead of one fever we shall have two." [3] All this, coupled

[1] Delaborde, pp. 534 f.
[2] Sanuto, *Spedizione di Carlo VIII*,
pp. 178 ff.; Comines, *Mémoires*, ed.

Mandrot, ii, pp. li–lxii, 205 ff.
[3] Delaborde, p. 538.

with Maximilian's other responsibilities, prevented the arrival of the vanguard of the imperial army in Italy until the late summer of 1495, after Charles had got back into the north of the peninsula; it was not until 1496 that Maximilian himself was able to lead an expedition across the mountains, and when it did finally arrive, it turned out to be a miserable failure.[1] Ferdinand in Spain was doubtless accurately informed of the Emperor's numerous embarrassments, and realized from the first that little military assistance could be expected from him. All the more reason why he should hasten his own preparations. By December, 1494, he had got ready a large fleet and 3500 soldiers, to be despatched, under Admiral Galceran de Requesens, to Sicily, to coöperate with the forces that were being mustered there.[2] Meantime, on March 31, 1495, the League was formally signed at Venice between the Pope, the Emperor, Spain, the Venetians, and the duke of Milan, "for the peace and tranquillity of Italy, the welfare of all Christendom, the defence of the honor and authority of the Holy See, and the rights of the Holy Roman Empire, . . . and the protection of its members against the aggressions of other potentates at that time possessed of states in Italy, even if those potentates should lose those states in the duration of the League."[3] The news of it reached Ferdinand in Spain either late in April or early in May; it caused him at once to send off to Sicily another detachment of 2100 men under Gonsalvo de Cordova, to support the troops of Requesens, who was already on the spot, and to bear aid to young Ferrante II in the recovery of the kingdom of Naples. The force was so small as to justify the verdict of Prescott that it was Ferdinand's intention "to assist his kinsman rather

[1] Ulmann, *Kaiser Maximilian*, chap. iii.

[2] Zurita, v, f. 52.

[3] Lünig, *Codex Italiae diplomaticus*, i, coll. 111–118.

with his name, than with any great accession of numbers;"
but when we remember what the ulterior objects of the Catholic King were, as well as the fact that he was holding another
army in readiness for a diversion in Cerdagne and Roussillon, we cannot wonder that it was not larger. It reached
Messina on May 24, and two days later was transferred to
Calabria, where Ferrante had already begun operations.[1]

The military events that followed can be recounted in
short space. On May 20, four days before Gonsalvo reached
Sicily, Charles VIII had quitted Naples, leaving the Count
of Montpensier with some 10,000 men to defend the kingdom as best he could. His retreat to France occupied
three months less than his descent into Italy. The two important events of it were the battle of Fornovo, on the Taro,
where his army succeeded in cutting its way through the
forces of his Italian foes assembled to oppose him, and the
treaty of Vercelli on the ninth of the following October,
by which he succeeded in detaching Lodovico il Moro from
the League of Venice.[2]   Meantime, in the kingdom of Naples,
Gonsalvo and Ferrante had come to blows with the French
forces that had been left to defend it. The first encounter
took place at Seminara, some twenty-five miles northeast
of Reggio; owing to the impetuosity of the young Neapolitan monarch, who insisted on fighting against the advice
of his more experienced ally, it resulted in a victory for the
French. The latter, however, were unable to follow up
their advantage. Gonsalvo managed to retreat in safety
to Reggio, while Ferrante boldly transferred himself to the
city of Naples by the ship of Admiral Requesens; and on

[1] Zurita, v, f. 65; Prescott, ii, pp.
281 f. Much light is thrown on the
Neapolitan policy of the Catholic Kings
by a series of letters from them to the
Great Captain, extending from February, 1495, to July, 1506, and published by L. I. Serrano y Pineda in
R. A., 3d ser. vols. xx–xxix, passim; cf.
here especially pp. 454 f. of vol. xx.
[2] Delaborde, pp. 608–651, 669.

July 11 he was able to effect an entrance into his capital. The rest of the year was occupied in ousting the French from the neighboring fortresses and in a fresh advance of Gonsalvo from southern Calabria. The Spanish commander was now seen at his very best. His army was still small, despite the arrival of reënforcements from Spain, but it was in perfect fighting trim; and the extraordinary rapidity of its movements rendered it impossible for the French to withstand him. One victory followed another in rapid succession; so that when at last, in the summer of 1496, Gonsalvo was called across to join Ferrante in besieging the town of Atella, he was saluted on all sides as 'the Great Captain', the title by which he was thereafter best known.[1] The capitulation of Atella, on July 20, virtually marked the end of the resistance of the French. Gaeta surrendered on November 19, and Taranto on the eighteenth of the following January. A little later Gonsalvo, at the invitation of the Pope, passed over to the Patrimonium Petri, expelled a French garrison which Charles had left in Ostia, and was subsequently accorded a most magnificent reception in Rome; in August, 1498, he was back in Spain. A series of raids and forays into French territory north of the Pyrenees had meantime been carried out by another army, under command of Enrique Enríquez de Guzman. Much damage was done and booty taken; and though the French retaliated by a counter-raid on Salsas, the enterprise demanded so many troops that were desperately needed elsewhere, that a truce soon terminated the struggle in that region.[2]

The League of Venice, in fact, had thoroughly accomplished the work that it had been organized to do, and the

[1] M. J. Quintana, *Vidas de los Españoles célebres*, i, p. 161.
[2] *Crónicas del Gran Capitán* in N. B.

A. E., x, pp. 29–50, 281–298, *passim*; Prescott, ii, pp. 282–309, and references there to the original authorities.

interests of its members had begun once more to diverge. Milan, as we have seen, had deserted at the treaty of Vercelli. The ridiculous failure of Maximilian's military demonstration in 1496 showed that nothing more was to be expected from him. Venice had forced Ferrante of Naples to deliver up to her some of the ports of Apulia in return for her aid against the French — an event which must have been most unwelcome to the king of Spain.[1] Finally, on October 7, 1496, the brave and vigorous, though cruel, Ferrante II of Naples, the ally of Gonsalvo, died most unexpectedly at the very moment of the recovery of his realm, and was succeeded by his weak and yielding uncle, Frederic. The latter was the fifth monarch to occupy the fatal throne of Naples within three years, and obviously far less competent to defend it than any one of his predecessors.[2] The significance of these events was not lost on Ferdinand the Catholic; they indicated that the time was ripe for a reversal of his policy. He had got rid of the French. He had no more use for his allies — indeed one of them, Venice, was actually in possession of a portion of the territory which he coveted for himself. The throne of Naples was at present occupied by a prince whom it promised to be easy to despoil. Now, if ever, was his chance to win the crown which Alfonso the Magnanimous had withheld from his father.

The first essential to the achievement of this purpose was to gain peace on the side of his quondam enemy, the king of France, and Ferdinand soon found that the latter was quite ready to meet him half way. Despite the resentment which he must have cherished against the Spanish monarch for his expulsion from Italy, Charles realized that

[1] Delaborde, p. 674. The principal ports were Trani, Brindisi, Otranto, and Gallipoli.
[2] Zurita, v, ff. 101–102.

he was in no condition to seek vengeance. Moreover, his fears of the hostility of the Catholic Kings were considerably increased in the winter of 1496–97 by the conclusion of the two Spanish-Hapsburg marriages, whose dangers to his own realm he had thoroughly realized, and which he had hitherto moved heaven and earth to prevent. On October 20, 1496, the Infanta Joanna became the wife of the Archduke Philip at Lille; on April 3, 1497, the Archduchess Margaret wedded the Infante John at Burgos: so that the two most powerful neighbors and rivals of France were now united by a double tie.[1] These same months also witnessed a revival of the negotiations for the marriage of the Infanta Catharine to Arthur, Prince of Wales, which had been almost abandoned after the conclusion of the Breton war. Encirclement, in fact, seemed to threaten the king of France, so that some sort of an understanding with his neighbors became almost a condition of existence. From Henry VII, as he well knew, he had little to fear. With Maximilian, as usual, negotiations dragged on for an interminable space without reaching any definite conclusion. But Charles's dealings with Ferdinand the Catholic determined the whole course of international relations during the next five years, and revealed for the first time to the world at large the schemes that had long lain hidden in the brain of the Spanish king.

Peace between the two sovereigns was simply and quickly attained. A suspension of hostilities was agreed to on February 25, 1497; on April 25, it was transformed into a seven months' truce, which was again extended and considerably amplified, on November 24, at Alcalá de Henares.[2] But an inquiry into the course of the negotiations that

---

[1] Zurita, v, f. 100; Prescott, ii, p. 327. Comines, *Mémoires*, ed. Mandrot, ii, p. 367, note.

[2] Sanuto, *Diarii*, i, coll. 866–868;

underlay these treaties shows that much more than a mere peace between the two kingdoms was under consideration. All through the year 1497 the ambassadors of Charles VIII, led by Guillaume de Poitiers, Seigneur de Clérieux, kept journeying back and forth between the courts of France and Spain; and in the course of their interviews with Ferdinand and Isabella a proposition for the joint conquest and partition of the kingdom of Naples came up for discussion.[1] Whether this proposal emanated ostensibly from the French or from the Spanish side, it is impossible to state. Comines tells us that it "was made by Ferdinand out of meere dissimulation to win time," notwithstanding, he thought, that the Spaniards "wished with all their harts the said realme of Naples to be their owne, and sure [sic] they had better title to it than they that possessed it."[2] Zurita, on the other hand, maintains that the idea of a division of Naples was first broached by the French. They began, so he tells us, by asserting that the whole of that kingdom unquestionably belonged to their master, and that he was resolved to have it, though he might consent to give up the realm of Navarre in exchange. Subsequently, however, they modified their demands, and were finally brought to suggest a partition, based on the cession of Calabria to the Catholic kings.[3] In view of what we know of the aims and ambitions of Ferdinand the Catholic, it is difficult to resist the conclusion that he was the real originator of the plan ; but we may well believe that he also succeeded in gaining the very considerable diplomatic advantage of making the other side propose it first. At any rate, it seems clear that the agreement at Alcalá de Henares,

---

[1] Zurita, v, ff. 118 ff., 132 ff. The footnotes to vol. ii, pp. 367–371, of Mandrot's Comines give valuable details in regard to Clérieux's negotiations.

[2] Quoted from Danett's translation of Comines, bk. viii, cap. xvi (vol. ii, pp. 346 f., in *Tudor Translations Series*).

[3] Zurita, v, f. 119.

signed November 24, 1497, was accompanied by an understanding of the sovereigns of France and Spain to the effect
that they should jointly invade Naples when the opportunity should arise, and divide it between themselves —
Calabria going to Spain, and the rest of the kingdom to
France. It also appears that the French ambassadors
on this occasion had various other proposals to make, all
of them indicating that Charles VIII was still so infatuated
with the idea of conquering Italy that he was willing to sacrifice everything else to the accomplishment of that end;
these, however, Ferdinand declined, on the ground that
they constituted an infringement of the rights of his allies
in the League of Venice.[1] As usual, the Catholic King
distrusted everybody, and wisely refused to commit himself
wholly to any one side as long as it was possible also to
maintain a foothold in the camp of the other. Nevertheless,
he had gone far enough to give a plain hint of the main
aim of his Italian policy in the immediately succeeding
years, though the incompetent monarch with whom he was
negotiating was totally unable to fathom its meaning. All
the preparations for the game that Ferdinand was to play
in Naples between 1500 and 1504, at first with the aid,
and then at the expense, of Louis XII of France, were made
before the death of Charles VIII, which occurred, as the
result of an accident, on April 7, 1498. Indeed, had it not
been for the various delays which the change of rulers inevitably caused, the climax of the Neapolitan drama would
not, in all probability, have been postponed nearly so long
as it was.

The new king of France was quite as anxious to conquer
Italy as his predecessor had been before him; but his first

[1] Zurita, v, ff. 132 f.

objective was the north rather than the south of the peninsula. From his grandmother, Valentina Visconti, Louis inherited a claim to the Milanese, which he was all on fire to vindicate against the Sforzas. At his accession to the French throne, he assumed the title of duke of Milan, and at once prepared to expel the usurper and set himself up in his place. For this enterprise, peace with his neighbors was, of course, indispensable; and he immediately took steps to assure himself of it in much the same way as Charles VIII had done on the eve of the raid of 1494, though not at so great a cost. In July he renewed the peace of Étaples with England. With Maximilian, who also had pretensions to Milan, he was unable to come to terms; but as the Emperor was deeply engaged at the moment in a war with the Swiss, his opposition did not promise to be serious, while his son, the Archduke Philip, was so amicably disposed that he actually did homage to the Chancellor of France for Flanders, Artois, and Charolais.[1] Ferdinand the Catholic also finally accepted Louis's friendly overtures, despite the fact that the Italian states, plainly foreseeing the intentions of the French king, urged the Spanish monarch to mediate between him and themselves. On July 31, 1498, the two sovereigns made a treaty of peace and of mutual aid in case of attack.[2] The business was transacted near Paris by Louis and certain Spanish ambassadors whom Ferdinand had despatched for the purpose, and a secret interview was apparently held at the same time, in which it seems probable that the partition of Naples was again discussed, though it is impossible to be certain.[3] At any rate, Frederic of Naples was so disturbed over the out-

---

[1] H. Lemonnier in Lavisse, op. cit., v, 1, p. 47.

[2] L. G. Pélissier, Louis XII et Ludovic Sforza, i, pp. 107–114; also, by the same, Documents sur la première année de Louis XII (Paris, 1890), p. 28.

[3] Zurita, v, ff. 146–149.

look, that he shortly afterwards sent an embassy to the
Spanish court to ask for the hand of one of the Infantas for
his son, the Duke of Calabria; the support and protection
of the Catholic Kings were doubly indispensable to him now,
because the Pope, together with the Venetians, was believed to be in league with the king of France.[1] Failing in
this, Frederic was constrained to draw close to Lodovico
Sforza, who was already in alliance with the Emperor; but
the trio were palpably inadequate to resist the mighty combination — including most of the rest of western Christendom — which had pledged itself to the support of
Louis XII.[2] The second act of the Italian drama was thus
opening with a change of scene and a considerable redis-
tribution of the powers concerned; but Ferdinand the
Catholic, though he shifted his methods according to the
needs of the moment, held steadily to the same ultimate
object which had animated him from the first. As before,
he planned to use the French king to weaken the king of
Naples, then to pick a quarrel with the invader and expel
him, and finally to seize the throne of Alfonso the Magnanimous for himself.

The war in northern Italy, during the years 1499–1500,
saw fortune alternate rapidly between the combatants.
Milan was taken, lost, and retaken by the French king and
the Venetians within the space of seven months, but Ferdinand the Catholic kept out of the struggle there. For the
time being his sole object seemed to be to lend aid to the
Venetians against the Turks. He made ready a large army
and a fleet for this purpose and appointed the Great Captain
commander of it; and in the winter of 1500–01 the allies
attacked and captured from the infidel, in a most gallant

[1] Zurita, v, f. 158.
[2] Pélissier, *Louis XII et Ludovic Sforza*, i, pp. 113 f., 373 ff.

action, the fortress of St. George in Cephalonia.[1]   Gonsalvo,
at the time of his departure on this expedition, was specially
warned not to take sides in any of the struggles between
Christian potentates which were at that time devastating
Italy;[2]   but in view of what subsequently occurred, it is
difficult to resist the conclusion that Ferdinand entered the
Turkish war largely as a means of getting his forces into
convenient proximity to Naples, in order that they might
be quite ready for action in that kingdom when the decisive
moment should arrive.   Meantime he vigorously pressed
forward his secret negotiations with the king of France concerning the partition of the realm they both coveted.
Frederic of Naples, foreseeing more plainly than ever the
fate that was in store for him, again attempted without success to engage the Spanish monarch to protect him against
his foes;   then, when his overtures were refused, he rashly
applied for aid to the Sultan, thus giving his prospective
enemies another excuse, which they did not fail to utilize,
for attacking him and seizing his dominions.[3]   Finally, on
November 11, 1500, by the famous treaty of Granada,
Ferdinand and Louis settled the details of the project for
the partition of Naples which they had cherished for so
long.   On the ground that they both had better right to it
than King Frederic, who had also imperilled the safety of
Christendom by alliance with the Turk, the kings of Spain
and France, in the interests of general peace and safety,
agreed jointly to invade the kingdom and to divide it between themselves.   Not only Calabria, but also Apulia, was

---

[1] Zurita, v, ff. 166, 177 f., 184, 189,
194, 199 f.; *Crónicas del Gran Capitán,*
in *N. B. A. E.,* x, pp. 63–72, 309–314;
J. Fuentes, *Gonzalo de Cordoba en
Cefalonia* (Madrid, 1909).

[2] Zurita, v, f. 179.

[3] Zurita, v, ff. 167–168.   Ferdinand

apparently attempted, at this stage of
the proceedings, to lure the French
ambassador Clérieux into his own service, by promising him the city of
Cotrone in Calabria, of which he was
titular marquis.

now to go to Spain, which had obviously increased its claims since the beginning of the negotiations; the profits of the crown pastures [1] in Apulia were equally divided; the rest of the realm was assigned to France; and any inequalities of income in their respective portions were to be so adjusted that the amount of revenue which the monarchs of both countries should derive from their new dominions should be the same.[2] The treaty was not to be made public until the high contracting parties had completed their military preparations, though the papal nuncio in France apparently wormed the secret out of King Louis before the close of the year. On the other hand, it seems that Lorenzo Suarez de Figueroa, who was now Spanish ambassador at Rome, "the very centre of all politics" in those days, was kept totally in the dark about it by his master, and therefore, when questioned, stoutly denied that any such pact existed.[3] It was a characteristic example of the methods of Ferdinand the Catholic.

The disparity of the forces of the allies and those of the king of Naples was such that an easy conquest was practically certain. The French troops, some 12,000 to 15,000 strong, under the lead of the Sieur d'Aubigny, left Milan June 1, 1501, and reached the Neapolitan frontier July 8. The French and Spanish ambassadors at Rome seized the moment when the invading armies were crossing the States of the Church to notify the Pope of the intentions of their masters, and to extort from him confirmation of their rights, and investiture in the territories to which they respectively laid claim.[4] No serious resistance was experienced from the forces of King Frederic, save at Capua. The city of Naples

---

[1] "Vulgariter nuncupatae, la Duana de la Pouille," as the treaty has it; cf. H. F. Pelham, Essays (Oxford, 1911), pp. 300–311.

[2] Text in J. Dumont, Corps universel diplomatique, iii, 2, pp. 445 ff.
[3] Zurita, v, f. 199.
[4] Zurita, v, ff. 214–215.

was surrendered without a blow, and the unfortunate
sovereign sent off to an honorable captivity in France, where
he died in 1504.[1] All the contemporary accounts of the
conduct of the French soldiers, during these first months
of the occupation of the kingdom, agree that it was atrocious. Murders and ravishings of the defenceless were the
order of the day, and a legacy of hatred was laid up for the
invaders of which the Spaniards were subsequently to reap
the advantage.[2] In the meantime, Ferdinand, having
finally refused to King Frederic the protection which the
latter had not ceased to hope for, ordered the Great Captain
to land his forces in the southern part of the peninsula;
thence they advanced northward and occupied within the
space of a month the bulk of the regions assigned to the
Spaniards. Taranto, commanded by Frederic's son the Duke
of Calabria, was the only place which defied them. It
was apparently too strong to be taken by assault, so that
Gonsalvo had to sit down to a siege. Only by transporting
a number of Spanish ships on rollers across a tongue of land
to the inner harbor directly under the walls of the town, was
he finally able to capture it, on March 1, 1502.[3] An ugly
incident of the capitulation was the fate of the young Duke
of Calabria. He had been solemnly promised his liberty
by Gonsalvo before he surrendered, but as a result of a
missive from Ferdinand, which arrived at the last moment,
the agreement was violated, and he was sent a prisoner to
Spain.[4]

[1] Prescott, iii, pp. 21 f.

[2] J. d'Auton, *Chroniques*, ii, pp. 55
ff.; C. Yriarte, *César Borgia*, ii, pp. 10–
13.

[3] *Crónicas del Gran Capitán*, in *N. B.
A. E.*, x, pp. 94 f., 322–326; Zurita, v,
f. 228; cf. also documents in *R. A.*,
3d ser., xxi, pp. 350–359. The difficulties in the way of capturing Taranto
were unquestionably very great, yet it
seems as if the operation need not have
taken quite so much time; and one is
tempted to ask whether Ferdinand did
not deliberately command the Great
Captain to prolong it, in order that a
greater share of the work and risk of
the conquest of Naples might be borne
by the French.

[4] Prescott (iii, pp. 24–32) follows an
excellent description of the siege of

The joint conquest concluded, the inevitable disputes and quarrels between the allies were not long in breaking out. Blood had been spilled in Rome months before, in a fight between some of the soldiers of the French army as it passed through, and certain Spaniards who were resident there, over the question as to whether the French or the Spanish king had the better right to the Neapolitan realm.[1] Now that the rivals were actually on the ground and in possession of the spoils, more serious trouble was bound to come. Ferdinand was of course amply prepared for it, though he urged Gonsalvo to postpone it as long as possible; and the accounts of the interviews of the Great Captain and the young French regent, the Duke of Nemours, concerning the limits of the possessions of their respective masters, read as though they also had become convinced that a breach was ultimately inevitable.[2] The precise cause of the quarrel — the question of the Basilicate and the Capitanate, which had perhaps purposely been left untouched in the treaty of Granada — is less interesting for us than the diplomacy by which the Catholic King sought to insure to himself the victory in the impending struggle. To Maximilian his ambassador represented that the conduct of the French, both in the north and south of Italy, indicated that they would be satisfied with nothing short of the control of the entire peninsula; and he urged the Emperor as lawful suzerain of Milan immediately to declare war upon them.[3] Though Maximilian did not accede to his desires, he was at

Taranto with a characteristic discussion of the "atrocious act of perfidy" by which the unfortunate duke was retained in captivity, and of the different arguments that have been advanced in palliation of it. Modern readers may perhaps be excused if they question whether present day political methods show as great an advance over the "laxity and corruption" then preva-

lent, as that singularly upright and high-minded historian is obviously inclined to attribute to them.

[1] D'Auton, *Chroniques*, ed. de Maulde, ii, pp. 32 f.

[2] Zurita, v, ff. 232–234; cf. also documents in *R. A.*, 3d ser., xxi, pp. 558–563, *passim*.

[3] Zurita, v, f. 241.

least kept practically neutral during the next few years; the treaty of friendship and alliance which it seemed probable that he would make with France in 1501 was postponed until 1504.[1] With the Pope and the Venetians also Ferdinand labored hard[2] and with good results. Alexander VI was not perfectly certain whether Spain or France was the safest repository of his political fortunes. He appeared at first to incline toward the latter, and his redoubtable son Caesar Borgia was hand in glove with Louis XII; but Spain had attractive proposals to offer in other directions, and at midsummer, 1502, it was believed in Venice that a rupture had been brought about between the Pope and the French. This was certainly an exaggeration; yet on the other hand the Borgias had been effectively prevented from breaking with Spain; and, lastly, the Venetians, who were becoming more and more alarmed every day by the preponderance of France in the north of the peninsula, maintained a neutrality which tended to be favorable to Ferdinand. If the Catholic King had not succeeded in winning allies for himself, he had at least made certain that they would not be secured by his foes.[3]

Meantime in the kingdom of Naples the rivals had at last abandoned all attempts at conciliation and begun to fight. The war was at first of the old-fashioned sort — a war of sieges, raids, and deeds of individual valor, rather than of decisive pitched battles in the open. Most characteristic and dramatic of all was the famous combat of eleven French against eleven Spanish knights outside the walls of Trani, in the winter of 1502–03 — the result of a

---

[1] H. Lemonnier, in Lavisse, *op. cit.*, v, i, pp. 56, 70 f.

[2] Though not hard enough, apparently, to satisfy Peter Martyr, who was passing through Venice at this junc-ture, on his way back from his famous embassy to Cairo. Cf. Mariéjol, *Pierre Martyr*, pp. 70 f.

[3] H. Lemonnier, in Lavisse, v, 1, pp. 59 f.

formal challenge issued by the Sieur d'Urfé. It was witnessed, so we are told, by over 10,000 persons, and is described in glowing colors by all the contemporary historians. The foremost champion on the French side was the Chevalier Bayard, the knight 'sans peur et sans reproche '; the most famous of the Spaniards — at least if his subsequent exploits be taken into account — was Diego García de Paredes, "who never had his equal in strength and courage," and lived on to the year 1533. The Spaniards gained the initial advantage by aiming their lances at the horses rather than at the persons of their foes; but when they attempted to ride down the dismounted Frenchmen and give them their *coup de grâce*, the most skilful of their adversaries leaped aside, and, catching the shafts of their spears as they rushed by, managed to disarm them. Night put an end to the fighting without conclusive results; the judges, who were Venetians, refused to give any verdict; before leaving the lists the combatants embraced one another, and all present agreed that it was a fair and equal feat of arms.[1]

More conclusive, if less heroic than these proofs of valor by renowned champions, were the first real battles of the war, in which the French at the outset obtained a decided advantage. In December, 1502, d'Aubigny won a considerable victory at Terranova in Calabria against an army which had recently been sent over from Spain to reënforce Gonsalvo; and the latter was obliged to rest on the de-

[1] *Crónicas del Gran Capitán*, in *N. B. A. E.*, x, pp. 120–125, 333–344, 506; Zurita, v, ff. 247–249; d'Auton, *Chroniques*, ed. de Maulde, iii, pp. 115 ff.; Gómara, *Annals of Charles V*, pp. 11, 94. All the accounts differ in detail: Zurita slides over the killing of the horses, but the number of dismounted Frenchmen seems to show that it occurred. A duel afterwards took place between Bayard and the Spanish cavalier Alonso de Sotomayor, in which the former, though weak from the effects of a fever, finally succeeded in slaying his redoubtable adversary. Those who are familiar with the characteristics of the historiography of the time will not be surprised to learn that this episode is not mentioned by any of the Spanish chroniclers.

fensive. In the beginning of 1503 there seemed a prospect of peace through the instrumentality of the Archduke Philip, who proposed the eventual cession of Naples to his son, the future Emperor Charles V, and the marriage of the latter to Claude, the daughter of Louis XII; the negotiations, however, proved abortive, owing to the refusal of King Ferdinand to ratify the terms which had been made for him in France. Indeed, the whole affair served chiefly to gain for the Spaniards much valuable time, and to enable Gonsalvo to be heavily reënforced; while on the other hand it lulled the French, who really believed that peace would be concluded, into a false sense of security, and rendered them unprepared for a continuance of the war. When in the end of April, 1503, Gonsalvo issued from his retreat at Barletta, intent on regaining the laurels which he had temporarily lost, his foes were in no condition to withstand him. He defeated Nemours at Cerignola. One of his lieutenants routed d'Aubigny at Seminara. On May 14, 1503, the Great Captain entered Naples in triumph; Gaeta alone in the whole kingdom held out for the French. Then indeed King Louis roused himself to desperate efforts to retrieve his fortunes. An army was sent into Cerdagne and Roussillon, and kept Ferdinand and Isabella busily occupied there. The French fleet revictualled Gaeta, and obliged Gonsalvo to raise the siege. Finally, a large force under La Trémouille was sent to retake Naples. As Alexander VI died (August 12, 1503) at exactly the moment the French general reached Rome, the latter wasted three months there in a fruitless effort to influence the cardinals in favor of the election of George d'Amboise; and when, in October, he finally reached his destination, Gonsalvo was fully prepared to receive him. A series of desperate combats along the river Garigliano ensued in the next three months, and were marked by a number of deeds of extraordinary valor and courtesy by the heroes of both armies. At first the French succeeded in throwing some troops across the stream, but they totally failed to dislodge the Spaniards from their main position; then, in a night attack, December 28, 1503, Gonsalvo suddenly assumed the offensive, seized the bridge by which the French army had crossed, and drove it back in headlong flight on Gaeta. This action practically marked the end of the war. Gaeta surrendered on January 1, 1504, and two months later a formal treaty was concluded between Louis and the Catholic Kings, in which the French sovereign definitely recognized the Spaniards as lawful possessors of Naples.[1]

Thus, after ten years of tortuous diplomacy and bloody war, the primary aim of the Italian policy of the Catholic King was at last triumphantly attained, and another rich territory added to the domains of the Spanish Empire. The Neapolitan contest in its different phases had exhibited Ferdinand at the very height of his powers. It was through it that Machiavelli became acquainted with his methods, which he described for the guidance of contemporary statesmen in *The Prince*. Into the question of the morality of those methods it is happily unnecessary for us to enter here; of their effectiveness there cannot be a shadow of doubt. It would be idle to deny that Ferdinand possessed many advantages in the struggle on which he had launched himself both against his own cousins and against the French. Tradition, on the whole, was distinctly favorable to him; for the memories of the union of Naples and Sicily under

---

[1] Full references to most of the principal contemporary authorities on these events may be found in the footnotes to Prescott, iii, pp. 48–156. Additional information may be gleaned from the notes to vol. iii of de Maulde's edition of d'Auton's *Chroniques*, and from the documents in *R. A.*, 3d ser., xxi, pp. 558–566; xxii, pp. 116–123; xxiii, pp. 497–505; xxv, pp. 124–133, and from the *Crónicas del Gran Capitán*, in *N. B. A. E.*, x, pp. 133–224, 344–421.

the Normans and Hohenstaufen counted heavily against the claims of the French as heirs of the house of Anjou, and of Ferrante and his successors as descendants of Alfonso the Magnanimous. Sicily, moreover, was of immense practical value to him throughout the contest as a base and source of supplies. The French had nothing to correspond to it, and their admiral, Prégent de Bidoulx, was unable, despite the most strenuous efforts, to wrest from his Spanish adversary the all-important control of the sea. Lastly, in Gonsalvo de Cordova the Spanish monarch possessed a general whom his enemies could not possibly hope to match. Prudent, yet immensely aggressive when the moment for action arrived; never over-elated by success or despondent in failure; liberal to his soldiers, courteous to his foes: he seemed to endow the cause he fought for with a certain moral elevation which made men forget the treachery of his master and contributed no small element towards its ultimate success. His diplomatic triumphs moreover must not be forgotten; his victories on the field of battle were scarcely more valuable to the Spanish cause than his manipulation of the leading Neapolitan families, who were wavering between the rival factions.[1] Yet after all, the conquest of Naples was primarily the work of Ferdinand the Catholic. It had been made possible chiefly because it had been planned for long before; it was largely the fruit of the Spanish monarch's ability to look ahead and work quietly and effectively towards the attainment of a distant goal. Moreover, it meant far more than the mere winning of a kingdom. It was Ferdinand's way of serving notice on his fellow sovereigns that united Spain intended to maintain and increase the Mediterranean empire which had been founded

---

[1] Cf., e.g., *R. A.*, 3d ser., xxiv, pp. 566–568; xxvii, pp. 514–517, 519–522; xxviii, pp. 111–115; also *N. B. A. E.*, x, pp. xxiii–xxv, xxviii.

by Aragon, as well as to assume all the responsibilities that she had inherited from Castile. In addition to setting her own house in order and developing and enlarging her possessions overseas, she proposed henceforth to play a leading part in the international politics of Western Europe.

The new master of the conquered kingdom made some changes in the system of government which he inherited from his predecessors. In the days of Alfonso the Magnanimous, there had been no attempt to subordinate Naples to the realms of the Crown of Aragon; if anything, the reverse had been the case, for the first conqueror of the Italian kingdom preferred it to his native land, fixed his residence there, and made it the centre of his dominions. Now, however, under Ferdinand the Catholic, Naples became a regular dependency of the Spanish monarchy, like Sicily and Sardinia before it; so that "a new Polity, new Magistrates and Laws agreeable to the Spanish Customs and Principles," were "introduced into the Kingdom."[1] The occasion of the initiation of these reforms was a visit which Ferdinand made to Naples during the winter of 1506–07 in a fit of jealousy and distrust of the Great Captain, who had continued to reside there as the royal representative after the completion of the conquest three years before.[2] The beginnings of the new régime were thus established under the supervision of the king himself.

The first evidence of the new order of things was that Naples "lost the Honour of being the Royal Seat,"[3] and was thenceforth governed, like the other Mediterranean dependencies, by viceroys sent out from Spain. These were, as elsewhere, appointees of the crown, and their average

[1] Giannone, *History of Naples*, tr. Ogilvie, ii, p. 475.
[2] *Crónicas del Gran Capitán*, in *N. B.*
A. E., x, pp. xxxviii–xlviii, 246–248, 436–453.
[3] Giannone, ii, p. 475.

term seems to have been about three years.   Many of them, however, held office for shorter periods, while a few extended their tenure to more than four times that length; the case of Ramón de Cardona, whose term began under King Ferdinand in 1509, and continued until his death in 1522, is a case in point.[1]   The powers of these Neapolitan viceroys were considerably greater than those of the corresponding officers in the other Mediterranean dependencies.   They were, from the first, the representatives of an absolute king; they did not reach back, as did the viceroys of Sicily and Sardinia, to the days of the more limited monarchy of the realms of the Crown of Aragon.   Their authority, moreover, was not restricted to the same extent as in the other Mediterranean dependencies by the rights of the local assembly; for the meetings of the ancient Neapolitan parliament had by this time degenerated into a mere formality, while the more important *Seggi* of the city of Naples found themselves more and more completely in the control of the central power as the years went by.[2]   So conveniently were these constituted, indeed, for the purpose of enabling the viceroy to divide and weaken the forces of his opponents, that Tommaso Campanella, writing in the early seventeenth century, hints broadly that the king of Spain might do far worse than to establish a similar institution at home, as a means of protecting himself against baronial encroachments.[3]   The great crown officers of Angevin days, the High Steward, Grand Chamberlain, and the rest, who had been maintained by Alfonso the Magnanimous, were now either dismissed or shorn of all their important functions; certain others 'after the

[1] Giannone, ii, p. 503; Stokvis, *Manuel*, iii, p. 708.

[2] A. von Reumont, *The Carafas of Maddaloni*, English translation, pp. 60–81, *passim*.

[3] Campanella, *A Discourse touching the Spanish Monarchy*, English translation (London, 1654), p. 63; Lea, *Inquisition in the Spanish Dependencies*, pp. 54 f.

Spanish fashion' were introduced to replace them, but Ferdinand took good care, as he had already done in Castile, that the central authority should not be overshadowed.[1] And finally, at the same time that he strove to weaken and divide all the forces from which opposition might be anticipated, Ferdinand took positive steps to fortify and Hispanicize the office of his representative in Naples. A special privy council, or *consulta*, of the viceroy, which soon came to be known as the *Consiglio Collaterale*, was instituted in 1507 at the time of the visit of the Catholic King, and at once took precedence of the Santa Chiara, the Sommaria, and all the other tribunals of the realm. Down to the end of the reign it was composed of two legists, a Sicilian and a Catalan, with a secretary or clerk, under the presidency of the viceroy. In later years a Neapolitan member was added, but the two senior councillors invariably came from outside the kingdom, and usually from Spain.[2] The significance of these arrangements was perfectly obvious. Besides being Spanish himself, the viceroy was to be advised and guided at every turn by a body dominated by Spanish influence. The Neapolitans were to be practically excluded from any real participation in the government of their own country.

One result of this system of administration was that Naples was overburdened with taxation to a far greater extent than any of the other Mediterranean dependencies of Spain. The home government expected its overseas possessions to pay for themselves and yield revenue besides; and as the power of the Neapolitan viceroy was virtually absolute, there was practically no limit to the number of tributes which he could impose.[3] There was, besides, a

[1] Giannone, ii, pp. 481 ff.   Kelly, p. 89.
[2] Giannone, ii, pp. 476 ff.; Ranke,   [3] Ranke, *op. cit.*, p. 90.
Ottoman and Spanish Empires, tr.

special reason why the inhabitants of Naples should be made to pay more heavily than the Sicilians or Sardinians; and that was the provision in the treaty of 1504, stipulating that the Angevin proprietors of the kingdom should be reëstablished in the possession of the estates from which they had been evicted in the course of the war. This difficult task was performed by Ferdinand himself, during his visit in the winter of 1506–07; and though every advantage was taken of such flaws as the ingenuity of the lawyers could discover to impugn the validity of the Angevin titles and evade the terms of the peace, a large number of the territories had either to be bought up or given back, and those who were deprived of them compensated by a grant of funds.[1]   All this was naturally very expensive, and necessitated fresh levies on the people : for a time it was not a question of making the new kingdom an asset but rather of preventing it from becoming a liability. Moreover, when the work of restoration and transfer was completed, the new imposts which it had called into existence were suffered to remain. What had been adopted as a temporary expedient was converted into a permanency, and Naples was given a long start on the road to financial ruin which she travelled to the bitter end. Other and most burdensome levies were invented and set in operation in the succeeding years, without the slightest reference to correct economic principles, or to the convenience or prosperity of the people. The pills were sometimes gilded, indeed, and their true nature disguised by the use of an attractive label; for men would often grant *donativos* which differed in no essential respect from the *tributos* at which they boggled; but of any serious or effective attempt to ease the burden we hear nothing at all. Needless to say the material prosperity of the kingdom

[1] Giannone, ii, p. 471; Prescott, iii, pp. 252 f.

suffered terribly under such a system as this. The sums which the government annually wrung from its subjects were multiplied seven or eight fold during the first hundred years of the Spanish administration, while agriculture, industry, and commerce dwindled away. It is, however, but fair to add that the blame for these unfortunate developments is to be laid less at the door of Ferdinand than at those of his Hapsburg successors. The Catholic King could plead the exigencies of the situation in Naples itself at the time of the conquest in partial justification for what he had done; but the sums derived from the far heavier exactions of the days of Charles V and the Philips were not utilized for the benefit of the Neapolitans, but were spent for the most part outside the realm, on the maintenance of other more remote and less subservient portions of the Spanish Empire.[1]

The ecclesiastical situation in Naples was peculiar and difficult, because of the kingdom's proximity to the States of the Church, the claims of the Pope to its feudal over-lordship, and the papal tradition of alliance with the hostile Angevin elements in the realm. Roman ambitions and encroachments had made trouble there before for the illegitimate Aragonese dynasty;[2] they were to do so again and in even more serious fashion in later years, particularly under Pope Paul IV. The strongest bulwark against these encroachments was the provision that no papal bull or other instrument could be promulgated in the realm without the special license or exequatur of the king or his representative; and no better proof could be desired of the firm resolution of the Spanish monarchs to eliminate Roman interference in the internal affairs of their dominions than

[1] A detailed account of these exactions may be found in L. Bianchini's *Storia delle finanze di Napoli*, lib. v, pp. 172–283, *passim*.

[2] Cf. J. Calmette, "La politique espagnole dans l'affaire des barons napolitains," in *Revue Historique*, cx, pp. 225–246.

the vigor of their resistance to any attempt to evade this regulation. In 1508 King Ferdinand gave orders to hang a papal messenger who carried a brief lacking the required indorsement of the king.[1]

The most interesting phase of the ecclesiastical history of Naples in this period, however, is the attempt and failure of King Ferdinand to introduce the Spanish Inquisition there. In 1503, Gonsalvo de Cordova, who desired to conciliate the Neapolitans, had made a solemn engagement that it should never be established in the kingdom;[2] but in the following year the influx of *conversos* from the other Spanish possessions became so great[3] that Ferdinand determined to ignore his general's promise and to try to set up the Holy Office in his new dominions. Jealousy of the papal Inquisition, which had meantime been introduced into Naples by Julius II, further strengthened the king's resolve; but the opposition of the Neapolitans was so outspoken that, fearing a revolution if he persisted, he postponed the fulfilment of his purpose until 1509.[4] When at last, at the very end of that year, all the preparations had been made, and the Inquisitors who had been appointed arrived, there was a terrible uproar in the capital. The populace rushed to arms and surged in fury through the streets. The Catholic King had unquestionably been prepared for some resistance, but the political situation in northern Italy, where the Pope needed Gonsalvo's veterans to fight his different foes, and was evidently prepared to make things extremely disagreeable for Ferdinand if he withdrew them to overawe the Neapolitans, convinced the Spanish monarch that, bitter as it was for him, he must

[1] Ranke, *op. cit.*, p. 88.
[2] Lea, *Inquisition in the Spanish Dependencies*, p. 52; L. Amabile, *Inquisizione in Napoli*, i, p. 93.
[3] Despite Ferdinand's order to Gonsalvo, of March 2, 1504, that they be expelled; cf. *R. A.*, 3d ser., xxiv, p. 568.
[4] Lea, *op. cit.*, pp. 54–57.

yield again. To cover his retreat he put forth two pragmaticas ordering the expulsion from the realm of all professed Jews and *conversos* before March 1, 1511, and thus
gave himself a plausible excuse for revoking the Inquisition
on the ground that there would be no more work left for it
to do. These pragmaticas, however, were not obeyed, as is
proved by the records of the papal Inquisition, which in
the meantime had continued its activities in Naples, and to
which, it seems, the inhabitants did not seriously object.[1]
The whole situation must have been gall and wormwood to
the Catholic King. The most recently acquired of his
dominions was honeycombed with unbelief; yet he was
prevented from using that means of arresting it which had
proved so terribly effective in Spain. His dissatisfaction,
moreover, must have been considerably enhanced by his
jealousy of the rival papal institution, subordinated though
it was to the authority of his viceroys. The whole affair
showed that the Neapolitans still retained some measure
of their pristine independence; and in this one matter at
least, they made good their contention to the very end of
the story, for the full-fledged Spanish Inquisition was never
permanently established within the kingdom.

[1] Lea, *op. cit.*, pp. 58–63; Amabile, *op. cit.*, i, pp. 97–121.

BIBLIOGRAPHICAL NOTE

See bibliographical notes at the end of Chapters XII and XIII, and add:
Sources and Contemporary Authorities.— L. Ildefonso Serrano y
Pineda, ed., " Correspondencia de los Reyes Católicos con el Gran Capitán," in *R. A.*, 3d series, vols. xx–xxix, *passim* — a series of 202 original
documents which throw much light on the relations of the sovereigns with
Gonsalvo during the Neapolitan campaigns. The study which was expected to accompany and elucidate them has not, so far as I am aware,
been yet put forth. Eleven other letters from Gonsalvo, most of them
written in 1499–1501, were also published in *R. A.*, 3d ser., xxxiv
(1916), pp. 300–316. The anonymous *Crónica llamada las dos Conquistas
del Reyno de Napoles*, sometimes called the *Crónica General del Gran
Capitán*, together with the *Breve suma de la vida y hechos de Diego García
de Paredes*, written by himself, the anonymous so-called *Crónica Manu-
scrita del Gran Capitán*, and also Paul Jovius's *Vita di Gonsalvo Fernando
di Cordova, detto Il Gran Capitano* (translated into Spanish in 1554 under
the title of *La Vida y Chrónica de Gonzalo Hernández de Córdova llamado
por sobrenombre El Gran Capitán*), were all published in 1908 by A. Rodríguez Villa in *N. B. A. E.*, vol. x. This volume also contains a number of
letters from Gonsalvo and other documents concerning him; and an
excellent introduction furnishes much useful critical and bibliographical
information. All these chronicles are primarily valuable on the military
side of the Neapolitan wars. Marino Sanuto's *Diarii* (Venice, 1879–
1903, 58 vols.) and his *La Spedizione di Carlo VIII in Italia*, ed. Rinaldo
Fulin (Venice, 1883), give a full account of the events of 1494–95. On
this most important annalist of the Italian wars and his work, see Henri
Hauser, *Les sources de l'histoire de France, XVIᵉ siècle*, vol. i (Paris, 1906),
pp. 53–55. Philippe de Commynes (Comines), *Mémoires*, is the work
of one of the keenest writers and diplomatists of the age, who possessed
unusual opportunities for knowing the facts; the best edition is that
of B. de Mandrot (Paris, 1901–03, 2 vols.); the English translation by
the Elizabethan Thomas Danett was edited by Charles Whibley, and
published at London in 1897. Jeán d'Auton, *Chroniques de Louis XII*,
ed. R. de Maulde La Clavière (Paris, 1889–95, 4 vols.), is also valuable.
On this work see Hauser, *op. cit.*, vol. i, pp. 126 f. Francisco López
de Gómara, *Annals of the Emperor Charles V*, Spanish text and English
translation, ed. R. B. Merriman (Oxford, 1912), contains several items
of interest in regard to the Neapolitan wars. Full references to Jovius,
Guicciardini, and the other standard Italian writers of the time will be
found in the footnotes to the pages of Prescott, where cited.

Later Works.—H. F. Delaborde, *L'expédition de Charles VIII en Italie* (Paris, 1888), is useful for a detailed account of the facts, though the thesis it attempts to prove is more than doubtful; cf. Henry Lemonnier in Lavisse's *Histoire de France*, vol. v, pt. 1, p. 13, and Joseph Calmette, " La France et l'Espagne," in *Revue des Pyrénées* for 1904. L. G. Pélissier, *Louis XII et Ludovic Sforza* (Paris, 1896, 2 vols.), gives a full and accurate account of France's foreign relations from April 8, 1498, to July 23, 1500. Wilhelm Busch, *England under the Tudors*, vol. i : King Henry VII, translated from the German by Alice M. Todd (London, 1895), is based on the sources, and contains valuable notes. Antonio Rodríguez Villa, *La Reina Juana la Loca* (Madrid, 1892), and " D. Francisco de Rojas, Embajador de los Reyes Católicos," in *Boletín de la R. A. H.*, vol. xxviii, pp. 180–202, 295–339, 364–402, 440–474 ; vol. xxix, pp. 5–69, are both valuable, and contain numerous original documents. Heinrich Ulmann, *Kaiser Maximilian I.* (Stuttgart, 1884–91, 2 vols.) ; J. H. Mariéjol, *Pierre Martyr d'Anghera* (Paris, 1887) ; Joseph Calmette, " La politique espagnole dans la guerre de Ferrare (1482–1484) " in *Revue Historique*, vol. xcii, pp. 225–253, and " La politique espagnole dans l'affaire des barons napolitains (1485–1492) " in *Revue Historique*, vol. cx, pp. 225–246, are all serviceable monographs.

On the changes in the government of Naples, see bibliographical note at the end of Volume I, Chapter XI, and add :

Tommaso Campanella, *A Discourse touching the Spanish Monarchy*, translated into English (London, 1654) ; on this man and his work cf. Andrea Calenda, *Fra Tommaso Campanella* (1895) ; Leopold von Ranke, *The Ottoman and the Spanish Empires*, translated by W. K. Kelly (Philadelphia, 1845) ; Luigi Amabile, *Il Santo Officio della Inquisizione in Napoli* (Città di Castello, 1892, 2 vols.) ; based on the sources ; vol. ii is largely composed of original documents ; H. C. Lea, *The Inquisition in the Spanish Dependencies* (New York, 1908), chapter ii.

CHAPTER XX

THE HAPSBURG PERIL, AND THE ANNEXATION OF NAVARRE

THE foreign policy of the last twelve years of the reign of Ferdinand the Catholic was largely shaped by that long series of family bereavements, which, beginning with the death of his son-in-law, Affonso of Portugal, in 1491, continued almost without interruption till near the end. Every single one of his dynastic ventures was attended with the most persistent ill fortune.

The marriage of Catharine of Aragon to Arthur, Prince of Wales, which had been arranged by the treaty of Medina del Campo in 1489, was not actually celebrated until 1501. The tender years of the children were the obvious reason for the long delay. In the course of it the original agreement of 1489 was abandoned, and another was substituted for it in 1496. Constant bickerings and manoeuvrings for diplomatic advantage characterized the relations of Spain and England during this period and in the succeeding years. Ferdinand and Isabella angered the Tudor king by coolly throwing over the treaty of Medina del Campo after they had got back Cerdagne and Roussillon. They declared, on the shallowest of pretexts, that the marriage which it had provided for could not take place.[1] They held out the prospect of a renewal of the negotiations for it, however, in order to induce Henry to join the League of Venice against France in 1495; and though the English king did

[1] W. Busch, *England under the Tudors*, pp. 91 ff.

not promptly accede to their desires, his position was so much stronger than it had previously been that the Catholic Kings felt it unwise to flout him again. A fresh marriage treaty, accordingly, was signed in October, 1496.[1] The haggling over details continued up to the proxy wedding, which was celebrated in May, 1499, and even beyond it, until the arrival of the princess in England in the autumn of 1501. The negotiations were at one time involved with the career of the pretender Perkin Warbeck, and also with the commercial and shipping rivalries between the two realms; and their outcome was powerfully affected by the conduct of the Spanish representative at London, Rodrigo de Puebla, who, in revenge for the nonpayment of his salary by the Catholic Kings, labored rather in the interests of England than of Spain.[2] Finally, however, the last difficulty was cleared away. On August 25, 1501, the princess sailed from Corunna, and, after having been driven back to Laredo by a storm, finally reached Plymouth, October 2. The wedding was celebrated at St. Paul's on November 14, and one half the large dowry of 200,000 scudi which had been agreed upon was paid over at the same time.[3]

Meanwhile the Catholic Kings had been cruelly stricken at home, as we have already seen, by the death of Prince John without heirs, October 4, 1497, six months after his union with Margaret of Austria, and again by the losses on August 23, 1498, and July 20, 1500, respectively, of the Princess Isabella and of her surviving child Prince Miguel.[4] The heiress to the thrones of Spain and the Spanish Empire was now the Princess Joanna, third child and second daugh-

[1] Busch, *op. cit.*, pp. 127–140 and ff.

[2] Busch, pp. 133 ff., 351 f.; Puebla was one of the first, if not actually the first resident ambassador in the annals of European diplomacy, not counting the representatives of the Italian states.

O. Krauske, *Die Entwickelung der ständigen Diplomatie* (Leipsic, 1885), p. 75.

[3] Busch, pp. 140, 353 f.

[4] *Ante*, pp. 267 f.

ter of the Catholic Kings, who had wedded the Archduke Philip the Handsome on October 20, 1496, at Lille, and had already given him two children, Eleanor, born November 16, 1498, and Charles, born February 24, 1500.[1] The latter on his father's side would inherit the Hapsburg domains in the Netherlands, Burgundy, Austria, and the Empire, and would probably ultimately be elected Emperor. If from his mother he received the Spanish thrones as well, the sovereignty of all the realms of Ferdinand and Isabella would be carried out of the peninsula to a foreign dynasty, which was already heavily loaded down with responsibilities in other parts of Europe, and cared far less for Spanish aims and aspirations than for the increase of its family dominions. Such was the really terrible catastrophe — threatening to undermine the foundations of all their splendid work — which now stared the Catholic Kings in the face. They had taken every reasonable precaution to prevent it, by the alliances which they had arranged for their two eldest children, but the hand of death had defied them. The double Hapsburg marriage, from which they had hoped to gain so much, promised now to spell the end of Spain for the Spaniards. And the worst part of the situation was that it seemed impossible to find any remedy. The rights of Joanna and her children, under the law of the land, were clear. The sovereigns had no hope of further offspring themselves, and no issue of any other marriage or of any collateral line could have a valid title to the thrones of both Aragon and Castile. Moreover, even if Ferdinand and Isabella were prepared to override all law and hereditary right in the interests of national independence, they could not well afford to insult and defy the house of Hapsburg, especially when they themselves were on such bad terms with

---

[1] A. Rodríguez Villa, *Juana la Loca*, pp. 33, 41.

France. It was a wonderful stroke of good luck for the future Charles V, as a contemporary historian sagely observed, that Prince Miguel, the sole remaining obstacle to his inheritance of the Spanish throne, should have died when the son of Philip and Joanna was but four months old;[1] and his very dynastically minded grandfather, Maximilian, did not propose that the infant should be robbed of even the tiniest portion of the fruits of his good fortune. The Spanish monarchs must have felt unutterable things at the way that their marriage policy had worked out, but for the moment there was little for them to do but to sit still and trust that something would turn up.

Common prudence, however, pointed to the wisdom of maintaining all existing ties with other friendly states, in order to be perfectly ready for whatever the future might hold; and this consideration was doubtless uppermost in the minds of Ferdinand and Isabella when, in April, 1502, their attention was once more focussed on England by the sudden and unexpected death of Arthur, Prince of Wales. The close bond that had united the two nations since his marriage with Catharine in the previous November was snapped; and it was essential for Spain that it should be promptly mended — the more so as she was obviously about to come to blows with France over the partition of Naples. The situation that had obtained at the time of the treaty of Medina del Campo was, in fact, almost precisely reversed: Spain, not England, was now in the position of suppliant, and Ferdinand and Isabella lost no time in despatching to London a special ambassador, the Duke of Estrada, to ask for a renewal of the previous treaty and a second marriage for Catharine with Arthur's younger brother, the future Henry VIII.[2] The Tudor sovereign

---

[1] Gómara, *Annals of Charles V*, p. 48.   [2] Busch, *op. cit.*, pp. 200 f.

was ready to negotiate, though he fully understood the strength of his own position, and gladly availed himself of it in later years to pay Ferdinand back for the humiliations which that monarch had previously inflicted on him. For the time being, however, all went smoothly. The new marriage treaty was drawn up, and ratified on June 23, 1503, providing for the celebration of the wedding in 1506, when young Henry should have completed his fifteenth year, and for the payment of the rest of Catharine's dowry at the same time.[1] Neither of these events, however, actually took place until after Henry VIII's accession in 1509. Though it was generally understood that Catharine's first marriage had never been more than a union in form, Ferdinand asked the Pope to grant the necessary bull of dispensation for her second, so phrased as to cover the case even if the previous one had been fully consummated, and the Pope acceded to his request. The final instrument, which arrived in England in the summer of 1505, did indeed introduce a faint element of uncertainty in the situation by speaking of Catharine's first marriage as *forsan consummatum*, but since the brief or preliminary summary of it which was sent to Spain in the previous year to comfort the dying Isabella omitted the word *forsan*, there could be no reasonable doubt of the papal intentions.[2] Both these documents were to play an important part twenty-five years later in the history of Henry VIII's divorce; and it seems to indicate an almost prophetic insight that the Spanish monarch should have taken such pains at this early date to safeguard the validity of his daughter's second marriage. Certainly the great energy and persistence displayed by Ferdinand in regard to the English match

[1] Busch, pp. 202 ff., 375 f. The first half of the dowry for Catharine's first marriage, paid on the occasion of her union with Arthur, was accepted as the equivalent portion of that for her second.

[2] Busch, pp. 202–205, 376–378.

shows that he was greatly disturbed over the state of his relations with the continental powers. He was at war with France. The Hapsburg alliances, from which he had hoped so much, actually menaced the independence of Spain; and the Portuguese marriages, by which he had sought to forestall this last danger, had turned out fruitless. No wonder, in view of all the circumstances, that he clutched at England.

Meantime the sovereigns had been reminded of the imminence of the Hapsburg peril through a visit from Philip and Joanna, who, after having been sumptuously entertained by King Louis of France, arrived in Castile from the Netherlands, in January, 1502.[1] The purpose of their coming was to receive the recognition of the Cortes as lawful heirs of the throne, and to enable the Archduke to become familiar with his future subjects. Ever since the death of Prince Miguel, Ferdinand and Isabella had begged them to come to Spain, they doubtless hoped that by approaching Philip while he was still young they might make him see things through their eyes, forget his Burgundian affiliations, become a true Spaniard and work primarily in Spanish interests.[2] But it was to be a long half century more before any real Hispanicization of the Hapsburgs was possible; certainly Philip was never susceptible to the process, and Charles V did not succumb to it until the end of his life. In the latter case it was dynastic ambition that stood in the way; with the Archduke it was mere shallowness and want of character. It had never been possible, in fact, to make him take a serious interest in anything, or pursue any plan to its logical conclusion. He had already got into difficulties with his mercurial father Maximilian in

[1] Prescott, iii, pp. 59 f., and references there.

[2] *Correspondencia de Gómez de Fuensalida*, p. xxviii.

the Netherlands; the sober energy and grandiose projects of the Spanish monarchs did not appeal to him at all. It is only too easy to see how utterly he disappointed the hopes of the Catholic Kings. The contemporary chroniclers give several instances to prove it,[1] and one can read much more between the lines. The conduct of the Archduke's Flemish attendants also elicited the most unfavorable comment. They had nothing in common with the Spaniards, and seemed solely intent on the acquisition of fat pensions for themselves. Moreover, Philip was most anxious to return as soon as possible to his native land. After his recognition, with his wife, by the Castilian Cortes at Toledo, and by those of Aragon at Saragossa,[2] he made his preparations to depart, despite the fact that Joanna, on account of an approaching confinement, was unable to accompany him. As on his journey to Spain, the Archduke determined to travel by way of France, toward whose monarch he had manifested a disposition far too friendly to suit either his father or his father-in-law; however, in view of the course of the war in Naples and the uncertainties of the situation in other parts of Europe, Ferdinand decided that it would do no harm to take advantage of Philip's offer to open negotiations for a peace. The result was the treaty of Lyons of April 5, 1503, which we have already noticed in connection with the Neapolitan war.[3] Philip had so grossly exceeded 'his instructions in arranging it that Ferdinand was not without justification for his refusal to ratify; and the only practical result of it, as we have previously observed, was to afford the Great Captain a precious respite in southern Italy, which he knew how to utilize far more effectively than did his foe. But the whole episode showed what the

[1] Cf., e.g., Peter Martyr, *Opus Epistolarum*, ep. ccl.
[2] Prescott, iii, pp. 61 f., and notes;
Rodríguez Villa, *op. cit.*, pp. 65 f.
[3] *Ante*, p. 306; Rodríguez Villa, pp. 72-81.

diplomacy of the years 1504–11 was to demonstrate more clearly still, that in view of the possibility of trouble with the house of Austria Ferdinand was prepared, at least temporarily, to seek an adjustment of his difficulties with France.

The next and perhaps the most stunning blow of all — not only in itself but also in the tremendous consequences with which it was fraught — was the death of Queen Isabella at Medina del Campo on November 26, 1504. By it the tie that had united the Spanish kingdoms was once more broken; for Isabella's will expressly provided that the thrones of Leon and Castile should descend to her daughter Joanna, as 'queen proprietress,' and to her husband Philip as king consort. Only in case Joanna should be absent from the realm, or "being present should prove unwilling or unable to govern," was her father to act as regent in Castile until the future Charles V should come of age; otherwise Ferdinand was henceforth to be nothing more than the king of the realms of the Crown of Aragon.[1] It was a bathos almost inconceivable for a man who had been so powerful, and Ferdinand's was not the sort of disposition that would submit to it without a struggle. Moreover he was not in all respects unfavorably situated for a contest against his daughter and son-in-law for the retention of the throne of Castile. The law of the land was indeed clearly against him; but on the other hand the national detestation of subjection to foreign authority would tell heavily in his favor. His war with France was over. Furthermore the Princess Joanna, who had given birth to her second son, the future Emperor Ferdinand, at Alcalá de Henares on March 10, 1502, had returned to the Netherlands in the

---

[1] Clause from the will of Isabella printed in Rodríguez Villa, *op. cit.*, pp. 429–431.

spring of 1504, eight months before her mother's death.[1] It is quite possible that her departure was hastened by ill-treatment at the hands of Ferdinand.[2] Certainly her absence from Spain at the time of Isabella's demise afforded her father a legal opportunity to act as regent in Castile until her return, without transgressing the provisions of her mother's will; it thus gave the Catholic King an enormous initial advantage over his children in the struggle for the throne of that realm. Finally, there were the very grave doubts raised by the phrase in Queen Isabella's will about Joanna's being "unwilling or unable to govern." We know that the possibility indicated by these words had been contemplated at least two years before Isabella's death and communicated to the Cortes; and the natural inference is that Joanna had already begun to show signs of the mental derangement which first became unquestioned and notorious after the death of her husband. There is, however, no documentary evidence to show that she was insane at this early date,[3] though she was certainly neurotic and hysterical. What seems most probable is that at the time of Philip's visit to Spain in 1502, Ferdinand and Isabella had made up their minds, if possible, to prevent her succession on account of the foreign rule which it would inevitably entail, and to utilize any signs of abnormality which the princess may have given as an excuse for setting her aside. At any rate the words in the queen's will gave Ferdinand a powerful weapon for a struggle against the harsh fate which the tragic consequences of the Hapsburg marriages had brought upon

[1] Rodríguez Villa, pp. 81, 92.

[2] Gómara, *Annals of Charles V*, p. 14: "His Majesty could never keep her here because of what he did and said to her."

[3] The tales of contemporaries, referred to in Prescott, iii, p. 162, are hard to substantiate. Fifty years ago, Bergenroth thought he had discovered proofs that Joanna was disloyal to the church, and that her father and mother had for that reason determined that she was not to be permitted to reign (*Calendar of State Papers, Spanish*, supplement to vols. i and ii, pp. xxvii ff.); his conclusions, however, have not been accepted.

him, and against the carrying of the sovereignty of Castile beyond the borders of Spain. If his conduct in the succeeding years seems deficient in parental solicitude, we must not forget that he was fighting for the cause of national independence as well as for his own hand.

There could be no question that Philip and Joanna intended to make all possible efforts to substantiate their claims to the Castilian throne. The Archduke assumed the title of king of Castile as soon as he had learned of his mother-in-law's death. He did everything in his power through his agent, Juan Manuel, to stir up disaffection against Ferdinand, particularly among the Castilian grandees. He wrote to his father-in-law to demand that he resign the Castilian regency and retire to his own domains. He even put forward claims to Naples on the ground that it had been conquered by the armies of Castile and was therefore a dependency of that realm, and strove to win away the Great Captain from his allegiance.[1] And at first King Ferdinand seemed to acquiesce in what he was powerless to prevent. He caused Philip and Joanna to be formally proclaimed as lawful sovereigns of Castile; he also summoned the Castilian Cortes to Toro on January 11, 1505, in order that the recognition might be confirmed.[2] But Ferdinand, like his father before him, was never so dangerous as when apparently at the end of his resources. He took good care that these same Cortes at Toro should ratify his title to the regency during the absence of his daughter; moreover he permitted the assembly openly to allude to Joanna's mental infirmities, and to the steps to be taken in view of them.[3] Still more important were his measures to strengthen his

---

[1] *Calendar of State Papers, Spanish,* supplement to vols. i and ii, pp. xxxiii, 73–75; Rodríguez Villa, p. 99; Prescott, iii, pp. 198–201.

[2] Zurita, vi, ff. 3–5; Rodríguez Villa, p. 96.

[3] Zurita, vi, ff. 5–7.

position abroad — his primary object being, of course, to
gain for himself at the expense of his son-in-law the friendship and alliance of France. To accomplish this some sacrifice, immediate or prospective, of the Spanish conquests
in Naples would inevitably be necessary, for Louis XII was
still very sore over the defeats that he had sustained there;
but Ferdinand was accustomed to rapid changes of front in
that quarter, and was prepared to bid high for the prize he
had set himself to win. The net result was a treaty, signed
by the French king and Ferdinand's representatives at Blois,
on October 12, 1505, providing for the marriage of the
Spanish monarch to Germaine de Foix, niece of Louis XII,
and granddaughter of Ferdinand's own half-sister Eleanor;[1]
this arrangement also incidentally strengthened the claims
of the Catholic King to Navarre, which had been held by
the senior branch of Germaine's family until it passed by
marriage to the Albrets in 1484. Louis XII at the same
time resigned all his rights to Naples to Germaine, to descend after her death to her children; he carefully stipulated,
however, that if she died without issue the French crown
was to get back those portions of the realm which had been
assigned to him by the treaty of Granada in 1500.[2]

Prescott, who is very severe on the "disgraceful and most
impolitic terms of this compact," points out that if Germaine
had had a son, he would have inherited all the realms of the
Crown of Aragon, and thus nullified the best results of the
marriage of Ferdinand and Isabella by once more severing
the destinies of the Iberian kingdoms; if, on the other hand,
she died childless, it was provided that a large share of
Spain's recent Neapolitan conquests should be surrendered.[3]
But if we fix our eyes on the immediate effects of the treaty,

[1] Cf. genealogical tables, p. 3, *supra*, and p. 340, *infra*.
[2] J. Dumont, *Corps universal diplo-*
matique, iv, 1, pp. 72–74.
[3] Prescott, iii, pp. 206 f.

rather than on the distant contingencies that were contemplated in it, we shall probably conclude that this verdict
is much too harsh. The all-important thing for Ferdinand,
at the moment, was to secure French support and the prospect of an heir — both of them indispensable weapons in
the impending contest for the Castilian throne and the
cause of Spanish independence of foreign sovereignty; and
with these the treaty provided him. The stipulation about
the partition of Naples in case Germaine should die childless was far too remote to cause him serious hesitation.
He had cheated Louis XII in that kingdom before, and
openly boasted that he would do so again; and as a matter
of fact, neither the French king nor his successors ever got
back the coveted lands. If, on the other hand, his new
queen had borne him a male child who had survived, there
is every probability that he would have labored with might
and main to set him on the Castilian throne to the prejudice
of the Hapsburgs, and at least a fair chance that he would
have succeeded. The treaty of Blois was not made merely
"in order to secure the brief possession of a barren authority"
or "to gratify some unworthy feelings of revenge." It was
a shrewd political move, virtually dictated by the needs of
the moment, but also calculated better than any other to
preserve the safety and independence of Spain at a serious
crisis in her career.[1]

[1] There is a story, accepted by
Gómara, Zurita, Sandoval, and later
Spanish historians, though apparently
not supported by any document, that
before approaching Louis of France,
Ferdinand attempted to drag la Beltraneja from the cloister and marry her,
"in order," so Gómara adds, "that with
her as his queen, he might reënforce his
claim to Castile as against King Philip."
Apparently the fact that he had loudly
proclaimed her illegitimacy thirty-five
years before did not trouble him in the
least; but his plan was wrecked on
the lady's firm refusal to entertain his
proposals. Cf. Gómara, p. 17; Prescott, iii, p. 204, note; Sitges, *Enrique IV*,
pp. 366 f. If any credence can be given
to this tale, it certainly shows that Ferdinand's principal object at this stage
was to keep the Castilian succession in
his own hands, and thus strengthens the
interpretation, which has been offered
above, of the reasons that subsequently
caused him to marry Germaine.

The marriage of Ferdinand and Germaine took place on March 18, 1506, at Dueñas near Valladolid; and six weeks later Philip and Joanna, who had this time been refused permission to cross France, arrived by sea at Corunna.[1] There had been much correspondence between the different parties during the previous year; in the course of it an arrangement had been evolved for the administration of Castile under the joint names of Ferdinand, Philip, and Joanna, and the handing over of one half the public revenues to the Catholic King.[2] This was obviously, however, merely a temporary makeshift, designed to tide things over until Philip and Joanna should reach Castile; a new settlement was inevitable as soon as the persons concerned could meet and talk things over. The interview finally took place, in the month of June, in the little village of Villafafila in the Galician mountains. Ferdinand arrived at the appointed place with a few faithful attendants mounted on mules, "with love in his heart and peace in his hands;" while his gorgeous son-in-law appeared at the head of a powerful army, and obviously enjoyed, for the moment, the support of the Castilian grandees.[3] And at first it seemed as if the cause of Philip and Joanna was to triumph all along the line; for Ferdinand signed an agreement in which he promised to retire to Aragon, and to surrender the government of Castile to his "most beloved children." An additional treaty, however, robbed Joanna of her share in the spoils on account of "her infirmities and sufferings, which for the sake of her honor are not specified"; Ferdinand and Philip bound themselves to use their united forces to prevent her from meddling in the government; the father betrayed his daughter and the husband his wife. Thus Philip thought

---

[1] Prescott, iii, pp. 208–211.
[2] Zurita, vi, ff. 38–42.
[3] *Calendar of State Papers, Spanish*, supplement to vols. i and ii, pp. xxxiv–xxxv.

to obtain the goal of his ambitions and to secure for himself undisputed control in Castile; but he little knew the man with whom he was dealing. On the afternoon of June 27, the very same day that the two treaties were signed, Ferdinand made a solemn protestation that he refused to recognize their validity, on the ground that they had been extorted from him under compulsion; and that he would never consent 'that his daughter should be deprived of her liberty or of her rights as hereditary proprietress of this kingdom.'[1] Prescott is at a loss "to reconcile this monstrous tissue of incongruity and dissimulation with any motives of necessity or expediency;"[2] but it is still more difficult to conceive of Ferdinand the Catholic as intriguing and deceiving without a definite purpose in view. The protestation was primarily valuable as a step toward disposing of his arch-enemy Philip; yet despite all its assertions that Joanna was lawful queen of Castile, it nowhere denied that she was mentally incapable of reigning, and consequently created no impediment to getting rid of her in case it should prove ultimately desirable to do so. Clearly Ferdinand wished to leave himself a free hand in Castile, in order that he might be able to act there in whatever way should seem most advantageous when the opportunity should arise; and the determining factor in the situation was the possibility of male issue by Queen Germaine. Prescott cannot seem to get rid of the idea that Ferdinand cared little or nothing for the cause of Spanish unity. He implies that the king's desire for male issue by his new wife is explained by his wish to deprive the Hapsburgs of the Aragonese realms and their dependencies, and that in order to attain that end he was willing to set up the old lines of cleavage within the Iberian

[1] *Calendar of State Papers, Spanish,* supplement to vols. i and ii, pp. 78–85.
[2] Prescott, iii, p. 219.

Peninsula.[1] But it seems far more consistent with the character of Ferdinand as we know it, to conclude that if the son whom Queen Germaine finally bore him, May 3, 1509, had survived,[2] the Catholic King would have strained every nerve to win for him the throne of Castile in defiance of the law of the land, and to hand down the united crowns to a Spaniard. The memory of his father's treatment of Charles of Viana was still fresh in his mind ; he had himself already been a party to one usurpation of the throne of the western kingdom in the interests of political expediency; why should he not have attempted it again ? The question is not susceptible of proof either one way or the other; but Ferdinand's conduct can be as adequately explained on the hypothesis of a somewhat unscrupulous patriotism as by assuming that his every move was inspired merely by personal jealousy and hate.

In any case, the Catholic King was powerless to give vent to his real feelings in the summer of 1506. He had another affecting interview with Philip on July 5, during which the most perfect apparent harmony prevailed between them; and he wrote him a letter from Saragossa on the twenty-ninth, urging him to treat Joanna lovingly, and that they should live together as a good husband and wife ought to do.[3] He not only fulfilled his promise to retire to Aragon ; on September 4, 1506, he embarked at Barcelona for Genoa on the way to settle the affairs of his kingdom of Naples.[4] But he had been only a few weeks on Italian soil when he was overtaken by the news of the sudden death of his son-

---

[1] Prescott, iii, pp. 206 f., 353.

[2] The child, who was named John, "only lived one hour," according to Gómara, p. 26. Cf. also Zurita, vi, f. 192, for a curious passage to the effect that the name John had almost always proved unlucky for kings and princes, in France and in England as well as in Spain.

[3] *Calendar of State Papers, Spanish,* supplement to vols. i and ii, pp. xxxvi-xxxvii.

[4] Prescott, iii, p. 240.

in-law Philip at Burgos, on September 25. The event was so convenient for his purposes that the accusation of poison was inevitable, as was the case with so many of the enemies of his redoubtable father. The physicians, however, were unanimous in declaring that the Archduke's death was due to natural causes, and they apparently convinced the contemporary historians,[1] though some modern writers incline to take the other view.[2] But whether or not King Ferdinand had any reason to expect that Philip would not long survive his departure for Italy, he certainly showed no impatience to return. Not until the late summer of 1507 was he back again in Castile. In the meantime he had settled the affairs of Naples, relieved the Great Captain, of whose popularity and independence he had become profoundly jealous,[3] from his duties as viceroy there, and held his famous interview with Louis XII of France at Savona, to which we shall return in another place.[4] Did the king deliberately stay away in order that suspicion and hostility might have a chance to cool down, and that the rebel barons might once more be brought into subjection for him by the iron hand of Cardinal Ximenes?[5] Or was his absence prolonged in the belief that his daughter's mental infirmities would increase the faster if she were left to bear her grief alone? There can be no doubt that Joanna became hopelessly insane immediately after her husband's death, though it was not till February 14, 1509, that she finally withdrew to the gloomy fortress of Tordesillas, to live out in dreary solitude the remaining forty-six years of her existence.[6] In the interim between her father's

[1] Zurita, vi, f. 80.

[2] *Calendar of State Papers, Spanish,* supplement to vols. i and ii, p. xxxvii; Burke, *History of Spain,* ii, p. 250. Prescott, iii, p. 243, and Rodríguez Villa, pp. 180 f., however, believe that the

Archduke died a natural death.

[3] *Crónicas del Gran Capitán,* in *N. B. A. E.,* x, pp. 244–249, 440–453.

[4] Prescott, iii, pp. 254–279.

[5] Rodríguez Villa, pp. 197 ff.

[6] *Calendar of State Papers, Spanish,*

return and her final retirement, she remained under the close supervision of Ferdinand. The latter had every reason to keep a strict watch upon her, for her hand was sought by various princes at the time, as a means of gaining title to the throne of Castile.[1] But all these proposals were firmly refused, on the plea of Joanna's insanity; and meantime her father left nothing undone which should serve to confirm his title to the administration of her kingdom. Some of the unruly barons, who had not forgotten how their ancestors had lorded it over the land during the periods of monarchical abasement, were inclined to raise their heads in revolt. Most of them, however, had been so thoroughly disciplined in the previous thirty years that they soon tired of anarchy and gave in their submission; and Ferdinand's final triumph over the factions was confirmed by the Cortes at Madrid, in October, 1510, when he solemnly took the oath as administrator of the realm in his daughter's name.[2] For the rest of his life, at least, the Hapsburgs were to be kept out, and Spain preserved to the Spaniards.

From this time onward the dynastic question falls into the background. Ferdinand's animosity to Philip transferred itself on the latter's death to his eldest son and heir, the future Emperor Charles V, who remained in the Netherlands until 1517, and certainly gave few signs in his early years of the abilities which developed so rapidly when he became possessed of his great inheritance. But the failure of male issue by Queen Germaine rendered it impossible for the Catholic King to turn his feelings to any practical account, and though the thought of the fate that awaited his kingdoms after his death must have embittered his de-

supplement to vols. i and ii, pp. xxxix–xli; Zurita, vi, ff. 178–179.

[1] One of the most prominent of her suitors was King Henry VII of England, the chief aim of whose later years was to pay off old scores against the Catholic King; cf. Busch, pp. 214 f.

[2] Zurita, vi, f. 233.

clining years, he was absolutely powerless to avert it. In only one way did he give any outward evidence of the feelings that burned within his breast, and that was by lavishing every sort of care and affection on Charles's younger brother, the future Emperor Ferdinand, who had been named for his maternal grandfather, and continued to reside in Spain until after the latter's death. The old king took an intense interest in his education, and made every effort to inculcate in him the Spanish point of view.[1] He would doubtless have been delighted to put him in his brother's place, and may possibly have laid schemes to that effect. Some historians have even thought that the real key to the old king's tortuous Italian diplomacy from 1509 to 1514 was his desire to create a new realm for his beloved youngest grandson out of Sicily, Naples, and any other states he might manage to acquire in the peninsula — the whole to be protected by the German, Austrian, and Spanish territories which would inevitably go to Charles.[2] Of all this there is no proof, for the Catholic King was a past master of the art of covering his tracks, and our only means of estimating the policy of the last part of the reign is the one definite achievement that resulted from it, namely, the acquisition of Navarre. To the story of this final conquest we now turn, but our picture of the latter years of the old king will be the more accurate if we bear in mind the gloomy prospect with which he was perpetually confronted at home : the assurance, growing stronger and stronger as time went on, that the empire which he had been at such pains to build up was destined to be inherited by a foreign prince.

From 1506 to 1511 the external policy of Ferdinand the Catholic continued to be based on friendship with France ;

[1] Galíndez Carbajal, *Anales Breves*,   Prescott, iii, pp. 364 f.
año 1516 (*D. I. E.*, xviii, pp. 338–350) ;   [2] Burke, ii, pp. 270–273.

the Hapsburg danger remained far too pressing for several years after Philip's death to admit of any other possibility. The Catholic King was constantly reminded of Maximilian's jealousy and hatred during this period by the visits to Spain of secret agents from the Netherlands, who did their utmost to fan the smouldering flames of discontent among the Castilian grandees and to persuade them to rise in revolt against his regency. One of these envoys had to be imprisoned; another was shown out of the realm directly after his arrival at Laredo.[1] Moreover, it was not merely a question of Ferdinand's maintaining his position as administrator in Castile. There is reason to believe, as we have already seen, that until the disappointment of his hopes of male issue by Queen Germaine he contemplated assuming the aggressive and ousting the Hapsburgs entirely. Clearly it would be impossible to fight both Hapsburgs and Valois at once. He had already scored heavily against the latter in the Neapolitan war, and prudence now dictated the maintenance of cordial relations with them, in order to be perfectly certain of their neutrality, and if possible of their alliance, in case Spain should come to blows with the former. Consequently, we find the rapprochement which began at the treaty of Blois, in October, 1505, continued and solidified in the succeeding years. In June, 1507, after his departure from Naples, Ferdinand met Louis at Savona near Genoa, where the latter had gone to suppress a revolt. The interview there lasted four days. Beneath the attendant festivities and the notable honors accorded to the Great Captain, it is difficult to determine what serious business was transacted on this occasion. Probably those who have seen evidences in it of a Franco-Spanish alliance against the Hapsburgs, or even of negotiations

---

[1] A. Walther, *Die Anfänge Karls V.*, p. 82.

preliminary to the league which was formed so shortly afterwards against the Venetians, have considerably exaggerated the importance of the whole affair. The only thing that the documents prove to have been definitely settled at Savona was the maintenance of the existing peace on the basis of the status quo for at least six months to come.[1] This, however, was quite enough to show that Ferdinand and Louis both realized that for the present neither was strong enough to be able to dispense with the support of the other.

In the following year, when France made peace with the Emperor, and joined with him and with Pope Julius II in the famous League of Cambray against Venice, the Spanish monarch seized the first opportunity to get himself included in the alliance.[2] To let Louis and Maximilian throw their united forces into Italy, while he stood completely aside, would mean danger to his new dominions in Naples; besides, if the king of France and the Emperor got a chance to lay their heads together while he was excluded from their deliberations, might it not result in the immediate sending of the Archduke Charles into Spain to claim the Castilian inheritance, the challenging of his regency there, and the upsetting of many other plans? There was also one positive advantage to be derived by Spain from entering the league against Venice, namely, the recovery of the Adriatic seaports of the kingdom of Naples, which had been intermittently in Venetian hands since 1495.[3] All these considerations combined to make Ferdinand throw in his lot with the allies; but he did so with little enthusiasm, and with a firm resolve, doubtless strengthened by the fact that the Great Captain was in retirement, to shirk the military

[1] R. de Maulde, "L'entrevue de Savone," in *Revue d'histoire diplomatique*, iv (1890), pp. 583–590.

[2] Walther, *op. cit.*, pp. 82 f.
[3] Prescott, iii, p. 312; and *ante*, p. 294.

duties assigned to him. The only part of the campaign that really interested him, the recovery of the Neapolitan ports, he accomplished with almost no effort at all; for Venice, comprehending the necessity of concentrating against France, virtually surrendered them without attempting a defence.[1] But the rest of the war the Spanish monarch left to his confederates, content merely to keep close enough in touch with them to make sure that they meditated no treachery. He knew the nature of Italian politics well enough to realize how rapidly the combinations changed, and doubtless foresaw that if Louis were permitted to gather in most of the spoils of the campaign, he would infallibly be made to pay for it in the near future. As usual his judgment was correct. Even before the Venetians had been brought to their knees, the allies had become so jealous of the preponderance of the French in northern Italy that everything was ripe for a complete diplomatic revolution.

By this time, moreover — that is, in the winter of 1510–11 — Ferdinand's own attitude towards the foreign situation had undergone a change. His hopes of male issue by Queen Germaine were practically gone. The ultimate succession of the Hapsburgs to the Spanish throne was consequently inevitable. On the other hand, there was no immediate prospect that the Archduke Charles would be sent to Castile. It seemed likely that his own regency in the western kingdom, which Maximilian had formally recognized on December 12, 1509,[2] would be permitted to continue unchallenged for many years to come. French aid, in other words, was no longer so indispensable for him in the dynastic problem, either for offensive or defensive purposes, as it had been before. And, finally, there was one more territorial conquest which he had ardently desired

---

[1] Zurita, vi, ff. 189–190.   [2] *Calendar of State Papers, Spanish*, ii, pp. 32 f.

since his boyhood, and was determined, if possible, to carry through before he died — a necessity for the attainment of Spain's natural boundaries on the north, yet scarcely to be accomplished without incurring the displeasure of France — the conquest of the little mountain kingdom of Navarre. When, therefore, the European powers, under the lead of Julius II, prepared to turn on Louis XII for the purpose of expelling him from Italy, Ferdinand was secretly rejoiced and promptly joined the confederates.[1] He had no more use for the Valois now; and if they were completely isolated, he might well derive territorial advantage from the fact in a region on which he had long had his eye. Into the well known story of the Italian campaigns of the Holy League we need not enter here, for though Gonsalvo's veterans formed the backbone of its armies, and Ramon de Cardona, viceroy of Naples, was on the whole its most successful general, Spain reaped no direct reward from its victories in that quarter. We must rather concentrate our attention on what is usually regarded as a side issue of the war, and see how Ferdinand utilized for his own purposes in the Pyrenees the fact that most of the French forces were engaged beyond the Alps.

Since the failure of John II of Aragon to get it away from the children of his first marriage, we have had no occasion to follow the fortunes of Navarre. Eleanor, the sister of the unfortunate Prince of Viana, and heiress, after his death, of the little Pyrenean kingdom, had carried it, as a result of a marriage which had been arranged for her in 1434,[2] into the possession of the powerful French house of Foix, whose principal domains, in Béarn and Bigorre, lay contiguous to Navarre on the northeast. Had she not had the good

---

[1] The league was formally consti-tuted on October 4, 1511.

[2] H. Courteault, *Gaston de Foix*, pp. 26 ff.

fortune to survive her treacherous father — though only for the short period of twenty-one days — her descendants would in all probability have been despoiled of their inheritance; but as it was, the kingdom passed, on her death in 1479, to her youthful grandson, Francis Phoebus, the eldest child of her eldest son Gaston, who had predeceased her.[1] Francis Phoebus, however, also died in 1483, leaving no children, so that Navarre was inherited on his death by his younger sister, Catharine, and was by her in turn transferred, through her marriage in the following year, to Jean d'Albret, son and heir of Alain le Grand, the most eminent of the feudal nobles of the south of France.[2] Navarre had thus been strengthened by dynastic unions with a number of adjacent states; but it had also been sadly shaken and disrupted by the frequent changes of its rulers; and, finally, it was seriously menaced by the jealousy of the neighboring powers. Ferdinand and Isabella had at one time planned to marry their son John to Catharine of

[1] Boissonnade, *La réunion de la Navarre à la Castille*, pp. 21–32. The following table will indicate the different relationships.

[2] A. Luchaire, *Alain le Grand*, chap. i.

CHARLES III (of Évreux)
King of Navarre (1387–1425) = Eleanor, dau. of Henry II of Castile

JOHN II of Aragon = Blanche, ob. 1441

Gaston IV de Foix=3. ELEANOR, ob. 1479 | 1. Charles, ob. s. p. 1461 | 2. Blanche = Henry IV of Castile

Gaston, ob. 1470 = Madeleine, dau. of Charles VII of France | John = Mary, sister of Louis XII of France

Gaston, ob. s. p. 1512 | Ferdinand the Catholic (2) = (1) Germaine

FRANCIS PHOEBUS, ob. s.p. 1483 | CATHARINE ob. 1517 = JEAN d' Albret, ob. 1516

Margaret, sister of Francis I of France = HENRY II, ob. 1555

JEANNE, 1555–1572 = Anthony of Bourbon

HENRY III (IV of France), ob. 1610

Foix,[1] and never really forgave the Albrets who had forestalled them; moreover, the younger line of the house of
Foix, represented at first by John, second son of Eleanor
of Aragon, and, after his death in 1500, by his children,
Germaine, the second wife of King Ferdinand, and Gaston,
the hero of the battle of Ravenna, insisted on treating the
Albret claims as a usurpation, and strove for a long time
to win the succession for themselves.[2]

Most important of all, however, was the effect on Navarre
of the newborn hostility between France and Spain. These
two states had now definitely entered upon a contest for
the supremacy in Western Europe. Navarre held the keys
to the passes of the western Pyrenees, Spain could not afford to let the destinies of the Albrets' realm be exclusively
guided by France, nor could France tolerate its permanent
subjection to the influence of Spain. The little mountain
kingdom, heretofore secluded and remote, became all at once
the battleground of opposing policies. In this long struggle
for the control of the Navarrese government, the Catholic
Kings, despite the fact that the local dynasty was rather
French than Spanish in its affiliations, were on the whole
victorious. By a series of eight treaties, between 1476 and
1500, they succeeded in reducing the Navarrese sovereigns to
the position of protégés of Spain. Their ultimate object
was doubtless annexation, but for this the time was not
yet ripe, and Ferdinand never did anything in a hurry.[3]
Besides, in the early years of the sixteenth century, a fresh
complication arose, when the Hapsburgs, in anticipation
of trouble with the Spanish monarchs, offered their alliance
to the sovereigns of Navarre in return for their support in
the successional quarrel in Castile. An understanding was

---

[1] Prescott, i, p. 415.   [2] Boissonnade, op. cit., pp. 57, 100, et passim.
[3] Boissonnade, p. 561.

reached between the houses of Austria and Albret, which
continued to be a thorn in the side of Ferdinand the Catholic
long after the death of Archduke Philip; it was also most
displeasing to Louis XII.[1] During the period immediately
preceding the war of the Holy League, the Navarrese managed to play off the ambitions of these different foreign
potentates against one another in such a way as to preserve
their independence. Finally, at the opening of the conflict,
they announced their intention of remaining strictly neutral,
in the belief that the hostile powers would so exhaust themselves during the course of it, that their own position would
ultimately become impregnable.[2]

These hopes were destined to be disappointed. Navarre's position between the two great rivals of the first
half of the sixteenth century, coupled with the military
value of the territory she possessed, rendered it inevitable
that sooner or later she should fall a prey either to France
or to Spain. It was during the spring of 1512 that her fate
was decided. The crucial event in the story was the death
in the battle of Ravenna, on April 11, of Gaston de Foix,
the representative of the claims of the younger branch of
his family against the Albrets, and the consequent passing
of his title to his sister Germaine, the wife of Ferdinand
the Catholic. Hitherto the French kings had tended to
support the Foix line, as a means of bringing pressure on the
existing dynasty; now it would be suicidal for them to
continue to do so, since the representative of the Foix
claims was the queen of Spain.[3] The only thing for Louis
XII to do was to draw near to the Albrets. On July 18,
at Blois, he concluded with them a secret treaty of alliance; this treaty, however, he purposely caused to be worded

---

[1] Boissonnade, pp. 206 ff.   [2] Boissonnade, pp. 266 ff.
                    [3] Boissonnade, pp. 279, 295.

in such ambiguous fashion as to deceive the Navarrese sovereigns themselves in regard to its true meaning. While they thought that they were only committing themselves to a defensive agreement — so loose as to be even consistent with the maintenance of their policy of neutrality — they really bound themselves to aid the king of France against attacks which he expected from the Spaniards and the English in the Pyrenees and in Guienne.[1] Ferdinand, in the meantime, sat still and watched events. He realized that the death of Gaston de Foix was ultimately bound to throw France into the arms of the Albrets, and that therefore the time had come for him to stop negotiations and make ready to attack; but, as usual, he wanted to make success as nearly certain as possible before he took the field. Consequently, while secretly preparing an army of invasion, he continued to negotiate with the Navarrese. He also brought every conceivable argument to bear upon that very magnificent young gentleman, his son-in-law, King Henry VIII, to induce him to send an English force into Guienne. Ostensibly the English were to go to war for the recovery of their ancient continental possessions; in reality, as Ferdinand plainly saw, the sole practical result of their expedition would be to help him to win his own game.[2] It must have given the old king great satisfaction to pull the wool over the eyes of the son of the one sovereign who had ever come near getting the better of him in the past; at one time he even had the effrontery to suggest that the only way for the English army to make certain of Guienne was to begin by attacking Navarre.[3] And Ferdinand's final act to justify the invasion which had been determined months before, was certainly one of the

[1] Boissonnade, pp. 316–321.
[2] *Calendar of State Papers, Spanish,*
ii, pp. 56 ff.; Boissonnade, p. 275.
[3] Boissonnade, p. 289.

most extraordinary pieces of duplicity that history records. He knew nothing whatever of the terms of the treaty which the Albrets made with the Valois on July 18, at Blois, but he realized that their rapprochement boded no good to him. To accomplish his own ends it was essential for him to forestall the confederates; but at the same time he well knew that the most telling possible vindication of the assault which he was now fully prepared to deliver, would be to spread it abroad that the Navarrese and the French had made an agreement to attack him. He accordingly concocted an abstract of a treaty, which he falsely represented as having been signed by Louis XII and Jean d'Albret, and published it as such on July 17; it purported to provide for a joint attack by the French and Navarrese on Guipúzcoa and the adjacent Castilian lands, and the settlement of all the details of an intimate offensive alliance between them, primarily directed against Spain.[1] However odious the deception, there can be no question of its effectiveness. The Spanish army of invasion, 17,000 strong, under the Duke of Alva, which crossed the Navarrese frontier from the westward on July 21, was persuaded that it was being employed for the purpose of national defence to anticipate a foreign attack, and not for aggression or spoliation; outsiders, too, were generally convinced of the justice of Ferdinand's cause.[2]

The Navarrese, it is almost unnecessary to add, were in no condition to resist. The fact that the Catholic King had continued to negotiate with them up to the very last moment, had lulled them into a false sense of security,

---

[1] All the older Spanish historians, and also Prescott, were duped, as were contemporaries, by the Catholic King, and accepted the absurd story of Peter Martyr, Bernáldez, and Zurita, that Ferdinand was really cognizant of the provisions of the treaty of Blois. It remained for M. Boissonnade, in 1893, to reveal the facts by an exquisite piece of destructive criticism. Cf. Boissonnade, pp. 289–294, 316–321.

[2] Boissonnade, pp. 325 ff.

so that no military preparations had been made; moreover, the English army, under the Marquis of Dorset, though it did not lend itself quite so obediently to Ferdinand's purposes as that monarch had hoped, created a most valuable diversion by threatening Guienne, and thus prevented the despatch of French troops to the aid of the Navarrese.[1] The Spanish invasion was, in fact, a triumphal procession. Jean d'Albret fled before it in early August into Béarn. Ten days later a subsidiary Aragonese army entered the southern part of the realm and besieged Tudela, which surrendered on September 9. Meantime (August 28) the Duke of Alva summoned the inhabitants of Pamplona to recognize Ferdinand as their lawful sovereign.[2] And the way in which the Catholic King defended his assumption of the crown of Navarre was certainly a fitting counterpart to the methods by which he had previously justified his invasion. Taking advantage of the fact that he was a member of the Holy League, he determined to make use of Pope Julius II to establish him in lawful possession of the territories he had won, just as he had previously utilized Alexander VI at the time of the discovery of America. On the plea that the Navarrese were heretics and schismatics, because they had adhered to the council which had been summoned to Pisa in the previous year at the instance of Louis XII, the Pope was induced to launch against them a bull of excommunication, dated July 21, 1512, which was solemnly published by Ferdinand exactly one month later in the cathedral church of Calahorra.[3] By it the Albrets

---

[1] *Calendar of State Papers, Spanish*, ii, pp. xlii ff.; Boissonnade, pp. 325, 335 f.

[2] Boissonnade, pp. 321–341.

[3] There has been a long controversy between French and Spanish historians over the authenticity of this and other papal bulls, put forth in connection with the conquest of Navarre. The whole affair is admirably elucidated in Boissonnade's book, pp. 341–370. The criticisms of his conclusions in Ruano Prieto's *Anexión del Reino de Navarra* are entirely unconvincing. Cf. *Revue Hispanique*, vii, pp. 264–269.

were declared to be deprived of their sovereign rights and their subjects absolved from their allegiance; on it, over and above all the claims which he could put forward on other grounds, Ferdinand based his seizure of the crown of Navarre, "which he had won with the full authority of the church . . . in a war for a just cause, as his Holiness had declared." [1]

Contemporary historians tell us that the usually unemotional Ferdinand actually wept for joy when he learned of the winning of Navarre.[2] We need not wonder at the depth of the old king's satisfaction. The conquest was not only the fulfillment of a duty bequeathed to him by his father, the realization of a dream that had haunted him from his youth; it rounded out his dominions on the north, just as the capture of Granada had done on the south, and was the *sine qua non* of national safety, whenever France and Spain should be at war. The military defence of his new frontiers was the problem which occupied Ferdinand's chief attention in Navarre during the remaining years of his reign. The French and the Albrets made a series of desperate efforts to recover it, down to the year 1521,[3] but none attained permanent success; for the Catholic King left no stone unturned to secure for himself undisputed control of the passes of the western Pyrenees. In the year 1514 he carried his conquests across the range, and obtained the complete submission of the small region of French Navarre, or 'Ultrapuertos,' as the Spaniards called it.[4] Moreover he entirely refused to listen to the advice of the counsellors who urged him to abandon it on the ground that it was not worth keeping; the Catholic King had been more than fourteen years in his grave before it was voluntarily

[1] Boissonnade, p. 339.
[2] Gómara, p. 34.
[3] Boissonnade, pp. 411–560.
[4] Boissonnade, pp. 408 f., 557.

relinquished by Castile, and the boundary between the two realms established where it is today. Constitutionally Ferdinand followed the traditional Spanish practice of suffering the conquered realm to retain complete autonomy. The national laws and liberties were scrupulously respected. The different organs of the local government — Cortes, Council, Exchequer, and the rest — were left virtually undisturbed. Every possible concession was made to win the loyalty of the Navarrese : so much so, in fact, that it is scarcely an exaggeration to say that the only change brought about by the conquest was the incoming of a new dynasty, which was represented on the spot by a Castilian viceroy.[1] On the other hand, the Catholic King did not propose to leave the realm which he had been at so much pains to conquer in any such state of independent isolation as would make it possible to tear it away from his successors. With the idea of committing the larger and more important portion of Spain to its protection and retention, he solemnly declared before the Cortes of Burgos, on July 7, 1515, that Navarre was united and incorporated with the kingdom of Castile.[2] It may well have cost him a pang not to turn it over to Aragon, with which it had certainly more intimate historical ties. Zurita tells us that he hesitated a long time before settling the difficult question ;[3] but there can be little doubt that his final decision was the wisest. Certainly Castile would have been threatened far more seriously than Aragon by the presence of the enemy in Navarre. It was but fair that she should reap the benefits of its annexation and undertake the onerous duty of its defence.

While the conquest of Navarre was being completed,

---

[1] Boissonnade, pp. 339 f., 562.
[2] *Cortes*, iv, pp. 249 f.

[3] Zurita, vi, f. 378; Colmeiro, *Introd.*, ii, p. 86.

the war against the French continued to rage with unabated violence in Italy. At one moment, just after the battle of Ravenna, there was a unanimous demand that the Great Captain be called forth from the retirement to which Ferdinand, after his return from Naples, had ungenerously consigned him. By him alone, insisted the allies, could the fortunes of the Holy League be restored. The Catholic King finally gave his consent, the less reluctantly because he plainly saw that a further advance by the French would endanger his Neapolitan dominions; and so great was the enthusiasm for service under the banner of Gonsalvo that it seemed, for a short space, wrote Peter Martyr, that Spain was to be drained of all her noble and generous blood.[1] But more favorable news was received from Italy before all the necessary preparations could be made. The Great Captain was ordered back into seclusion on his estates at Loja, and died at Granada on December 2, 1515, without having been able to render the last service which his country demanded.[2] Other generals carried the work of the League to its triumphant conclusion. The French were soon expelled from Milan; peace was made before the end of 1514, and Louis XII died on the last night of the year. His brilliant young successor, Francis I, immediately returned into Italy, won 'a battle of the giants' at Marignano, reoccupied the Milanese, and before he had been a year on the throne regained all, and more than, the prestige which his predecessor had lost; but Ferdinand, save for making a fresh alliance with Henry VIII of England,[3] seems to have remained quite indifferent to the conquests of the French. The old king's days were numbered,

---

[1] Peter Martyr, *Opus Epistolarum*, ep. ccccxxxvii.

[2] Galíndez Carbajal, *Anales Breves*, in *D. I. E.*, xviii, p. 338; *Crónicas del Gran Capitán*, in *N. B. A. E.*, x, pp. 252 f., 463–466, 583.

[3] *Calendar of State Papers, Spanish*, ii, pp. 268–270; Zurita, vi, f. 398.

and he knew it; of his principal contemporaries, whom he had fought and outwitted, only one, the Emperor Maximilian, was still alive; a new generation had arisen; he had done his work and was probably not sorry to go.   Death came to him at last, on January 23, 1516, in the little village of Madrigalejo in Estremadura; and Adrian of Utrecht, the envoy of the Hapsburg Charles, hovered about like a bird of evil omen all through his final illness,[1] as if to remind him in his last moments of the detested Fleming, who was to reap the reward of his labors and to inherit his hard-won domains.   Certainly it was the bitterest irony of fate that at the very moment when Spain's national unity had been attained, her national independence should have been lost.   Ferdinand and Isabella had earned the everlasting gratitude of their country by giving her the one, and by increasing, beyond the most ambitious dreams of their contemporaries, the wealth and extent of her dominions overseas.   Yet their reign had also resulted in depriving her of the other, and in bequeathing her the almost insoluble problem of reconciling the national interests with the dynastic ambitions of a race of alien kings.

[1] Galíndez Carbajal, *Anales Breves*, in *D. I. E.*, xviii, p. 341.

BIBLIOGRAPHICAL NOTE

See bibliographical notes at the end of Chapters XII, XIII, and XIX, and add:

Sources. — *Calendar of Letters, Dispatches, and State Papers relating to the Negotiations between England and Spain*; edited for the British government by G. A. Bergenroth; vols. i and ii, and supplement to them (London, 1862–68). This is cited in the notes as *Calendar of State Papers, Spanish.* It is a source of primary importance, which throws light on much else besides the relations of England and Spain. It is supplemented, especially on the side of the Low Countries, by the *Correspondencia de Gutierre Gómez de Fuensalida*, ed. the Duke de Berwick y de Alba (Madrid, 1907).

Later Works. — Prosper Boissonnade, *Histoire de la réunion de la Navarre à la Castille* (Paris, 1893); the definitive work on the subject with which it deals. Fernando Ruano Prieto, *Anexión del Reino de Navarra en tiempo del Rey Católico* (Madrid, 1899), adds nothing of importance; cf. *ante*, note to p. 345. Andreas Walther, *Die Anfänge Karls V.* (Leipsic, 1911), is valuable.

INDEX
TO VOLUMES I AND II

INDEX

TO VOLUMES I AND II

References are to volumes and pages, Roman numerals indicating the former, Arabic the latter. In a compound item, each volume reference carries until it is superseded by another. The abbreviations 'f.' and 'ff.' indicate that the reference is to the page designated and, respectively, to that next following or to the two next following. (In the footnotes to the text, on the other hand, 'ff.' is not restricted to the two pages following, but may include a larger number.)

353

persecutes the Granadan Moors, 95 f.;
provisional regent of Castile (1506–
07), 333; founds the University of
Alcalá, 161 f., 253; in the North African
campaigns, 241–255, 259; his
Complutensian Polyglot Bible, 155;
regent of Castile (1516–17), 241.
Xucar, the, *see* Jucar.

Yaakub, Merinite king of Morocco
(1258–86), i, 304.
Yahya I, Hafside king of Tunis (1228–
49), i, 315.
Yantares, i, 247, 248.
Yolande, *see* Violante.
Yusuf I, king of Granada (1333–54), i,
127 f., 129, 302.
Yusuf, Merinite ruler of Morocco (*c.*
1265), i, 108 ff., 114.
Yusuf, Merinite king of Morocco (1286–
1306), i, 126, 127, 300.

Yusuf, descendant of Okba, chosen ruler
of Spain by the army, i, 17.
Yusuf Ibn Tashfin, Almoravide leader,
i, 22 f.

Zafra, Hernando de, ii, 73.
Zahara, ii, 63.
Zallaka, battle of (1086), i, 22, 70.
Zalmedina, i, 463.
Zamora, i, 62; ii, 51, 52.
Zapata, Luis, Castilian councillor, ii, 227.
Zarauz, Biscayan town, i, 264.
Ziyán, king of Valencia (1229–38), i,
294, 295.
Zoraya, queen of Granada, ii, 64.
Zulil, i, 12, n. 4.
Zúñiga, Juan de, grand master of
Alcántara, resignation of (1494), ii, 108
Zurita, Jerónimo, Aragonese historian, i,
341, 358, 400, 406, 418, 422, 434, 446,
448, 464, 507; ii, 60 f., 183, 296, 347.